RETHINKING WRITING EDUCATION IN THE AGE OF GENERATIVE AI

Bringing together leading scholars and practitioners, *Rethinking Writing Education in the Age of Generative AI* offers a timely exploration of pressing issues in writing pedagogies within an increasingly AI-mediated educational landscape.

From conceptual and empirical work to theory-guided praxis, the book situates the challenges we face today within the historical evolution of writing education and our evolving relationship with AI technologies. Covering a range of contexts such as L2/multilingual writing, first-year writing, writing centers, and writing program administration and faculty development, the book examines various AI-informed writing pedagogies and practices. Drawing on interdisciplinary perspectives from writing studies, education, and applied linguistics, the book bridges theory and practice to address critical questions of innovation, ethics, and equity in AI-supported teaching.

This book is essential for writing educators and researchers looking to leverage AIs to facilitate the teaching and learning of writing in critical and transformative ways.

Chaoran Wang is an Assistant Professor of Writing and a Multilingual Writing Specialist at Colby College, USA. Her research examines multilingual literacy and the role of technology through the intersecting perspectives of applied linguistics, writing studies, and educational technologies.

Zhongfeng Tian is an Assistant Professor of Bilingual Education at Rutgers University–Newark, USA. His research, grounded in translanguaging theory, focuses on collaborating with pre- and in-service teachers to foster equitable, inclusive, and socially just learning environments for bi/multilingual students in ESL and dual language bilingual education contexts.

RETHINKING WRITING EDUCATION IN THE AGE OF GENERATIVE AI

Edited by Chaoran Wang and Zhongfeng Tian

Routledge
Taylor & Francis Group

NEW YORK AND LONDON

Designed cover image: © Getty Images

First published 2025
by Routledge
605 Third Avenue, New York, NY 10158

and by Routledge
4 Park Square, Milton Park, Abingdon, Oxon, OX14 4RN

Routledge is an imprint of the Taylor & Francis Group, an informa business

ISBN: 978-1-032-73142-1 (hbk)
ISBN: 978-1-032-72765-3 (pbk)
ISBN: 978-1-003-42693-6 (ebk)

DOI: 10.4324/9781003426936

Typeset in Galliard
by SPi Technologies India Pvt Ltd (Straive)

CONTENTS

CONTRIBUTORS

Christopher Basgier is the Director of University Writing at Auburn University, where he works with faculty on teaching through writing and consults with departments on integrating writing throughout undergraduate and graduate curricula. His research, which spans writing across the curriculum, genre, threshold concepts, digital rhetoric, and artificial intelligence, has appeared in venues like *Across the Disciplines*, *The WAC Journal*, *The Writing Center Journal*, *Composition Forum*, and *Studies in Higher Education*.

Brenta Blevins is an Associate Professor of Writing Studies and Digital Studies at the University of Mary Washington. She teaches and researches multimodal and digital literacy, rhetoric, and pedagogy with particular interest in virtual (VR) and augmented reality (AR). Her publications have addressed digital media and pedagogy, multimodality, and multiliteracy centers in *Computers and Composition*, *The Peer Review*, and various collections.

Curtis J. Bonk is a professor at Indiana University Bloomington who specializes in research on nontraditional and informal learning at the intersection of psychology, technology, education, and business. Across his career, Curt Bonk has over 430 publications including 20 books and over 175 journal research articles. He has given presentations around the globe related to online teaching and learning, generative AI pedagogy and language learning, and self-directed online learning, including hundreds of keynote and plenary talks. Curt Bonk co-hosts the weekly award-winning podcast show, Silver Lining for Learning (https://silverliningforlearning.org/). He can be reached at cjbonk@iu.edu or http://curtbonk.com/.

Suresh Canagarajah is the Evan Pugh University Professor at Penn State University. He publishes on translingualism, decolonization, embodiment, and disability studies. He teaches courses on sociolinguistics, rhetoric and composition, and language teaching in the departments of English and Applied Linguistics.

Luciana C. de Oliveira (Ph.D.) is an Associate Dean for Academic Affairs and Graduate Studies in the School of Education and a Professor in the Department of Teaching and

Learning at Virginia Commonwealth University. Her research focuses on issues related to teaching multilingual learners at the elementary and secondary levels, including the role of language in learning the content areas. She served in the presidential line (2017–2020), served as President in 2018–2019, and was a member of the Board of Directors (2013–2016) of TESOL International Association. She was the very first Latina to serve as President of TESOL.

Allessandra Elisabeth dos Santos is an English language teacher and a researcher in Brazil with a PhD in Education. Her research focuses on Generative Artificial Intelligence and its impact on writing. She is the vice leader of TECLA (Technologies, Education, and Linguistics) research group at the Federal University of Sergipe (UFS). Over the past 28 years, Allessandra has served as a teacher, teacher educator, and academic coordinator in TESOL/TEFL. She was also a visiting research scholar at the School of Education at Virginia Commonwealth University (VCU). She holds a Post-Baccalaureate Diploma in Education from the University of Winnipeg, Canada.

Whitney Gegg-Harrison is an Associate Professor in the Writing, Speaking, and Argument Program at the University of Rochester. Dr. Gegg-Harrison's work integrating insights from linguistics and cognitive science into the first-year writing classroom is featured in a 2021 article in the Journal of Teaching Writing (Vande Koppel Memorial Issue). Along with colleagues, she co-wrote *A Multidisciplinary Exploration into Flow in Writing* (Routledge, 2024). Dr. Gegg-Harrison's writing on Medium in early 2023 brought attention to the issues with automated AI detection, and since then, she has been an advocate for students falsely accused of submitting AI-generated text.

Ghada Gherwash, Ph.D., is the Director of the Farnham Writers' Center and Assistant Professor of Writing at Colby College. Her research focuses on the intersectionality of second language writing and writing center theory, intercultural communication, second language acquisition, qualitative research methods, language teaching, and policy. She has published work on topics related to literacies and second language writers, language variation, sociolinguistics, and cross-cultural composition, contributing to a deeper understanding of language and communication in diverse contexts.

Robert Godwin-Jones, Ph.D., is Professor in the School of World Studies at Virginia Commonwealth University (VCU). His research is principally in applied linguistics, in the areas of language learning and technology and intercultural communication. He writes a regular column for the journal Language Learning & Technology on emerging technologies.

Emily Hellmich (PhD, University of California, Berkeley) is the Associate Director of the Berkeley Language Center. Her research focuses on the impacts of digital technologies on language, language use, and language education, with particular interest in how language learners use (and don't use) digital technologies to support their language learning.

Amir Kalan is an Assistant Professor in the Department of Integrated Studies in Education (DISE) at McGill University. His work aims to create a sociology of writing that provides insights into historical, cultural, political, and power-relational dimensions of textual practices. He is interested in multimodal composition, critical writing studies, critical genre theory, and intercultural rhetoric.

Joshua M. Paiz, Ph.D., is a Teaching Assistant Professor of English for Academic Purposes (EAP) at George Washington University. He holds a doctorate in Applied Linguistics/ELT from Purdue University. He specializes in the intersections of Machine Learning, Natural Language Processing, and Applied Linguistics, focusing on generative AI in English Language Teaching (ELT). Dr. Paiz has also published extensively on LGBTQ+-inclusive practices in ELT.

Shawna Shapiro is a Professor of Writing and Linguistics at Middlebury College. Her research focuses on college transitions for immigrant/refugee students and on innovative approaches to working with multilingual/L2 writers. Dr. Shapiro's work has appeared in many peer-reviewed journals, including *College Composition and Communication*, *Research in the Teaching of English*, and *TESOL Quarterly*. Recent books include *Cultivating Critical Language in the Writing Classroom* (Routledge, 2022; see also https://clacollective.org/) and *Fostering International Student Success in Higher Education* (TESOL/NAFSA, 2024). She has also written for Inside Higher Ed and The Conversation. More information at https://sites.middlebury.edu/shapiro

Paulo Boa Sorte is an Associate Professor of TESOL, Educational Technologies, and Applied Linguistics at the Federal University of Sergipe, Brazil. He holds a Doctorate in Applied Linguistics from the Pontifical Catholic University of Sao Paulo. He worked as a Fulbright Visiting Scholar at the University of Michigan and the University of Miami. His academic interests include TESOL, digital literacies, generative artificial intelligence, GPT algorithm, virtual, augmented, and mixed realities.

Xiao Tan is an Assistant Professor of English at Utah State University. She has received her Ph.D. in Writing, Rhetorics, and Literacies from Arizona State University. Her research focuses on multimodal writing for second language/multilingual writers. She is an editorial board member of *Computers and Composition*, and her works appear in *Computers and Composition*, *Journal of Second Language Writing*, and *Journal of English for Academic Purposes*.

Kimberly Vinall (Ph.D., University of California, Berkeley) is the Executive Director of the Berkeley Language Center (BLC) at the University of California, Berkeley. With publications in the fields of SLA and CALL, her research explores the critical potentials of digital tools, like machine translation, to support language/culture learning and the development of digital literacy skills.

Marc Watkins is an Assistant Director of Academic Innovation and Directs the Mississippi AI Institute for Teachers at the University of Mississippi. His writing has been awarded a Pushcart Prize and his teaching has been awarded a Blackboard Catalyst Award for Teaching and Learning.

Wei Xu received her Ph.D. in Second Language Acquisition & Teaching from the University of Arizona. She is joining Northern Illinois University as an Assistant Professor of English in 2025 fall. Her research revolves around genre studies, multimodal composing, and generative AI and writing, especially for multilingual writers. Her works appear in journals such as Journal of Second Language Writing and Computers and Composition.

FOREWORD

What ChatGPT Says About Writing

Suresh Canagarajah
Penn State University

Since ChatGPT broke into our lives two years ago, both scholars and ordinary people have been debating the benefits and dangers for us. Leading scholars like Noam Chomsky and Steven Pinker have weighed in on alternate sides of the debate on whether AI can replicate or exceed human thinking and communication. Doomsday scenarios proliferate both for our social life and for our writing—i.e., that AI will lead to writers plagiarizing ChatGPT products; people losing their literacy skills; texts and media proliferating impersonal and unethical ideas generated by machines; and, hence, AI taking over life and humans becoming extinct!

As scholars of writing, we can adopt the pragmatic position that the answer to concerns about responsible writing depends on the attitudes and strategies of the writers themselves. This makes it all the more incumbent on writing instructors and scholars to cultivate attitudes and practices that treat AI as a useful resource, with writers engaging with it in critical and creative ways to negotiate shared and mediated outcomes. Though AI is a technology that comes with seemingly superhuman capabilities, the fears it generates are not dissimilar to what other technologies such as printing, word processing, and social media have generated in the past. The editors and contributors of this book bring the expertise to address these concerns by situating AI and writing in a historical context and drawing from empirical and practical work to articulate effective ways to incorporate AI into writing pedagogy, with suitable changes in educational policy, curriculum, and program management. They demonstrate how AI might be used by students to enhance their voice and meanings, develop their communicative proficiencies, and adopt an ethical positionality on using AI.

It is important to note that AI has implications for all teachers beyond those who are specialists in technology and choose to adopt it in their instruction. AI is so imbricated into all areas of our life that we cannot think of it as an option anymore. Scholars have started talking about a "post-digital condition" in life when online/offline and human/technology are not separate domains in our everyday activities.

More importantly, the debates around AI teach us something fundamental about what writing is. Technologies, material resources, and objects have always been part of writing. We have to critique the ideologies and communicative theories that have made us think that human communication is individual, cognitive, and autonomous and that any mediation by objects is treated as a threat to our voice, agency, and originality. I use this space to draw our attention to this broader question about the nature of writing so that we can treat the place of AI in our composing life with greater balance.

From the beginning of writing, the inscription of meanings has involved material spaces, objects, and technologies. Though the technologies in the past might have been analog, they were still important in shaping communication. Consider Quipus when Incas made knots in strings to keep a record of transactions or events, theorized by many as the beginning of literacy. Or the rune stones of Vikings where they carved historical information and ownership rights on stone tablets. Or the cave etchings by aborigines in Sri Lanka to represent their spiritual and aesthetic interests. Or the "dreaming" of Aborigines in Australia when they left paintings and images in the environment to communicate about their patterns of mobility and habitation across lands. The technology they used for these inscriptions are not mere instruments, they actively shaped the messages. Different inscription tools allow people to represent messages in different ways. Consider how in calligraphy the choice of different brushes or pens with different nibs is part of the message. In addition to these technologies of representation, material resources are involved in the medium on which inscriptions are made—such as stones, strings, caves walls, or soil. These materials also shape the message. Consider how the proximate landmarks in "dreaming" relate to the messages left there on habitation patterns. Where these inscriptions are recorded is part of the meaning. In that sense, writing involves the whole material ecology for meaning.

Furthermore, these ancient inscriptions required the distributed practice and collaborative work of both readers and writers to make meaning. In fact, the reader/writer distinction falls apart. In cases such as cave painting, quipus, and dreaming, the messages are "layered" by subsequent readers who add their own experiences or thoughts to the initial inscriptions, expanding the message. Since these inscriptions are non-alphabetical, the participants in these literacy events couldn't have treated the writing as having an easy one-to-one indexicalization of signifiers and signifieds. (Not that there is such a one-to-one connection even in alphabetical literacy, despite claims to the contrary in modern society, as I will discuss next.) For example, my previous mention that the instrument is part of the message, or that the whole material ecology is part of the message, implies that we cannot isolate the signifier and signified from the whole assemblage. From all these perspectives, writing has always been a material, ecological, and social activity where meanings are constructed continuously by diverse participants across different spaces and times. It is in this sense that the recent sociolinguistic term entextualization is a better word to describe writing. That is, while writing makes us think of the finished product as containing the meanings of a writer, entextualization makes us treat writing as an ongoing activity that involves diverse material resources, contexts, technologies, and social participants, constructing and negotiating the continuous production of meanings. In treating writing as entextualization, ancient people probably held complex and nuanced notions of voice, ownership, and originality, treating these as emerging from shared, distributed, and negotiated practices with other bodies, both human and nonhuman.

So, what made us forget or disregard these understandings of how writing and literacy work? Modern theories and pedagogies of literacy are influenced by a more recent orientation stemming from 16th-century European Enlightenment epistemologies. Brian Street has labeled this new orientation autonomous literacy. This orientation treated the inception of alphabetical literacy as the beginning of modern civilization, as these texts allowed people to depersonalize meanings and thinking by inscribing them on a page, with alphabets treated as a superior or more rational symbolic system for writing. The finished text was valued for its portability, transporting the meanings across space and time, presumably transcending diverse contingencies to keep the textual meanings permanent and universal. Social and material mediations on writing were disregarded as autonomous literacy adopted a conduit model of meaning whereby ideas are transferred from the writer's mind to the text, and decoded by readers, to communicate meanings in a transparent text. Thus, this orientation disregarded the role of objects, material resources, and technologies in shaping textual meanings. Also, the finished textual product stops the trajectories and co-constructions of meanings, treating them as inscribed with finality in the text. This orientation thus allows for writing that is owned by the individual who produces the text, ensuring their agency and presumed authentic voice. At a broader level, autonomous literacy plays into important ideologies emerging around 16th-century Europe, such as the importance of mind over body, individual over environment, and humans over objects. It also plays into many social movements emerging at that time, such as the market economy and the capitalist valuation of individual ownership of intellectual and material products.

An unintended benefit of ChapGPT is that it jolts us out of the myth of autonomous literacy to confront us with the agentive role of material objects and technologies in writing, calling for more nuanced views on human agency, voice, and ownership. We can draw from notions such as Bruno Latour's "hybrid agency" to consider how human writers can work with material and social partners to generate meanings. We are also now familiar with social constructionist definitions of voice as not pure, spontaneous, and inner, but co-constructed and emerging out of an assemblage of semiotic resources. In fact, even in the most dependent or passive uses of ChatGPT, human agency is always present. We have to consider the prompts given by the writer, and the choices made to accept one among several versions or variations of output, as indications of a writer's agency and creativity. If our personal role in generating texts through ChatGPT is always present, we can educate students to be more responsible, critical, strategic, and creative in their engagement with technology for richer outcomes.

The authors in this book do exactly that. They offer suggestions for diverse areas of writing instruction, such as classrooms, program management, curriculum, policy, and assessment to cultivate more responsible uses of AI. This book will be an important resource for scholars of multilingual writing for years to come.

INTRODUCTION

Chaoran Wang and Zhongfeng Tian

It has been two years since OpenAI's release of ChatGPT, a large language model that sparked widespread debates and renewed interest in artificial intelligence (AI). AI, in its many different forms, has a long history of application in writing education: intelligent tutoring systems, chatbots, machine translation, automated written evaluation, and other AI technologies have been used to support students in learning to write and to help teachers evaluate and gain insights into students' writing behaviours (Link et al., 2022; Jeon, 2021). Generative AI, as its name suggests, is a type of AI capable of generating new content—such as text, images, or music—that mimics patterns from its training data though it does not simply repeat what it has learned. This distinguishes generative AI from predictive AI, which typically focuses on tasks like classification, labelling, or predicting outcomes. This capacity to generate—typically viewed as a cognitive skill tied to human intelligence and creativity—has a profound impact on education and society, with generative models advancing rapidly to handle increasingly complex tasks across modalities.

In Western logocentric traditions, writing itself has long been viewed as a technology—a tool for capturing spoken words and extending mental capacities. Unlike natural speech, writing requires the use of equipment such as pens, inks, word processing tools, and alike, making it, as Ong (1995) describes, "completely artificial" (p. 82). In educational settings, writing has similarly been treated as a cognitive tool for students to articulate, organize, and discover their ideas in a way that makes thinking visible and learning assessable. Unfortunately, when writing is limited to serving as a textual representation of students' knowledge in a subject area or as a structural demonstration of one's familiarity with certain academic discourse conventions, it becomes more susceptible to replication by AI's generative capabilities. Yet, writing teachers know that writing holds—and should hold—more purposes beyond these functional roles. As a literacy *practice* (e.g., Heath, 1983; Street, 1995), writing also encapsulates cultural, socio-political, emotional, and embodied meanings to both writers and readers. It is these multiplicities embedded in a writer's lived experiences that make each piece of writing unique. When writing is reduced to singular, abstract, and structural forms, it risks falling into AI's replicable domains, leading to what many writing instructors and educators see as a new "literacy crisis" posed by generative AI.

DOI: 10.4324/9781003426936-1

Noam Chomsky (2023) critiques ChatGPT as "basically a high-tech plagiarism" and "a way of avoiding learning." Disagreeing with Chomsky, Sarah Eaton (2023) believes that we are entering a postplagiarism era in which we have to transcend the historical notion of plagiarism as "hybrid human-AI writing will become normal" (p. 3). These contrasting views are just one of the many differing perspectives at this critical moment in writing education where AI challenges our long-held notions of authorship and intellectual integrity, as well as our relationships with technology as writers and educators. Are we truly in opposition to AI, or could these technologies become allies that enhance students' writerly voice and rhetorical agency? What elements of writing are irreplaceable by machines and algorithms at all, regardless of the advancement of these technologies? What is missing in our current pedagogy that results in misunderstandings of writing as replicable products? How might we incorporate AI ethically to foster joy, authentic expression, deep learning, criticality, creativity, and justice? This volume is an initial attempt to explore these questions and to rethink writing education in the age of generative AI, through three main approaches delineated below.

First, it is essential to situate the challenges we face today within the historical evolution of writing education. Amir Kalan (Chapter 1) particularly critiques and examines the historical groundings of writing pedagogy that promoted "machine-like, decontextualized writing" that is highly compatible with AI. Kalan's tracing of Western rhetorics and writing pedagogies provided a compelling perspective of how students have long been encouraged to produce "textual hallucination" that resembles AI's innerworkings. Also from a historical lens but taking a different route, Brenta Blevins (Chapter 3) revisits the major writing pedagogies established in the field, discussing how their core principles are still valuable yet can be adapted differently in light of the challenges of AI. It is in a similar spirit that Kimberly Vinall and Emily Hellmich (Chapter 4) and Marc Watkins (Chapter 8) draw on their extensive work with machine translation and AI-powered reading tools to reexamine concepts of authorship, originality, accessibility, and ethics. Together, these perspectives provide a way to see AI's affordances and challenges not as newly invented but as a continuity in our historical and evolving relationship with AI technologies and our writing pedagogies.

Second, resonating with Johnson (2023), we believe that "technologies must be taught" (p. 171). It is not out of pragmatism that we make this claim (e.g., "because students will enter a professional world of AI so we have to make them ready and competent"). Rather, it is the inherently social and political nature of both writing and technology that compels us, as writing educators, to engage students with the reality of an increasingly AI-mediated world—where their words, art, text, social media interactions, and the natural resources and environments they inhabit are exploited as the very "blood" of AI (Anderson, 2023). They— and all of us—have already been implicated, without being given a choice in the first place. As argued by Whitney Gegg-Harrison and Shawna Shapiro (Chapter 2), both "teachers and students are experiencing a lack of *agency* regarding these emergent technologies." In fact, what can be even more harmful is a simplistic "banning or policing approach" that robs our students of the critical opportunities to participate in and investigate issues of "access, justice, and power" in relation to AI and writing. Thus, adding to Johnson's call, technologies must be taught, not only to students but also as part of writing instructors' evolving pedagogical repertoire so they can better empower both their students and themselves. This underscores the importance of writing teacher professional development, given the range of teachers' readiness, familiarity, positionality, and experience with effective pedagogies around AI, as shown in Wei Xu and Xiao Tan's nationwide survey of second language writing instructors in American higher education (Chapter 5).

Third, we recognize that it is important to contextualize AI writing pedagogies and reflect on the practices within our institutional settings and specific writing programs. With this in mind, we bring together diverse approaches to praxis in various contexts such as writing program administration and faculty development in a Writing Across the Curriculum setting (Chapter 6 Christopher Basgier), writing centre practices and tutors' professional development (Chapter Ghada Gherwash and Joshua Paiz), first-year writing (Chapter 8 Marc Watkins), and multilingual academic writing (Chapter 9 Allessandra Elisabeth dos Santos, Paulo Boa Sorte, and Luciana de Oliveira). These praxes not only showcase how theories inform pedagogical practices but also offer reflective stances toward theories in light of evolving AI technologies, providing practical implications for writing instructors, administrators, and education practitioners.

The volume is organized into two parts: Voices from the Field (Chapters 1–5) and Praxis in Context (Chapters 6–9), grounded in the North American higher education context. From conceptual and empirical work that reexamines our historical relationship with writing pedagogy and technology to theory-guided praxis, we hope that this volume at least offers some resources for further discussions and practices in a wider range of educational and cultural contexts. Below we briefly introduce each chapter.

In Chapter 1, Amir Kalan critiques writing education's long-standing focus on formalist approaches and its neglect of writing for authentic expression, social action, and identity. Kalan argues that the anxiety and fear of chatbots in educational settings stem from these traditional pedagogies, which promote decontextualized writing that can be easily mimicked by AI chatbots. In this sense, AI resembles Frankenstein's Monster, which reveals the uncomfortable truths about the problematic aspects of traditional writing education that undervalue writing's social functions and students' authentic expressions. Kalan's analysis reveals the limitations of a pedagogy that prioritizes "correct" form over communicative intent, critical thinking, and identity expression. The chapter encourages educators to adopt "use theories of language," which focuses on *what writing can achieve* and prioritizes the communicative impact of writing, advocating for writing as a space for personal expression, identity negotiation, civic dialogue, and social impact.

In Chapter 2, Whitney Gegg-Harrison and Shawna Shapiro argue that fear-driven, restrictive responses to generative AI—such as institutional bans and the development of AI-detection tools to monitor academic integrity and policing the use of AI-generated text—are not only ineffective but also harmful. They contend that such measures undermine both student and teacher agency and may lead to a counterproductive, dehumanizing rhetoric around AI use in educational settings. Drawing from Critical Language Awareness (CLA) and Critical AI Literacy (CAIL), Gegg-Harrison and Shapiro advocate for a shift from punitive towards empowering practices. The intersection of CLA and CAIL opens new avenues for writerly agency, fostering critical engagement with AI technologies. The authors propose a series of principles and strategies for writing instructors to offer students learning opportunities that are inclusive, critical, and socially aware.

In Chapter 3, Brenta Blevins reviews established composition pedagogies and discusses how each offers valuable insights into navigating the complex changes AI brings to writing classrooms, particularly those that view writing and technology as interlinked. Blevins points out that while GAI technology raises questions about current writing instruction, educators need not abandon established principles; instead, they can adapt them to help students use AI effectively and responsibly. Rather than overhauling writing education, she argues that process and post-process pedagogies, collaborative writing, genre awareness, second language and multilingual writing pedagogy, and disability studies pedagogy, among others, offer insights for guiding students to use AI thoughtfully. Blevins also highlights the ethical dimensions of using AI, emphasizing that teachers should foster discussions on when and how AI might be suitable for writing tasks. In the end, she suggests that while GAI tools will reshape writing, educators can guide students to develop the skills needed to navigate this evolving landscape thoughtfully and ethically.

In Chapter 4, Kimberly Vinall and Emily Hellmich reexamine the concept of authorship in the age of AI. Drawing upon their research with language instructors and students, they explore whether translated texts can be "owned" by students and how authorship is challenged by the use of machine translation (MT) in language learning. Building on Pennycook's exploration of Western views on authorship, they contrast the modernist emphasis on originality and individual authorship with a postmodern view of language as inherently intertextual, drawing from multiple cultural and linguistic sources. Using examples from their own research, they reveal three major "faultlines" in language learning: where meaning resides, the originality of text, and ownership of words. The authors conclude that rethinking authorship in light of AI and MT should move beyond a simplistic focus on ownership of words, fostering a more nuanced and reflective learning process that utilizes AI as a resource for meaning-making.

In Chapter 5, Wei Xu and Xiao Tan examine L2 writing teachers' initial responses to ChatGPT, the leading generative AI tool at the time of the study, within their instructional practices. By surveying 122 teachers and interviewing 13, the research reveals the teachers' varied levels of familiarity and use experiences with ChatGPT, highlighting perceived benefits such as enhanced linguistic input, support for brainstorming, and reduced student anxiety. The study also addresses ethical complexities, particularly around using ChatGPT for feedback and grading, underscoring the need for professional development and clear guidelines. Xu and Tan advocate for AI's transparent, supportive role in classrooms to responsibly enrich learning and conclude with pedagogical recommendations and a call for further empirical research to refine AI guidelines in writing education.

In Chapter 6, Christopher Basgier discusses his approach to using the literacy crisis prompted by generative AI as an opportunity to advance evidence-based writing pedagogies in a Writing Across the Curriculum (WAC) program. Basgier draws upon Sandra Tarabochia's (2017) relational ethic as a framework to engage faculty in constructive discussions about AI in disciplinary writing education. In addressing faculty anxieties around AI, Basgier discussed specific pedagogical practices, such as "Generative AI Playground" and workshops, that demystify AI's capabilities and limitations, encouraging faculty to examine AI within their disciplinary contexts. Basgier also extends Tarabochia's relational ethic by highlighting the importance of "acknowledging different values, centering intellectual commitments, and recognizing different comfort levels." He advocates for open dialogue about these elements, which fosters empathy and facilitates curricular adaptations across disciplines in response to AI's educational impacts. Through this nuanced approach, Basgier provides a means to guide writing instructors towards a proactive, ethically grounded engagement with generative AI, rather than succumbing to the "crisis" narrative.

In Chapter 7, Ghada Gherwash and Joshua Paiz explore the integration of generative AI in writing centres, focusing on its implications for tutor development and student support. They discuss how AI demands a recalibration of essential tutoring skills and argue that writing centres should adapt to AI's role in reshaping educational practices, positioning themselves as proactive environments that influence broader academic conversations around AI and students' ethical use in writing and communication. By ethically embedding AI, writing centres can help tutors critically engage with AI tools and guide student discussions on AI use in writing.

Adopting a socio-ecological perspective to understand AI's role in writing, Gherwash and Paiz show how AI opens new paths for peer tutor professionalization. They conclude with practical, dialogic training scenarios that Writing Center Administrators (WCAs) can implement to help tutors engage with generative AI tools in ways that support their ongoing professional development.

In Chapter 8, Marc Watkins explores the use of AI-powered reading assistants to support students' reading in a first-year writing class, particularly for those facing challenges such as disabilities, language barriers, or academic underpreparedness. Through a pilot study, Watkins examines how these tools enhance accessibility for diverse learners by simplifying complex texts, providing vocabulary support, and offering multilingual assistance, aligning with Universal Design for Learning principles. Using the "DEER" (Define, Evaluate, Explore, Reflect) praxis (Cummings et al., 2024) to guide students in the ethical and effective use of AI, Watkins discusses how AI-powered reading assistants promote student metacognition and responsible usage. Watkins highlights the potential of AI tools to reduce anxiety, improve focus, and increase information retention. However, he also raises concerns about overreliance, which could undermine close reading skills essential for learning and raise important questions about artistic intent and copyright implications.

In Chapter 9, Allessandra Elisabeth dos Santos, Paulo Boa Sorte, and Luciana de Oliveira examine integrating ChatGPT into writing instruction for multilingual learners in higher education, with a focus on fostering critical questioning skills. Aligning their approach with Freirian critical pedagogy and the multiliteracies framework, dos Santos et al. use ChatGPT as a scaffolding strategy to develop students' critical thinking through active engagement, questioning, and reflection. The chapter details an inquiry process to incorporate ChatGPT into course design, lesson planning, and student learning. Dos Santos et al. introduce a "Prompt Creation Reference Chart" for effective prompting, highlighting essential elements like *author*, *request*, and *purpose*. By exemplifying how to guide students in writing review articles, the authors demonstrate ChatGPT's potential as a collaborative tool and argue that effective interaction with AI cultivates students' ability to ask meaningful questions and critically analyze AI-generated responses. Concluding with the ethical implications and practical value of integrating generative AI into educational contexts, dos Santos et al. suggest that it is essential to cultivate adaptive and reflective writers who are equipped to engage with evolving digital technologies in higher education.

References

Anderson, S. S. (2023). "Places to stand": Multiple metaphors for framing ChatGPT's corpus. *Computers and Composition, 68*, 102778. https://doi.org/10.1016/j.compcom.2023.102778

Cummings, R., Monroe, S., & Watkins, M. (2024). Generative AI in first-year writing: An early analysis of affordances, limitations, and a framework for the future. *Computers and Composition.* https://doi.org/10.1016/j.compcom.2024.102827

Eaton, S. E. (2023). Postplagiarism: Transdisciplinary ethics and integrity in the age of artificial intelligence and neurotechnology. *International Journal for Educational Integrity, 19*. https://doi.org/10.1007/s40979-023-00144-1

Heath, S. (1983). *Ways with words: Language, life and work in communities and classrooms.* Cambridge, UK: Cambridge University Press.

Jeon, J. (2021). Chatbot-assisted dynamic assessment (CA-DA) for L2 vocabulary learning and diagnosis. *Computer Assisted Language Learning, 36*(7), 1–27. https://doi.org/10.1080/09588221.2021.1987272

Johnson, G. P. (2023). Don't act like you forgot: Approaching another literacy "crisis" by (re)considering what we know about teaching writing with and through technologies. *Composition Studies, 51*(1), 169–175.

Link, S., Mehrzad, M., & Rahimi, M. (2022). Impact of automated writing evaluation on teacher feedback, student revision, and writing improvement. *Computer Assisted Language Learning, 35*(4), 605–634. https://doi.org/10.1080/09588221.2020.1743323

Noam Chomsky on ChatGPT: It's "basically high-tech plagiarism" and "A way of avoiding learning". (2023, February 10). Open Culture. Retrieved October 23, 2024, from https://www.openculture.com/2023/02/noam-chomsky-on-chatgpt.html

Ong, Walter J. (1995). *Orality and literacy: The technologizing of the word.* New York: Routledge.

Street B. (1995). *Social literacies: Critical approaches to literacy in development, ethnography and education.* London: Longman.

Tarabochia, S. L. (2017). *Reframing the relational: A pedagogical ethic for cross-curricular literacy work.* CCCC/NCTE.

PART I

Voices from the Field

1

CHATBOTS, FRANKENSTEIN'S MONSTER OF DOMINANT WRITING EDUCATION

Amir Kalan

The accessibility and ease of AI text generation have created a debate among educators and researchers about the challenges and opportunities for academic writing practices and pedagogies in the age of chatbots such as ChatGPT (Adiguzel et al., 2023; Dennehy et al. 2023; Dwivedi et al., 2023; Halaweh, 2023; Liebrenz et al., 2023; Macdonald et al., 2023). This debate is partly a response to the panic displayed by teachers and educational administrators on news programmes and social media (Li et al., 2023). Anxieties about the emergence of chatbots are expressed in a number of different ways. One reaction has been rather apocalyptic, predicting the demise of school and college composition. Some, for instance, have warned about the "end of high school English [because of] what ChatGPT can produce" (Herman, 2022, para. 1) and pictured AI as a "threat to the future of college essay" (McDermott, 2023, para. 1). In a different response, some educators have reported how they are using chatbots in the process of teaching and learning writing in an attempt to incorporate the technology into their everyday pedagogy (Barrot, 2023; Baidoo-Anu & Ansah, 2023; Kasneci et al., 2023; Su et al., 2023). In this chapter, I take a different stance from these two major positions to argue that the panic created by ChatGPT, and other chatbots, is partly the result of the uncomfortable encounter with the problematic nature of our own writing pedagogies. The emergence of chatbots is an unpleasant reminder that the writing practices that we require our students to perform can easily be delivered by a machine because for long we have engaged in pedagogies that treat writing as an "autonomous" activity that "disguises the cultural and ideological assumptions that underpin [text] so that it can then be presented as though [writing] is neutral and universal" (Street, 2003, p. 77). The process of hiding the ideological foundation of writing has largely happened because of disregarding the human networks that use writing as a means of communication about issues that impact their lives and communities. AI is a Frankenstein's Monster that mirrors the writing practices that we have promoted. The monster has now risen only to remind us that, obsessed with formalistic features of writing, we have ignored engaging with the most important function of writing: human communication. Thanks to the emergence of chatbots, and the sense of unease that they have caused among writing teachers, this shortcoming of dominant writing pedagogies has become more visible than ever.

DOI: 10.4324/9781003426936-3

Writing education for long has actively engaged in what Trimbur (1990) called *the rhetoric of deproduction*. In order to project a sense of "objectivity" and "rigour," dominant Anglo-American rhetoric invites students to *de-produce* the writing process, or to remove traces of human involvement, positionality, perspective, and doubt from the text. In a sense, writing teachers often ask students to write like a machine by avoiding the representation of the complexities of human knowledge generation. Thus, it is not surprising that the ability of AI-based machines to outperform our students has created panic among us. This is particularly true about writing in English as an additional language where the dominant pedagogies have traditionally focused on English learners' interlingual "interferences" to create "error-free" texts with little interest in creating space in writing for these students' cultural beliefs, worldviews, and discourses. Language learners' native rhetorical practices are considered "mistakes" that undermine the objectivity of their arguments. Or worse, language learners can be treated as "not ready" to propose an argument or share ideas until they can create formalistically perfect texts (Kalan, 2014, 2021a, 2022).

In this chapter, I discuss how the availability of chatbots is an opportunity for language teachers to reflect on their practice to provide students with writing activities that invite expressions of identity and subjectivity by challenging pedagogies of deproduction. I explain that in a rhetoric of deproduction, we define "quality" through a formalist lens, with a focus on syntax, rhetoric, and style. We promote pedagogies that remove traces of positionality, devalue the message in favour of the form, and prioritize report-writing over genre exploration and experimentation. While recognizing current attempts to create alternative multimodal, translingual, expressive, and embodied writing pedagogies, here I focus on the historical roots and philosophical foundations of Anglo-American rhetoric, which still impact much everyday writing education:

> Despite these expansions in resources and approaches for teaching academic writing to multilingual students, and doing so with sensitivity to the language repertoires students bring with them, the dominant L2 pedagogies still take graphocentric literacy as the norm for highstakes academic writing. Critical thinking, voice, or rhetorical diversity are allowed to enter the text in a controlled manner without deviating from what compositionists call "standard written English" (SWE).
>
> *(Canagarajah, 2024, p. 294)*

In order to conceptualize an alternative theoretical foundation for engagement in writing practices that cannot be easily replicated by chatbots, I embed Trimbur's theory of the rhetoric of deproduction in a larger network of concepts that have, for long, explained that language use, including the act of writing, cannot be understood properly when studied as detached from its social function. I discuss *"use" theories* of language as an alternative to formalistic approaches that have dominated everyday teaching and assessment practices. Now that AI can create formalistically acceptable textual products, "use" theories of language can help us shift our focus from "how texts are constructed" to "what texts can do," for example, to the impact texts can have on learners and their communities. After introducing this alternative theoretical orientation, I write about its pedagogical implications including the possibility of writing as a means of exploring new discursive horizons, launching writing projects with meaningful social agendas, collaboration with out-of-school writing mentors, and creating space for hybrid genres and translingual practices.

Rhetoric of Deproduction and the Pedagogy of Correction

When we use the word "writing" in scholarly conversations that focus on students' writing practices in educational structures, our concern is not usually all forms of writing. In this context, the word "writing" often refers to "essayist literacy" (Farr, 1993; Gee, 1986; Scollon & Scollon, 1981) as the main textual medium of academic communication within schools and universities. More recently, Aull (2024) has also discussed how "correct" written English has been narrowly defined over the past 150 years. The dominance of this tendency can explain why most areas of writing studies, including second language writing research, rarely pay attention to non-essayist genres such as poetry, memoirs, and social media posting. The main interest is often essayist academic writing as the language of schooling because "expository essays [have] become evaluation metrics in coursework and testing" (Schleppegrell, 2001, p. 434).

Even the use of the word "essay" is not an accurate description of the genre of school assignments. "The essay" as a writing genre was developed by Montaigne in France in the 16th century. The genre was later adopted by other European thinkers, including British philosophers such as John Lock and David Hume, and thus found its way into intellectual and scientific exchanges in the English language. The Montaignian essay was a literary genre for sharing personal reflections with ample rhetorical flexibility that even allowed translanguaging. Montaigne's essays host a large number of quotations from other languages, especially Latin. As a literary genre, the Montaignian essay was meant to communicate personal reflections and thoughts about cultural, social, and political issues. Over time, the word "essay" in Anglo-American schooling has changed connotations to mean a form of academic report-writing in educational settings, typically written for an audience of one: the teacher.

The transformation of the nature of the essay from a literary genre to the main medium of school writing was not an organic development. It was guided by intentional institutional attempts to create a communicative vehicle for the British Empiricist movement as part of a larger positivist doctrine that dominated post-Renaissance Europe. The Royal Society of London made a concerted intervention against the dominant rhetorical culture of the time, which it deemed complex, decorative, and ambiguous. Thomas Sprat (1667) famously formulated the vision of this rhetorical campaign in his book *The History of the Royal Society*:

> [T]he only remedy ... [is] a constant resolution, to reject all amplifications, digressions, and swellings of style: to return back to the primitive purity, and shortness, when men deliver'd so many *things*, almost in an equal number of *words*. They have exacted from all their members, a close, naked, natural way of speaking; positive expressions; clear senses; a native easiness: bringing all things as near the mathematical plainness, as they can.
>
> *(pp. 112–114)*

The Royal Society's push for "mathematical plainness" was the rhetorical expression of the philosophical vision of positivism and scientificism. In this tradition, mathematical rhetoric was deemed the best tool for capturing the "truth." Since this period in Anglo-American history, writing teachers' main enterprise has become the identification and correction of students' "amplifications, digressions, and swellings of style" in order to make their text meet expectations for scientific objectivity. As I highlighted in the introduction, Trimbur (1990) called this approach "the rhetoric of deproduction," or a rhetoric that hides references to the production of the text:

> [E]ssayist literacy ... teaches our students a rhetoric which removes traces of authorship and the circumstances of production from essayist prose. Essayist literacy, that is, depends on a form of persuasion which convinces our students that when they read, they are not subject to persuasion but only decoding the words on the page. In this sense, the practices of essayist literacy can be explained as a legitimation strategy which authorizes statements by concealing their production. What enables essayist literacy to appear to stand apart and speak for itself is a strategy for naturalizing the text I will call the rhetoric of deproduction.
> *(Trimbur, 1990, p. 75)*

The pedagogical implication of this rhetorical regime, centuries later for today's teachers and students, is unfortunately a pedagogy of correction in which writing teachers are tasked with the job of correcting, in Sprat's words, "swellings of style."

The dominance of the pedagogy of correction has long been identified in sociology, a field where there can be more attention to the humans involved in the process of text production and their sociomaterial contexts. Bourdieu, for instance, explained that what we consider "legitimate language" is always a semi-artificial language that needs to be protected by institutions that employ "grammarians, who fix and codify legitimate usage, and ... teachers who impose and inculcate it through innumerable acts of correction" (Bourdieu, 1991, p. 60). Recent scholarly movements such as translanguaging and multimodality have created more room for alternative writing practices; however, there are still concerns about what constitutes "legitimate language" in recent literature, particularly in publications interested in decolonizing academic writing (Canagarajah, 2024; Flores & Rosa, 2015; Garcia & Baca, 2019; Kubota, 2021; Motha, 2014). With the availability of chatbots, the pedagogy of correction is, all of a sudden, irrelevant, and institutions are stripped of this traditional role. Drawing on large pools of written text, chatbots identify and produce popular linguistic performances that can appeal to the largest audience, including language and writing teachers.

The pedagogy of correction not only imposes itself on students' writing style—by restricting them from expressing complexity, sharing subjective understandings of phenomena, and rhetorical experimentation—but also is used to control the content of students' texts. The content of student writing is often a repetition of concepts and discourses offered in the curriculum. Written assignments are typically used as a means of measuring students' familiarity with the topics taught in the classroom. Writing at school is typically used as an assessment tool to verify students' contact with discourses they are exposed to in the classroom and their readings. Writing in this sense is an activity that requires students, like chatbots, to constantly incorporate discourses that they may not deeply understand into their texts. Bourdieu et al. (1994) conducted a well-cited research project in France that showed college students used specialized vocabulary in their essays without fully comprehending them. The researchers found that instructors observed shallow understanding of terms and discourses in their students' assignments but accepted the delivery as long as their students' use of words indicated that they were willing to echo the instructors' concepts and discourses:

> The traditional instruments of communication between teachers and students—presentations and essays—thus appear to have the latent function of preventing a precise measure

of student comprehension and of distinguishing this from the mnemonic repetition (écho-lalie) of professional words which mask misunderstanding. Most students are unable to define terms which appear with high frequency in the language of lecturers and essays. This shows that the illusion of being understood, the illusion of understanding and the illusion of having always understood are mutually reinforcing, and supply alibis to each other. Student comprehension thus comes down to a general feeling of familiarity … [through the use of] technical terms and references, like "epistemology," "methodology," "Descartes," and "sciences."

(Bourdieu et al., 1994, p. 15)

Thus, next to rhetorical regulation, the school essay is also a venue for showcasing "legitimate" discourses. Chatbots can easily echo discourses of interest by capturing frequently used academic terminology from online databases while appearing as if they understood the meanings associated with the terms. Similar to college students, chatbots create an "illusion of understanding" (the term used by Bourdieu et al. to describe student academic writing). In this sense, textual communication of academic discourses, both on AI applications and in college writing, resembles a state of *hallucination*, in which chatbots and students appear to understand the concepts that their readers, AI users and teachers, are interested in seeing in their texts. While this lack of real perception occurs among students because of the reduction of writing to an assessment tool, with chatbots, it is the result of the fact that in their process of text generation "no actual language understanding is taking place" (Bender et al., 2021, p. 615).

Here I am intentionally using the word "hallucination" in association with Bourdieu's concept of "illusion." AI experts use the word "hallucination" as a key term in their descriptions of how chatbots write (Alkaissi & McFarlane, 2023; Daniel, 2023; Ji et al., 2023; Reuters, 2023; Weise & Metz, 2023). Similar to Bourdieu and his colleagues' findings about college writing, chatbots' texts sound confident, factual, and objective, while chatbots, being machines, cannot in any way understand what they write. They select concepts and themes from piles of texts through lexical connections and collocation chains rather than any meaningful understating of words and subjects. Then, they combine the themes and present them in frequently used genres such as several-paragraph essays. The semantic, pragmatic, and personal detachment from discourses and concepts allows chatbots to go as far as inventing citations, names of experts, and even words that do not exist in order to produce polished final written products that contain all the expected components of "legitimate" written language. This manner of presentation resembles hallucination. Technically, "hallucination" is the result of a chatbot's attempt to estimate the correct response to a question by predicting the best next words in association with the words in a prompt without actually knowing the right response. The imposition of a rhetoric of deproduction in educational structures, reinforced by a pedagogy of correction, has pushed students to perform the same form of textual hallucination: echoing required discourses in a sterilized style that hides students' ideologies, positionalities, doubts, and unique linguistic performances.

Although this pedagogical regime impacts all students; it, more aggressively, targets additional language writers and speakers of "non-standard" varieties of the dominant language because their language practices can be significantly different from those in standardized English. These students' linguistic and rhetorical "errors" become an easy target for "correction." At the same time, these students' ideas, personal stories, expressions of identity, histories, and languages become completely irrelevant as their technical development is prioritized.

Pedagogical Implications of Prioritizing Deproduction and Correction

Interest in formalistic gimmicks that can project objectivity in writing has had serious implications for everyday writing pedagogies. It is important to reflect on some of these implications to realize why, with the rise of AI, the current pedagogical regime feels under threat.

Removing traces of subjectivity and positionality. As previously explained, the Royal Society of London's vision of reducing written communication to a mathematical representation of facts happened in response to the rise of positivism and empiricism with their emphasis on scientific objectivity. An important part of this intellectual wave, with a direct impact on Anglo-American rhetoric, was the emergence of British Empiricism in a philosophical rivalry with French Rationalism and German Idealism (Vanzo, 2016). The British empiricists sought to establish a rhetoric that avoided the speculative, reflective, rhetorically complex, and polemical nature of German and French writing of the time. The Royal Society, thus, paved the way for the appearance of a scientific rhetoric that centred on clarity, avoided exaggeration, and presented empirical data as evidence. Although this rhetorical orientation was originally promoted as a style suitable for reporting the findings of empirical research projects, over the past centuries, it has dominated English writing in most educational structures, even in teaching "English as a Second Language" settings.

Part and parcel of this rhetoric has been the removal of all traces of human subjectivity and positionality to create an ambiance of objectivity in the text. As I explained, Chatbots are capable of constructing a veneer of factuality even when they hallucinate and fabricate evidence for their assertions. Also, chatbots do not need to worry about expressions of human subjectivity in their writing because, being machines, they do not possess human positionality (unless they are designed to reflect their creators' perspectives) (Ferrara, 2023; Rozado, 2023). Beyond potential debates over the merits or flaws of empiricist academic writing, the emergence of AI writing, with its ability to imitate essayist literacy, provides an opportunity to focus on how prevailing writing pedagogies have overlooked the potential for incorporating students' personal perspectives and lived experiences into writing activities.

Anglo-American rhetoric has discouraged expressions of subjectivity and positionality to the degree that students are typically prevented from, and sometimes punished for, using the first-person pronoun "I" in their essays (Hyland & Jiang, 2017; Pho, 2008). Nevertheless, in most non-expository genres, writers are in the centre of the text. In poetry, memoirs, most forms of fiction, and other forms of creative writing, writers draw on their lived experiences and are transparent about their positionality and how it forms their view of the world. The same also applies to some academic genres such as the personal essay, ethnography, narrative inquiry, oral history, and the diary study. These qualitative academic genres allow more presence of the writer in the text, yet, compared to persuasive and argumentative essays, they remain underutilized in writing classes. They are also absent from standardized tests such as TOEFL and IELTS, examinations whose writing modules constitute language learners' first experiences with English writing and their first impressions of English rhetoric.

A remedy for anxieties about students' unwarranted use of chatbots can be bringing "I" to the centre of writing. As I will explain in more detail later, such an approach will allow writing teachers to humanize writing. The dominant rhetoric has, particularly, prevented language educators who are in contact with English learners from regarding their students' histories and identities as major components of writing and composition classes. Centring students' experiences in writing can encourage them to move away from using chatbots.

Chatbots are not aware of our students' unique histories, circumstances, and issues. Chatbots can project a sense of objective analysis in their texts, but they cannot fabricate our students' lived experiences.

Devaluing the message in favour of form. Most organic out-of-school writing is used and mobilized to facilitate communication between humans about genuine cultural, social, and/or political issues (Chun, 2019; Kitchin, 2014; Lysaker, 2014; Yagelski, 2012). In contrast, a rhetoric of deproduction trains students to centre its recommended writing style as a criterion for scientific rigour. In this rhetoric, the credibility of a message lies within the form of presentation rather than the content. This characteristic makes teachers shift their attention from "what is said in a text" to "how it is said." This shift requires adopting a pedagogy of correction in teaching writing. A regime of pedagogical correction is not interested in the message, in the content that a group of humans share an interest in or are curious about. It does not treat students as knowledge holders and intellectuals capable of exchanging important and valuable discourses. In the case of students who write in an additional language, a focus on style will lead to treating minoritized and racialized students' views as irrelevant or even worthless (Curtis & Romney, 2019; Fecho, 2018). Valuing the content of writing in the classroom can change the status of English learners from writers in need of linguistic correction to communicators who possess unique discourses that their teachers and peers may not have had access to.

A focus on students' discourses will also facilitate connecting students' writing with the communities from which students have inherited their discourses, beliefs, and perspectives (Kalan, 2022). The advantage provided by focusing on students' content of writing, in particular, is conducive to culturally responsive pedagogies in language classes, for instance, with students with immigrant and refugee backgrounds (Galloway et al., 2019; Lee, 2010; Polat et al., 2019). This pedagogy of highlighting marginalized discourses can create collective conversations about the concerns and struggles of our students' communities, an important feature of any authentic communication.

Writing assessment rubrics do not typically award students for centring their concerns and their communities' discourses. We often treat a well-formed written text as the ultimate object of writing whereas authentic writing is often only the beginning of a collective conversation or a catalyst for communal thinking to address real issues that are impacting human lives. By ignoring the potential of writing to circulate our students' discourses, we have prevented ourselves from tapping into dimensions of writing that cannot be reproduced by chatbots. Chatbots can generate text, but not the human interactions, sensitivities, and sensibilities that are triggered by and surround the text. To create a productive post-AI writing pedagogy, we might need to pay more attention to content that is locally created by our students and their communities and that can facilitate further conversations among them.

Prioritizing reporting over exploration and experimentation. Not only do dominant writing pedagogies devalue students' discourses, but also, with a focus on the style of writing, they discourage the use of writing as a tool for learning and exploring new topics and issues. A focus on the presentation of "evidence" in prescribed genres fails to promote writing as a form of thinking that allows experimentation with new concepts and semantic horizons. Essayist rhetoric is by nature a rhetoric of assertion and argumentation (Kent, 1999; Olson, 1999), whereas writing can be employed to express uncertainty, curiosity, possibility, and creativity without necessarily reaching a persuasive conclusion in a polished finalized text. There is a solid body of literature that focuses on writing as a tool of learning, exploration, and experimentation as opposed to assertion (see for instance, Klein & Boscolo, 2016; Newell, 2006). When we write to learn, writing as a craft is only of secondary importance. We use writing in search of, or to create, new meanings. From this perspective, the writer, as a learning subject, is superior to text. Text is used to nurture intellectual growth.

Changing the function of writing from assertion to exploration typically requires rhetorical experimentation (Kalan, 2021b). The dominance of the scientific writing regime has resulted in elevating the status of report-writing and report-writing genres at the expense of marginalizing more flexible rhetorical practices. We train students to use writing to "objectively" report evidence and/or findings to assert their theses and prove their hypotheses. The dominance of a rhetoric of reporting is sustained by genre control through the creation of genre templates that can be immediately recognized by hierarchical structures that report writers are required to report to. Academic articles are typically reports for supervisors in different capacities: teachers, professors, editors, grant committees, promotion committees, or a particular research community. Although there are different varieties of report-writing genres, in our current institutional practices, most of them share the same essence: essayist reporting with its emphasis on objectivity, and clarity of the organization of the text for supervisors to navigate the text easily and rapidly.

Whereas in writing for exploration, we can engage in flexible rhetorical practices that organically serve our curiosity or imagination, in the process of reporting we need to strictly control the genre for creating a sense of immediate communication of rigorously excavated hard data. The former leads to a rhetoric of experimentation and the latter to rhetorical control. Regardless of the advantages and disadvantages of each approach, with chatbots reproducing established genres in very little time, in the age of AI, we can start thinking of the possibility of awarding genre and rhetorical deviation as proof of human involvement in textual production in a way that cannot be replicated by machines. Obviously, an appreciation for genre complexity as a sign of human involvement in the process of writing should not be viewed as an assessment strategy. Genre creativity should be regarded as an organic development aimed at facilitating students' creative expression.

In conclusion of this section, a rhetoric of reproduction and a pedagogy of correction have nurtured writing practices, which now seem to be performed much more quickly and effectively by chatbots than human learners. We ask students to paraphrase and combine already existing texts, as references or examples to support a thesis, without creating a meaningful and long-lasting connection between our students and the discourse communities that they borrow their evidence from. We ask students to write in fixed genre templates such as the five-paragraph essay. We teach them to employ rhetorical gimmicks to project a sense of objectivity and rigour. The students share the writing with an audience of one, the teacher, while they imagine an unreal universal audience. We require students to follow standardized writing conventions ranging from formulated topic sentences to using connectors and punctuation formats. Also, we ask them to create texts individually as a task for a school grade. Chatbots can perform almost all of these tasks, propelling us to think of alternative approaches.

Theoretical Frameworks for Writing Pedagogies of Human Interaction

With the ability of chatbots to produce the formalist elements that educational settings have traditionally valued, we might now have the opportunity to pay more attention to some of the other dimensions of writing that we have often ignored. As I discussed, we have, for long, focused on the text itself, the way the text has been constructed, and the way it is presented. With the rise of AI, it might be an appropriate time to confidently shift our attention from "what the text looks like" to "what a text can *do*" in order to engage in writing practices that (at least for now) cannot be copied by chatbots. In this section, I discuss a theoretical tradition that, in contrast with essayist deproduction, has highlighted the communicative nature of writing, the uses of writing, and the social impact of writing.

In the field of philosophy of language, there has been a rich tradition of philosophical exchange that defines language as what it *can do*, as opposed to what *it is*. The theories that emerged from this tradition are often referred to as "use theories of language" in that they seek to define the meaning of language by its use and what it achieves in human interactions and in society. Use theories were a response to logical positivism, an earlier school of philosophy that, somehow similar to the Royal Society's project, intended to turn language into mathematically abstract logical statements, believed to be required for an objectivist representation of "the truth." The major philosophers who contributed to this project were Russell (2005), earlier Wittgenstein (1961), and Carnap (1937). After the failure of these philosophers' plan to reduce language to logical statements, the philosophy of language had to come to terms with the reality of the social nature of language and, thus, recognized the significance of the everyday use of language. Accordingly, this later trend has gained the label of *ordinary language philosophy (OLP)*. OLP explored how humans used language to get things done, accomplish tasks, and achieve objectives. Major contributors to this intellectual backlash were Austin (1962), Searle (1969), and later Wittgenstein (1961).

Austin, in his *How to Do Things with Words* (1962), described his theory of "speech acts." He argued that there is an inherent connection between "speech" (language) and "acts" (what can be achieved with language). In this book, he developed the idea that uttering words is a form of action; thus, language and its use cannot and should not be treated as two separate entities. The real meaning of our utterances is their use: "To say something is in the full normal sense to do something—which includes … the utterance of certain words in a certain construction" (Austin, 1962, p. 99). When we apply this notion to writing, we can see that to write is to perform a social act. Searle (1969) developed Austin's theory of speech acts, highlighting that the fundamental question in language studies should be how human beings make linguistic noises and utterances that have remarkable social consequences. After a revision of his ideas, Wittgenstein (1958), in the same manner, illustrated that "the meaning of a word is its use in the language" (p. 20). He explained that language should not be treated as marks on a page that express a relation to objects in the world, or to abstract entities such as propositions; instead, language is what people *do*. To assess linguistic performance, we need to evaluate its social outcome.

In writing studies, there has been an area of research that focuses on writing as a form of "social action" (see for instance, Cooper & Holzman, 1989; Kitchin, 2014; Lysaker, 2014; Yagelski, 2012), a notion that is theoretically harmonious with the philosophical proposition of "speech acts." The advocates of writing as social action emphasize that in authentic writing contexts, writers never write for writing's sake but to achieve a communicative, cultural, social, or political goal. Similarly, we can prioritize a writing pedagogy that invites students to write as a form of social action. One major example of writing as social action in educational settings is facilitating students' engagement in writing projects that can create social impact and achieve societal change. In these projects, students are invited to write in order to address issues debated in the communities that surround them, and they are assessed based on their involvement in creating texts that impact society. In this approach, writing functions as a catalyst to bring students together in the form of writing communities with certain sociocultural and political agendas. In these writing communities, students collaboratively work on writing projects of their interest. Highlighting the significance of writing as a collective act will also allow teachers to invite students' friends, family, and community members into their writing classes, especially when students write about their communities.

Running a writing class through the lens of "writing as social action" will allow teachers to regard the act of writing as much more than creating the text itself. The text is only part of a larger intellectual performance that includes human interaction, collaboration, research about social discourses, debates about political issues, and engagement in different forms of activism. Writing, in this sense, is a form of praxis that allows "reflection and action upon the world in order to transform it" (Freire, 2005, p. 51) because writing is the best way "to name the world, to change it. Once named, the world reappears to the namers as a problem and requires of them a new naming" (p. 69).

This perception of writing can change our view of the impact of AI on teaching writing. Chatbots can churn out texts about different subjects, but they cannot create writing communities that centre local issues and human interactions in their activities. Although not usually made use of in dominant writing pedagogies, there are well-developed pedagogical traditions that can help ease the feeling of anxiety about the impact of chatbots by proposing alternative visions of the purpose of writing. For instance, *community literacy* and *community writing* movements have long advocated for writing practices that are used by and for communities (see for instance, Flower, 2008, Higgins et al., 2006; Long, 2008; Peck et al., 1995).

> Community literacy [is] "a search for an alternative discourse," a way for people to acknowledge each other's multiple forms of expertise through talk and text and to draw on their differences as a resource for addressing shared problems (Peck, Flower, and Higgins 205). Thus, we [are] not describing an existing community but aspiring to construct community around this distinct rhetorical agenda, to call into being what Linda Flower has more recently described as "vernacular local publics."
>
> *(Higgins et al., 2006, p. 9)*

Thus, in a community literacy approach, "talk and text" are mainly a means of creating an "alternative discourse" as a local contribution to larger political dynamics. In this form of writing, the goal is not writing, but creating discourses that impact and form local publics.

With overlap with the field of community literacy, there is an area of writing studies that promotes "writing as civic dialogue" (Pough, 2002). Writing projects that aim to create civic dialogue insert students' voices, as citizen activists, into societal debates through their writing. They treat students as stakeholders in social issues, especially those that affect their communities, with the purpose of impacting the process of policy-making and social-planning in different forms.

A very important component of most projects that resemble community literacy and civic dialogue approaches is community publishing (Mathieu et al., 2012; Downing, 2000). Civic dialogue through writing can only happen when students write for an authentic audience and publish and circulate their ideas as a community. Community publishing allows writing communities to take control of communicating and disseminating their message. It allows community members to bypass gatekeepers who modify texts to censor discourses.

In terms of our concerns about the appearance of chatbots, community writing and publishing can broaden our understanding of the writing process by adding a component that cannot be performed by AI technology: intense human interaction and collaboration to make collective decisions about rhetorical performances, discursive strategies, and editorial processes. Community writing and publishing can push our focus towards a post-textual space, propelling teachers to ask, what can we do with the text when it is created? How should we present the text? How do we distribute it? Who is our audience? How do we engage in a dialogue with the audience after they read our publication? A community writing and publishing approach changes the status of the text from the end component of the writing process to the initial stage of a process of social engagement. The use and community theories of writing require literate and intellectual activities that cannot be performed by chatbots and are, thus, a great source of alternative forms of teaching writing.

Possible Post-AI Pedagogical Practices

Now that AI can produce texts rapidly and effortlessly, how can we use writing-as-action theories as a source for alternative pedagogies that offer our students a broader vision than grammatical and lexical correctness? In this section, I list some of the pedagogical implications of use and community theories of writing to conclude the chapter with some practical suggestions for educators. Although useful for all writing courses and programmes, the approaches that I suggest here can particularly transform additional language classes with emergent multilingual writers. Language learners' writings are constantly scrutinized for formalistic errors. As learners of a new language, these students are subject to longer periods of rhetorical and mechanical training before the content of their writing is seriously paid attention to. Moreover, racial and cultural differences between language educators and their students can create power relations that might impact teachers' views of students' capacity to mobilize writing in authentic intellectual and social contexts. Teachers might even find comprehending multilingual writers' discourses difficult because they were developed in different linguistic and cultural contexts. The emergence of AI can hopefully encourage more engagement with some of the following underutilized approaches.

Writing as exploring discursive horizons. Writing classes at college and university levels are offered as "service courses," severed from students' core and specialized subjects. International students typically take extra pathway courses or other support classes to practice writing in the institutional language and thus are moved even further from the "real" university venues where exchange of ideas, thoughts, and discourses occurs. In most ESL (English as a Second Language), ESOL (English for Speakers of Other Languages), EAP (English for Academic Purposes), and ESP (English for Specific Purposes) programmes, writing is taught as a separate skill from speaking, listening, and reading, which reduces writing classes to a space for rhetorical practice only. As I have explained elsewhere in more detail, this compartmentalization has rendered writing classes contentless (Kalan, 2021a, 2021c). As a result, students have been prevented from using writing for the purpose of generating, exchanging, and exploring discourses. Although creative teachers attempt to address this problem, institutional cultures often regard students as incapable of producing and sharing ideas before they can produce errorless texts. With the presence of chatbots, it is more commonsensical than ever to doubt the usefulness of this approach.

In authentic social contexts, the main purpose of writing is communicating ideas, thoughts, and discourses. It is possible to prioritize pedagogies that value this important dimension of writing and award students not only for "how they write" but for "what they write." Teachers can treat writing classes as writing communities where learners exchange discourses as well as writing skills. Teachers, hence, can facilitate and evaluate students' discursive engagement as well as their rhetorical performances. Discursive engagement activities include researching textual repertoires and social venues for discourses, sharing discourses with peers, and collectively analyzing and critiquing them. In classes with speakers of minority languages, this approach will allow and encourage the presentation of students' native discourses to challenge the dominant culture in the spirit of respect for epistemological diversity. Such an approach requires meta-textual activities that chatbots cannot replicate. For instance, chatbots cannot participate in pre-writing oral conversations in student groups about the discourses that international students are exposed to in their host countries. Nor can they debate the best genre examples for textual representation of these discourses in available literature as part of a writing project. Teachers who incorporate such activities can expand understandings of the writing process by including collaborative exercises that introduce students to new discourses.

Launching writing projects with meaningful social agendas. Connections with humans and their local discourses as a remedy for the interference of chatbots can also happen when students use writing to create a dialogue with the communities they come from or larger society. Teachers can invite students to develop agendas for their writing projects that allow them to identify and address social issues that impact them and their families. Through writing, students can add their voices to societal debates. AI is not able to create or lead projects of this nature because they require lived experiences and being embedded in local social contexts. Chatbots do not have access to online data about most of our students' communities and their everyday local issues. They cannot engage in a dialogue with local stakeholders. They cannot generate text that contain community members' experiences with injustice and discrimination in their unique contexts. As highlighted in the previous section, such writing agendas require engagement with publishing so that students can address authentic local audiences. Chatbots cannot print booklets and zines and hand them out in the streets. They cannot engage in face-to-face community conversations that emerge from such grassroots publishing efforts.

Such an approach is particularly empowering in classes with additional language learners. The dominant institutional deficit mentality regards language learners as technically deficient in their ability to communicate in an additional language. A focus on voice for social impact can change the status of international, minoritized, and racialized students into knowledge holders with valuable outlooks because these students are often immersed in social contexts where they experience intense forms of injustice and discrimination. From this perspective, additional language writers are *cosmopolitan intellectuals* (Campano & Ghiso, 2011) with much to teach us about the world through their writing, with or without formalistic errors.

Writing with out-of-school mentors. Engaging with writing projects that seek to establish a dialogue between students and society will provide students with the opportunity to work with community members outside of the classroom and the institution. These collaborators could be students' friends, family members, community elders, community leaders, and local culture workers such as writers, journalists, artists, and publishers. Once writing teachers welcome these individuals into the writing process, they can play the role of students' organic mentors. Some of them might already have intellectual connections with the students, and some mentorship relationships can develop as a result of opening the writing project to community members.

Chatbots are not able to create these human networks, which are an important feature of authentic forms of writing. Unlike school writing, authentic textual performances do not occur in a vacuum but are part of larger communal interactions and activities. These human networks facilitate the exchange of ideas and discourses. They also foster non-aggressive editorial processes in which students' mentors discuss language issues without the intention of punishing students with a lower grade for their errors. When teachers make use of this communal mentorship, they step down from their role as "error correctors" and allow the out-of-school mentors to address technical shortcomings as equal collaborators rather than assessors or graders. In this context, errors facilitate more human communication and exchange.

Hybrid genres and translingual practices. As I previously explained, an important form of reinforcement of the rhetoric of deproduction is the use of genre templates, such as the five-paragraph essay, and traditional genre developmental models, such as argumentative and persuasive models. Adherence to these genre templates and models is often awarded in writing classes as rhetorical mastery. Chatbots are trained to follow dominant genre structures based on available digital text (Chang et al., 2023; Floridi, 2023). Hence, chatbots' genre performances are currently based on a limited number of recognized genre structures. Most of the essays produced by ChatGPT, for instance, are written in different variations of the Anglo-American academic essay, with the introduction, body, and conclusion structure, and with central topic-sentence-based paragraphs that support a thesis. Similarly, creative writing produced by ChatGPT still does not show a great genre variety. ChatGPT poems are often rhymed and rarely experimental. Chatbots can become more creative as they consume more text with a diversity of genres. Nevertheless, since the foundation of chatbots is large language models (LLMs), it is likely that their genre performances will remain limited to imitating frequently used genres. LLMs are advanced artificial intelligence models designed to understand and generate human-like text. They are trained on vast amounts of text data, learning the statistical patterns and structures of language including genres. Thus, they might always produce genres that they are already given.

If educators are concerned about the interference of chatbots in student writing, they need to recognize that investment in teaching fixed genre templates in the age of AI is hardly reasonable or productive. Instead, they can invite students to engage in hybrid genre practices and genre experimentation. Genre fluidity is in fact a significant feature of all authentic writing because writers constantly tweak genres based on communicative circumstances (Kalan, 2021b, 2023).

In previous sections, I wrote about the possibility of mobilizing writing classes as spaces for discursive dialogue, social action, and expression of identity. Such an approach often requires genre flexibility and experimentation. Students who are involved in a project that seeks to create civil dialogue with an authentic readership often need to create genres and media that can help them achieve their communicative objectives based on the community that they intend to address and available forms of dissemination. Chatbots are not able to construct unique hybrid genres, especially those that, besides text, include images, sounds, videos, and other semiotic features. Examples of such hybrid genres include illustrated text, prose and poetry mixtures, and polyphonic forms of writing such as dual-ethnography and wiki-writing.

On the other hand, if projects are designed for students to express their identities and write about their lived experiences, genres are required that embrace subjectivity and reflexivity; for instance: storytelling, poetry, autobiography, autoethnography, and the personal essay.

The more a teacher allows students to insert their own lives into their writing, the more different their writing style will become from what chatbots can offer. An important component of expression of identity for language learners can be the use of their mother tongues, and other languages they know, in their writing alongside their learned languages. Thus, English teachers who are worried about the encroachment of AI can allow students to create genres that embrace translanguaging. It is easier for students, than for chatbots, to write about themselves and use their mother tongues, and their own accents, within English texts. Chatbots have no access to students' personal lives and (at least so far) cannot create meaningful multilingual texts with languages and dialect varieties that our students bring into the classroom.

Conclusion: AI as an Opportunity for Collective Cultural Production

Current anxieties about the impact of AI on writing education are by no means an unprecedented trend. There were similar waves of panic about the emergence of the Internet, Wikipedia, digital correctors, and Google Translate. The scepticism about these digital technologies has been mainly expressed as a form of concern about plagiarism. However, reducing the AI debate to a question about plagiarism might prevent us from engaging with larger issues about traditional pedagogies, which might inadvertently push students towards practices such as meaningless repetition of ideas (sometimes in the form of plagiarism) and rhetorical formats. In this chapter, I tried to illustrate that a less noticeable cause of teachers' anxieties about chatbots might be the fact that AI has made mainstream teaching approaches, which function according to a rhetoric of deproduction and a pedagogy of correction, irrelevant. With the entrance of chatbots into our writing classes, an emphasis on rhetorical and formalistic perfection may not any longer make much sense to our students. If AI can do what we have traditionally viewed as the focus of teaching writing, what are some alternative theorizations about textual engagement that can make writing classes relevant again?

In response to this question, I listed a number of use and community theories of writing that are more interested in "what writing can achieve" than "what a text should look like." I also suggested a number of models that can help teachers to create writing communities that aim to use writing for expression, experimentation, identity negotiation, civic dialogue, and social impact. I explained that this alternative approach will allow us to treat writing classes as venues for the exchange of discourses within texts rather than focus on the rhetorical make-up of texts. In this approach, writing classes are led by meaningful projects that aim to address social issues that impact students' lives. These projects can bring different people together in different forms of collaboration, a function that chatbots cannot perform. Also, projects of this nature legitimize genre hybridity and translingual practices, which may not be what chatbots were originally designed for. In brief, with the emergence of chatbots, we now have the opportunity to move beyond the rhetoric of deproduction towards a rhetoric of collective intellectual production for social impact.

References

Adiguzel, T., Kaya, M. H., & Cansu, F. K. (2023). Revolutionizing education with AI: Exploring the transformative potential of ChatGPT. *Contemporary Educational Technology, 15*(3), ep429.

Alkaissi, H., & McFarlane, S. I. (2023). Artificial hallucinations in ChatGPT: Implications in scientific writing. *Cureus, 15*(2), e35179. https://doi.org/10.7759/cureus.35179

Aull, L. (2024). *You can't write that: 8 myths about correct English*. Cambridge University Press.

Austin, J. L. (1962). *How to do things with words*. Oxford University Press.

Baidoo-Anu, D., & Ansah, L. O. (2023). Education in the era of generative artificial intelligence (AI): Understanding the potential benefits of ChatGPT in promoting teaching and learning. *Journal of AI, 7*(1), 52–62.

Barrot, J. S. (2023). Using ChatGPT for second language writing: Pitfalls and potentials. *Assessing Writing, 57*, 100745.

Bender, E. M., Gebru, T., McMillan-Major, A., & Shmitchell, S. (2021, March). On the dangers of stochastic parrots: Can language models be too big? In *Proceedings of the 2021 ACM conference on fairness, accountability, and transparency* (pp. 610–623).

Bourdieu, P. (1991). *Language and symbolic power*. Harvard University Press.

Bourdieu, P., Passeron, J. C., & Saint Martin, M. de. (1994). *Academic discourse: Linguistic misunderstanding and professorial power*. Stanford University Press.

Campano, G. and Ghiso, M. P. (2011) Immigrant students as cosmopolitan intellectuals. In S. Wolf, P. Coates, P. Enciso and C. Jenkins (Eds.), *Handbook of research on children's and young adult literature* (pp. 164–176). Lawrence Erlbaum.

Canagarajah, S. (2024). Decolonizing academic writing pedagogies for multilingual students. *TESOL Quarterly, 58*(1), 280–306.

Carnap, R. (1937) *The logical syntax of language* (K. Paul Trans.). Trench, Trubner.

Chang, K. K., Cramer, M., Soni, S., & Bamman, D. (2023). Speak, memory: An archaeology of books known to ChatGPT/gpt-4. arXiv preprint arXiv:2305.00118.

Chun, C. W. (2019). Writing as resistance in an age of demagoguery. *Writing & Pedagogy, 11*(3), 311–328. https://doi.org/10.1558/wap.40490

Cooper, M., & Holzman, M. (1989). *Writing as social action*. Boynton/Cook.

Curtis, A., & Romney, M. (Eds.). (2019). *Color, race, and English language teaching: Shades of meaning*. Routledge.

Daniel, W. (2023, April 17). Google CEO Sundar Pichai says "hallucination problems" still plague A.I. tech and he doesn't know why. *Fortune*. Retrieved June 13, 2023 from https://fortune.com/2023/04/17/google-ceo-sundar-pichai-artificial-intelligence-bard-hallucinations-unsolved/

Dennehy, D., Griva, A., Pouloudi, N., Dwivedi, Y. K., Mäntymäki, M., & Pappas, I. O. (2023). Artificial intelligence (AI) and information systems: Perspectives to responsible AI. *Information Systems Frontiers, 25*(1), 1–7.

Downing, J. D. (2000). *Radical media: Rebellious communication and social movements*. Sage.

Dwivedi, Y. K., Kshetri, N., Hughes, L., Slade, E. L., Jeyaraj, A., Kar, A. K., Baabdullah, A. M., Koohang, A., Raghavan, V., Ahuja, M., Albanna, H., Albashrawi, M. A., Al-Busaidi, A. S., Balakrishnan, J., Barlette, Y., Basu, S., Bose, I., Brooks, L., Buhalis, D., ... Wright, R. (2023). Opinion paper: "So what if ChatGPT wrote it?" Multidisciplinary perspectives on opportunities, challenges and implications of generative conversational AI for research, practice and policy. *International Journal of Information Management, 71*, 102642. https://doi.org/10.1016/j.ijinfomgt.2023.102642

Farr, M. (1993). Essayist literacy and other verbal performances. *Written Communication, 10*(1), 4–38.

Fecho, B. (2018). *Is this English? Race, language, and culture in the classroom*. Teachers College Press.

Ferrara, E. (2023). Should ChatGPT be biased? challenges and risks of bias in large language models. arXiv preprint arXiv:2304.03738.

Flores, N., & Rosa, J. (2015). Undoing appropriateness: Raciolinguistic ideologies and language diversity in education. *Harvard Educational Review, 85*(2), 149–171.

Floridi, L. (2023). AI as agency without intelligence: On ChatGPT, large language models, and other generative models. *Philosophy & Technology, 36*(1), 15–22. https://doi.org/10.1007/s13347-023-00621-y

Flower, L. (2008). *Community literacy and the rhetoric of public engagement*. SIU Press.

Freire, P. (2005). *Pedagogy of the oppressed* (30th anniversary ed., trans. Myra Bergman Ramos). New York: Continuum.

Galloway, M. K., Callin, P., James, S., Vimegnon, H., & McCall, L. (2019). Culturally responsive, antiracist, or anti-oppressive? How language matters for school change efforts. *Equity & Excellence in Education, 52*(4), 485–501.

Garcia, R., & Baca, D. (Eds.). (2019). *Rhetorics elsewhere and otherwise*. NCTE.

Gee, J. P. (1986). Orality and literacy: From the savage mind to ways with words. *TESOL Quarterly*, *20*(4), 719–746. https://doi.org/10.2307/3586522

Halaweh, M. (2023). ChatGPT in education: Strategies for responsible implementation. *Contemporary Educational Technology*, *15*(2), ep421. https://doi.org/10.30935/cedtech/13036

Herman, D. (2022, December 9). The end of high-school English. *The Atlantic*. Retrieved June 13, 2023, from https://www.theatlantic.com/technology/archive/2022/12/openai-chatgpt-writing-high-school-english-essay/672412/

Higgins, L., Long, E., & Flower, L. (2006). Community literacy: A rhetorical model for personal and public inquiry. *Community Literacy Journal*, *1*(1): 9–42.

Hyland, K., & Jiang, F. (2017). Is academic writing becoming more informal? *English for Specific Purposes*, *45*, 40–51.

Ji, Z., Lee, N., Frieske, R., Yu, T., Su, D., Xu, Y., … & Fung, P. (2023). Survey of hallucination in natural language generation. *ACM Computing Surveys*, *55*(12), 1–38.

Kalan, A. (2014). A practice-oriented definition of post-process second language writing theory. *TESL Canada Journal*, *32*(1), 1–18. https://doi.org/10.18806/tesl.v32i1.1196

Kalan, A. (2021a). *Sociocultural and power-relational dimensions of multilingual writing: Recommendations for deindustrializing writing education*. Multilingual Matters. https://doi.org/10.21832/9781788927819

Kalan, A. (2021b). Writing in times of crisis: A theoretical model for understanding genre formation. In E. B. Hancı-Azizoğlu, & M. Alawdat (Eds.), *Rhetoric and sociolinguistics in times of global crisis* (pp. 214–234). IGI Global. https://doi.org/10.4018/978-1-7998-6732-6.ch012

Kalan, A. (2021c). COVID-19, an opportunity to deindustrialize writing education. In I. Fayed, & J. Cummings (Eds.), *Teaching in the post COVID-19 era: World education dilemmas, teaching innovations and solutions in the age of crisis* (pp. 511–519). Springer. https://doi.org/10.1007/978-3-030-74088-7_50

Kalan, A. (2022). Negotiating writing identities across languages: Translanguaging as enrichment of semiotic trajectories. *TESL Canada Journal*, *38*(2), 63–87. https://doi.org/10.18806/tesl.v38i2.1357

Kalan, A. (2023). Genre as a product of discursive fusion: A theoretical framework for interdisciplinary academic rhetoric. In L. Buckingham, J. Dong, & F. Jiang (Eds.), *Interdisciplinary practices in academia: Writing, teaching and assessment* (pp. 9–27). Routledge.

Kasneci, E., Seßler, K., Küchemann, S., Bannert, M., Dementieva, D., Fischer, F., … & Kasneci, G. (2023). ChatGPT for good? On opportunities and challenges of large language models for education. *Learning and Individual Differences*, *103*, 102274.

Kent, T. (Ed.). (1999). *Post-process theory: Beyond the writing-process paradigm*. Southern Illinois University Press.

Kitchin, R. (2014). Engaging publics: Writing as praxis. *Cultural Geographies*, *21*(1), 153–157. https://doi.org/10.1177/1474474012462535

Klein, P. D., & Boscolo, P. (2016). Trends in research on writing as a learning activity. *Journal of Writing Research*, *7*(3), 311–350.

Kubota, R. (2021). Critical antiracist pedagogy in ELT. *ELT Journal*, *75*, 237–246.

Lee, J. S. (2010). Culturally relevant pedagogy for immigrant children and English language learners. *Teachers College Record*, *112*(14), 453–473.

Li, L., Ma, Z., Fan, L., Lee, S., Yu, H., & Hemphill, L. (2023). ChatGPT in education: A discourse analysis of worries and concerns on social media. arXiv preprint arXiv:2305.02201.

Liebrenz, M., Schleifer, R., Buadze, A., Bhugra, D., & Smith, A. (2023). Generating scholarly content with ChatGPT: Ethical challenges for medical publishing. *The Lancet Digital Health*, *5*(3), e105–e106.

Long, E. (2008). *Community literacy and the rhetoric of local publics*. Parlor Press LLC.

Lysaker, J. (2014). Writing as praxis. *The Journal of Speculative Philosophy*, *28*(4), 521–536. https://doi.org/10.5325/jspecphil.28.4.0521

Macdonald, C., Adeloye, D., Sheikh, A., & Rudan, I. (2023). Can ChatGPT draft a research article? an example of population-level vaccine effectiveness analysis. *Journal of Global Health*, *13*, 01003.

Mathieu, P., Parks, S., & Rousculp, T. (Eds.). (2012). *Circulating communities: The tactics and strategies of community publishing*. Lexington Books.

McDermott, M. (2023, March 14). Does ChatGPT pose a threat to the future of the college essay? *Utah Public Radio*. Retrieved June 13, 2023, from https://www.upr.org/utah-news/2023-03-14/does-chatgpt-pose-a-threat-to-the-future-of-the-college-essay

Motha, S. (2014). *Race and empire in English language teaching*. Teachers College Press.

Newell, G. E. (2006). Writing to learn. In C. A. MacArthur, S. Graham, & J. Fitzgerald (Eds.), *Handbook of writing research* (pp. 235–247). The Guilford Press.

Olson, G. A. (1999). Toward a post-process composition: Abandoning the rhetoric of assertion. In T. Kent (Ed.), *Post-process theory: Beyond the writing process paradigm* (pp. 7–15). Southern Illinois University Press.

Peck, W. C., Flower, L., & Higgins, L. (1995). Community literacy. *College Composition and Communication*, *46*(2), 199–222.

Pho, P. D. (2008). Research article abstracts in applied linguistics and educational technology: A study of linguistic realizations of rhetorical structure and authorial stance. *Discourse Studies*, *10*(2), 231–250.

Polat, N., Mahalingappa, L., Hughes, E., & Karayigit, C. (2019). Change in preservice teacher beliefs about inclusion, responsibility, and culturally responsive pedagogy for English learners. *International Multilingual Research Journal*, *13*(4), 222–238.

Pough, G. D. (2002). Empowering rhetoric: Black students writing black panthers. *College Composition and Communication*, *53*(3), 466–486.

Reuters. (2023, February 11). Google cautions against "hallucinating" chatbots, report says. *Reuters*. Retrieved June 13, 2023 from https://www.reuters.com/technology/google-cautions-against-hallucinating-chatbots-report-2023-02-11/

Rozado, D. (2023). The political biases of ChatGPT. *Social Sciences*, *12*(3), 148–156.

Russell, B. (2005). On denoting. *Mind*, *114*(456), 873–887. https://doi.org/10.1093/mind/fzi873

Schleppegrell, M. J. (2001). Linguistic features of the language of schooling. *Linguistics and Education*, *12*(4), 431–459. https://doi.org/10.1016/S0898-5898(01)00073-0

Scollon, R., & Scollon, S. (1981). *Narrative, literacy and interethnic communication*. Ablex.

Searle, J. R. (1969). *Speech acts: An essay in the philosophy of language*. Cambridge University Press.

Sprat, T. (1667). *The history of the Royal Society of London, for the improving of natural knowledge*. Royal Society.

Street, B. (2003). What's "new" in new literacy studies? Critical approaches to literacy in theory and practice. *Current Issues in Comparative Education*, 5(2), 77–91.

Su, Y., Lin, Y., & Lai, C. (2023). Collaborating with ChatGPT in argumentative writing classrooms. *Assessing Writing*, 57, 100752. https://doi.org/10.1016/j.asw.2023.100752

Trimbur, J. (1990). Essayist literacy and the rhetoric of deproduction. *Rhetoric Review*, *9*(1), 72–86.

Vanzo, A. (2016). Empiricism and rationalism in nineteenth-century histories of philosophy. *Journal of the History of Ideas*, *77*(2), 253–282.

Weise, K., & Metz, C. (2023, May 1). When A.I. chatbots hallucinate. *The New York Times*. Retrieved June 13, 2023 from https://www.nytimes.com/2023/05/01/business/ai-chatbots-hallucination.html

Wittgenstein, L. (1958). *Philosophical investigations* (G. E. M. Anscombe, Trans.). Macmillan.

Wittgenstein, L. (1961). *Tractatus logico-philosophicus*. Routledge and Kegan Paul.

Yagelski, R. P. (2012). Writing as praxis. *English Education*, *44*(2), 188–204.

2

FROM POLICING TO EMPOWERMENT

Promoting Student Agency in the Context of AI Text-Generators and AI-Detection Tools

Whitney Gegg-Harrison and Shawna Shapiro

Introduction

In November 2022, we educators were entering our fifth semester of pandemic teaching. We had been in crisis mode, working harder than ever to adapt our pedagogy in ever-changing conditions. We learned how to teach over Zoom, including with asynchronous formats (and got good at spelling the word "asynchronous"!); we adjusted to the reality of hybrid teaching in masked, distanced classrooms; we adapted our classes to account for frequent absences and missing work due to illness and loss. And we did all of this while dealing with our own losses, and the precarity that results from being in contingent positions during a crisis that affected institutions' budgets. In short, we were exhausted and stretched thin. We were crawling our way to Thanksgiving break and looking with longing toward the longer Winter break ahead.

Enter ChatGPT and the larger phenomenon of Large Language Model (LLM)-based text-generators, colloquially described as "Generative AI." Suddenly we began seeing articles like "The College Essay Is Dead" (Marche, 2022), and studies showing how easily these tools could generate work that would receive at least passing scores, if not better, on college-level assignments (Choi et al., 2023; Leffer, 2023; Terwiesch, 2023). We were confronted with a myriad of ethical, pedagogical, and even existential questions: *What is our job as writing teachers? Will AI be replacing us—and when? What even counts as "writing," anyway?*

Much of the initial response to these concerns has been driven by fear. Some large public school districts chose to ban AI text-generation tools (Yang, 2023). Some higher education institutions did the same (Castillo, 2023). And many individual instructors began to share statements of "zero tolerance" for these technologies. Underlying these swift and broad responses was a (desperate) hope that perhaps classroom instruction could continue as usual, instead of requiring yet more pedagogical adaptation: perhaps the use of AI could simply be banned and treated as an academic honesty violation.

With the bans, of course, arose the need for enforcement mechanisms—a need many companies have capitalized on. Developers like Edward Tian of GPTZero and companies like Turnitin raced to create tools that would "detect" whether a tool like ChatGPT had

DOI: 10.4324/9781003426936-4

been used to generate a given text. These detectors added to the growing arsenal of automatic surveillance tools such as Proctorio, which many institutions had adopted during the pandemic in hopes of making it more difficult for students to cheat on remote learning assessments. The use of these tools has risen steadily, despite established concerns about algorithmic bias (Meaker, 2023) and anxiety for student test-takers who had to use them (Harwell, 2022).

It has become clear that both teachers and students are experiencing a lack of *agency* regarding these emergent technologies. Many students worry that their privacy is being invaded, and that some instructors or institutions care more about "catching" misbehavior than about supporting their learning and growth (Jimenez, 2023). Many teachers feel pedagogically disempowered, playing whack-a-mole in response to technologies and to the policies their institutions may have made without their input. And in our current political environment, when curricula are already being policed by many state governments for evidence of content deemed too "woke" or "progressive" (Moody, 2023), many teachers rightly feel the desire to control *something* about what and how they teach. It is no wonder that the introduction of AI text-generators raised concerns about the security and meaning of our jobs as teachers.

But concerns about AI go beyond pedagogical control. There are also very real concerns about student engagement and learning. As writing teachers, we know that the point of writing is not (just) the creation of a beautiful final draft: We write to figure out what we think, to attempt to wrangle those thoughts into an organized structure, and in the process, rethink those thoughts and even come up with entirely new ones. (We did a lot of that while writing this chapter!) If technology does this work of writing (and thinking) for students, how can we scaffold their intellectual engagement and encourage their growth as communicators? Of course, this is a question that teachers have been wrestling with for years, with the increased use of tools like Grammarly, the integration of editing and text completion features into word processing programs, and the ease with which students can purchase essays from online "paper mills." Although ChatGPT may be cheaper and faster at doing work for students, the concern about barriers to learning is longstanding.

However, when we approach these conversations from a place of fear, we miss the very real pedagogical opportunities that these emergent technologies can create. We miss the potential for empowering students as writers—and increasing our own sense of efficacy and relevance as teachers. *What would it look like if we approached generative AI with the goal of enhancing learning and agency—both our students' and our own?* This is the central question of this chapter. To answer it, we draw on two conceptual frameworks: Critical Artificial Intelligence Literacy (CAIL) and Critical Language Awareness (CLA).

We begin with a brief introduction to the two frameworks. Then, we discuss the motivations and dangers of a fear-based orientation that focuses on banning and/or policing the use of AI-generated text, drawing on CLA and CAIL to understand the ways in which this orientation harms students. We then present a set of principles and strategies for promoting agency, informed by these two frameworks.

Foregrounding Agency: Critical Language Awareness (CLA) and Critical AI Literacy (CAIL)

Both CLA and CAIL aim to promote a critical orientation, which we define here as the recognition of issues of power, privilege, identity, and agency. Combined, these frameworks provide a lens for understanding biases within and about language and AI, so that we can foreground agency in how we work with writers and with these new technologies.

CLA is a framework that dates back to the late 1980s, developed by linguists and literacy scholars in the UK who wanted to attend to social and political aspects of language within English curricula in primary and secondary schools (Carter, 1997; Shapiro, 2022). Underlying most CLA-informed approaches is an ideology of critical pragmatism (Pennycook, 1997; Ruecker & Shapiro, 2020)—a commitment to teaching students what they need to be successful linguistically today, while also engaging students in critical examination and envisioning a more linguistically just and inclusive world in the future.

What brought Shawna to CLA was a recognition of perceived dichotomies around language differences in writing—between assimilation and resistance, between pragmatism and progressivism, and between teaching the norms that exist today and promoting more inclusive norms in the future. The question she hopes to answer with CLA is not "Which side should we be on?" but rather "How do we help students navigate the tensions within these dichotomies?" (Metz, 2019; Shapiro, 2022; Weaver, 2019). One concept central to CLA is rhetorical agency, which can be defined as the ability to make informed decisions around language use, with an awareness of the context and potential consequences for those decisions (Shapiro, 2022). Centering our work on agency helps to ensure that students' goals, needs, and assets remain at the core.

CAIL is a still-developing framework with interdisciplinary roots in work exploring the social, ethical, and environmental implications of "artificial intelligence" as well as media and information literacy. While the name "Critical AI Literacy" is relatively new (Bali, 2023; Mills & Goodlad, 2023), the concerns that are central to CAIL are not. CAIL focuses on reducing our vulnerability to misleading AI hype through building public literacy around how generative AI works, with critical attention to the potential impacts on marginalized populations, both in terms of how the tools are trained and how they are deployed. In particular, CAIL asks us to question the intuition that algorithms are inherently fairer than human judgment, drawing attention to the issue of algorithmic bias, which occurs when algorithms make decisions that systematically disadvantage particular groups of people, as we've seen in cases where automated tools are used in policing, hiring, and healthcare (Butler et al., 2021).

What brought Whitney to CAIL was a lifelong interest in AI combined with deep concerns about the ways in which tools that learn from human-generated input might perpetuate and even exacerbate the biases embedded in that input. Since 2010, Whitney has taught a first-year writing class centered on questions about language and the mind. In these classes, discussions of developments in language-related technology occur alongside discussions about language from a psychological and social perspective. Over the years, the scholars whose work these classes have explored have included many whose perspectives now inform CAIL: Cathy O'Neil, Joy Boulamwini, Abeba Birhane, Safiya Umoja Noble, and Emily Bender.

We think that CLA and CAIL make a good team (just like Whitney and Shawna!). Neither framework would suggest that banning generative AI tools is an agentive choice for students or teachers. Both approaches would encourage curiosity and some healthy skepticism about these tools, as well as about the "detectors" that claim to police students' use of them. Most importantly, CLA and CAIL invite us to think about power and privilege in relation to AI text generation, with questions such as:

- What biases about language (and about writing processes) do these tools perpetuate? How can those biases be lessened?
- Who benefits most from the development and use of these tools? Whose voices are often left out of the conversation?
- How can these tools be empowering to writers—and in what ways might they be disempowering?

The Problem(s) with Banning + Policing

Before we unpack our approach to AI text generation in writing classes, it is worth addressing a question raised earlier: If we're concerned about the potential harm that AI text-generators might have on learning, why not ban the use of AI text-generators altogether, and simply treat all uses of these tools as academic dishonesty? This approach might seem like a simple solution. But CLA and CAIL help us to understand that such an approach is in fact mis-guided, ineffective and, most importantly, likely to cause the most harm to students who are already marginalized.

The first complication is that it is often unclear what even "counts" as AI text generation. Though ChatGPT is relatively new, other related tools such as spell-check, autocomplete, and grammar-check (which draw similarly upon language models) have been around for a while and are even built into the word processors that students use. Are we to ban these as well? Some instructors have indeed called for a return to pencil-and-paper work, completed in class, in order to ensure that students get no help whatsoever from technology (Klein, 2023). However, this approach severely limits the kinds of assignments or assessments that we can use and is not a particularly viable option for classes that are taught online or in a hybrid format. Importantly, it also raises accessibility concerns, particularly for students who need to use computers as a disability accommodation.

A second concern is that "AI-detectors" are often inaccurate and/or inconsistent (Edwards, 2023a; Fowler, 2023). It turns out that distinguishing human versus machine-generated text is quite a difficult endeavor! One reason for this is that detection tools use predictability as an indicator of AI use, so text that follows common linguistic patterns is more likely to get flagged as AI-generated (Edwards, 2023b). However, we know from a great deal of research in psycholinguistics that human language processing is also rooted in prediction (e.g. Martin et al., 2018). Language only works for communication *precisely because* it is governed by conventions and norms, and while some genres have less constrained norms than others, the only kind of writing that is *truly* unpredictable is word salad.

Thus, a feature the detectors are looking for is in fact inherent to everyone's language use, to some extent. Two particular patterns often used to distinguish ChatGPT output are the use of generalizations (e.g., "In today's society") and boosters (e.g., "very" or "absolutely"). But empirical research on student writing has found that novice writers tend to use these patterns frequently as well; they need to learn over time how to offer more contextualized and cautious claims, using hedging language such as "might" or "possibly" (Aull, 2020). This is just one way in which the work of less experienced writers may be flagged as "likely AI-generated."

Students for whom English is an Additional Language are especially vulnerable to having their writing falsely identified as AI-generated. As Warschauer et al. (2023) point out, while any student perceived to be using generative AI is vulnerable to accusations of academic dishonesty, those risks are heightened for those writing in English as an Additional Language. Not only are these students more likely to be viewed with suspicion when submitting work that seems "too good to be true," but even automated tools are more likely to flag their writing as "AI-generated." A study by Liang et al. (2023) found that automatic detection tools tend to flag students' written responses on TOEFL exams (the most commonly used English language exam in the United States) as "AI-generated" much more often than writing on similar topics from native English speakers.

Studies also find that humans—even linguists—are not any better at reliably distinguishing AI from human writing (Casal & Kessler, 2023). If the output of AI text-generation tools *cannot* be reliably distinguished from human writing, then whatever we say about AI-generated text we're also saying about the human-written texts that are falsely identified as AI-generated. So, it's worth paying attention to the rhetoric used to describe AI-generated text and ways of detecting it.

Indeed, the discourse around "detectability" perpetuates numerous inaccurate, dehumanizing, and unjust assumptions about language and writing—for example, the idea that each writer has a unique "voice," that "formulaic" writing is inherently bad, and that "error-free" writing is suspect, especially if it comes from a student from a linguistically marginalized background. These misguided notions can lead to "false positives" whether the AI-detection is being done by an automated tool or a fellow human. These false accusations are incredibly hurtful to students whose writing gets read as, quite literally, "not human."

The contradictory assumptions about AI-generated writing are on display in a recent CNN video in which "suspiciously perfect" text is described by professors as the primary giveaway that students have submitted AI-generated text (CNN Business, 2023). In effect, students are put in a bind—their work needs to be "good, but not too good" to be read as human-written. In that same video, professors claim they can detect AI-generated text because the writing sounds "robotic" and "like a 50-year-old compliance lawyer." These criticisms tend to overlook the fact that many forms of writing—particularly within technical and professional writing—use a genre and style that are highly routinized. Some students (and compliance lawyers!) may need to write in those ways to achieve their communicative goals, and when we use rhetoric that describes this kind of writing as "robotic," we dehumanize them.

This dehumanizing rhetoric can be particularly harmful to neurodivergent writers, as we can see in the recent case of the autistic Purdue professor Rua Williams, whose email was falsely believed by a reader to be AI-generated because it supposedly "lacked warmth" (Pollina, 2023). In their response to the accusation, Williams points out that "[t]he panic over what generated text means for society has made people suspicious, and without proof they label anything that feels different as fake. But there's a huge diversity in linguistic expression and fear of difference leads to discrimination" (Williams, 2023). To that we say an emphatic YES.

Moreover, the tools themselves often perpetuate a dehumanizing rhetoric. For example, one AI detector provides the following message to students whose text is identified as AI-generated: "Did you write this yourself? Unfortunately, it reads very machine-like. If you write like a robot, you're going to get graded like a robot" (Content @ Scale, 2023). Accusations like this can be alienating to any writer but are particularly harmful to those from linguistically marginalized backgrounds, who, as illustrated in the aforementioned study from Liang et al. (2023), are also disproportionately likely to have their writing falsely flagged as AI-generated.

CAIL helps us to see AI-detection tools as yet another example in which algorithmic bias exacerbates existing prejudice, while CLA helps us to better understand the linguistic biases underpinning both detection tools and our own assumptions about detectability. In sum, our two frameworks help us understand why banning and policing are not productive, agentive paths forward, and why many of the claims made about AI text generation and detection are misguided and problematic.

Principles and Strategies for Agency and Empowerment around AI Text Generation

But even if we put aside all the issues we've just covered with AI-detection, there is a larger issue at stake for us as instructors: Do we really want to turn our jobs from teachers to police? Do we want to be part of ushering in a world where every piece of writing our students share with us is met with immediate suspicion, suspected of non-human provenance? What does that do to our students, and what does it do to us as teachers?

With an increased sense of agency, we can decide where to invest our energies and our sense of control. This in turn allows us to maintain a sense of purpose and joy in our work as teachers, readers, and evaluators of writing in the face of the changes that are taking place. We can embrace our responsibilities and rights—and those of our students—when it comes to use of AI text-generators and other tools. We recommend Conrad's (2023) "Blueprint for an AI Bill of Rights for Education" as an excellent starting point for thinking about these responsibilities and rights. This document outlines rights for educators, including the right to have input on AI-related decisions, resources, and policies at their institutions, and rights for students to consult and receive guidance on AI use without fear of punishment, as well as a process for appeal if they are accused of academic misconduct in use of AI.

In the remainder of this chapter, we present a set of principles and strategies, informed by CLA and CAIL, for promoting student and instructor agency in the face of AI text generation and the efforts to "detect" the use of it. We follow each principle with a pedagogical strategy that represents uptake of that principle in our teaching praxis. Readers may adopt the principles but come up with different pedagogical strategies in applying them.

Principle #1: Ignoring (and AI Ignorance) Is Not the Solution

Recognizing the difficulties and dangers of "policing" student use of AI tools, some instructors might be inclined to try to ignore these emergent technologies altogether, in the hopes that not talking about these tools will prevent students from using them. But when has censoring information ever empowered students to make better choices? (see, for example, the dismal success rate for abstinence-only sex ed—for example, Stanger-Hall & Hall, 2011).

Moreover, if we don't talk about AI text-generators with our students, we may actually exacerbate student inequities in terms of knowledge of and access to these tools (e.g., Warschauer et al., 2023). Students from privileged backgrounds, who already have resources not available to others (e.g., parents willing to "proofread" their papers, even if this is technically a violation of most academic honor codes), are also more likely to be "in the know" about AI text-generators and about methods for "thwarting" any AI-detection tools that their teachers might be using. We don't eliminate these inequities by avoiding the issue: we reinforce them.

Whether we like it or not, AI is part of our students' rhetorical future. Many experts are predicting that the ability to work with generative AI tools will become a valuable asset in the job market—possibly a skillset that is eventually required for some professions (Dell'Acqua et al., 2023). If we wish to prepare students to navigate the world as it actually is—a key tenet of both CLA and CAIL—then we cannot overlook this reality.

That said, talking about AI text generation does not mean uncritically promoting the use of these tools. There is a parallel here with how we talk about "standardized English" from a CLA perspective. We highlight the prevalence of prescriptivist ideologies that suggest that what is "standard" is linguistically superior to what is "non-standard" (e.g., Watson & Shapiro, 2018; Weaver, 2019). Here, the goal is not to force students to assimilate to unjust prescriptivist expectations but rather to prepare them to decide for themselves when and how they might wish to conform with or resist those expectations, as a manifestation of their rhetorical agency (Shapiro, 2022).

Likewise, talking with our students about AI need not suggest that we approve of everything about how these tools (and the companies building them) operate, nor that we think their use in educational settings is necessarily appropriate. The goal is not to force students to use AI tools but to prepare them for a world in which both generative AI and tools for "detecting" the use of it exist. Framing the conversation in terms of AI literacy and language awareness helps to hone in on rhetorical agency through informed decision-making.

Strategy #1: Be Transparent About Our Approach to Generative AI

CAIL and CLA would suggest that transparency—rather than avoidance—should be our aim, when it comes to addressing AI text generation. We may invite students to use AI text-generation tools, or even require the use of those tools for some activities or assignments (though we should always have an opt-out alternative; see Conrad's "Blueprint for an AI Bill of Rights for Education"). Or we may choose to recommend against the use of those tools, offering a clear rationale rooted in student learning rather than fear (e.g., Bjork-James, 2023). One place we can articulate our approach is in our course syllabi. Shawna's syllabi for Fall 2024 include the following blurb:

> I am open to your using AI text-generation tools like ChatGPT to aid your learning, similar to how you might use an internet search engine to find information or examples for an assignment. But please be advised that these tools have many weaknesses, including inserting inaccurate information and made-up sources. If you would like to use one of these tools for a class assignment, please **notify me in advance** so we can make sure you use the tools to *enrich rather than inhibit* your learning.

Whitney has a much longer note in her syllabus that begins as follows:

> There are a number of apps and tools (AI-based and otherwise) that may be useful to you as a writer, but it's important to make sure that you are using them in ways that are ethical and that do not compromise your own learning or the development of your writing skills but instead help you deepen your understanding of what you're doing when you write. If you think of these tools as tech-based "peers," this can help you understand when and how to use them ethically. **Remember: the principle is that YOU need to be the one making decisions about everything in your writing**.

Whitney goes on to delineate some ethical and unethical uses of the technology, informed by principles of academic honesty—for example, that passing off the ideas or work that came from elsewhere (human or machine) as your own is dishonest, whether it be generating content, proofreading, or translating work from other languages.

Although our blurbs are different in some ways, both emphasize writerly agency: We are neither banning the use of these tools nor adopting an "anything goes" approach. Rather, we attempt to promote a critical orientation by making students aware of the complexities around these tools, so that students can make an informed choice about whether, when, where, and how to use them ethically and effectively.

Having a general syllabus policy is a great place to start. But we also need clear, assignment-specific policies that take into account our learning goals. There are ways of using AI text-generation tools that would not necessarily hinder learning for some kinds of assignments and might even enhance learning (Anderman & Xie, 2023; Mollick & Mollick, 2023), but this is not true of *every* kind of assignment. For example, if we are asking students to reflect on their own experiences or their own process, this reflective writing really does need to come directly from the student in order for the learning goals to be met—a policy decision that should be clearly communicated to students.

In Whitney's class, each assignment for which AI use is permitted has an accompanying document that starts like this:

> If you want to use generative AI tools for this assignment, here are my suggestions for things to try. If you want to try something that's not listed here, check with me in advance. And as always, make sure you document the chat transcript(s) from whichever tool(s) you use.

This statement foregrounds student agency by presenting use of generative AI tools as an option but not a requirement. The document then goes on to offer a few suggested uses of AI tools that are designed to be specific to the assignment. In a research proposal assignment involving secondary sources, for example, students are provided with suggested prompts to use a tool like Perplexity.AI, Elicit, or Google's NotebookLM (all of which enable students to ask questions about an existing collection of sources), such as "What ideas connect these 4 articles?" or "What are some possible research questions I could ask, as a first-year college student, that build on these 4 articles?" or "Help me understand the research methodologies used in these 4 articles," along with guidance on how to make the questions even more specific and how to ask good follow-up questions.

For instructors who don't feel equipped to create bespoke prompt recommendations for each assignment, another valuable approach that centers student agency is the "flipped interaction pattern" (White et al., 2023) adapted by Whitney's colleague Yu Jung Han, who provides this template prompt that students can use with any generative AI chatbot:

> I want you to ask me questions to help me (TASK). Ask me questions until you have enough information to generate (OUTPUT). When you are ready, generate (OUTPUT) by mainly using my responses. Ask me one question at a time. Ask me the first question.

For example, a student working on brainstorming may use "brainstorm ideas for my paper" as TASK and "a list of ideas for my paper" as OUTPUT, whereas a student working on outlining their paper may use "create an outline for my paper" as TASK and "a structured outline" as OUTPUT. No matter what aspect of the writing process the students are working on, this approach encourages students to remain engaged participants, with the chatbot assuming the role of an assistant guided entirely by the goals and input of the student.

The approaches described here provide both scaffolding and guardrails: Students who are curious about the tools but do not know where to start receive some scaffolding so that they can explore the tools productively. Those who are afraid that trying the tools might get them into trouble, moreover, have guardrails in the form of clear communication about which uses are in-bounds and what to do if they want to try something outside of those bounds.

Whitney also emphasizes transparency by giving students explicit guidance on documenting their usage of AI tools (as well as other contributors to their process, such as conversations with peers and tutors) in a "Writer's Memo" that they produce for each assignment. This has the benefit of helping students build good habits for keeping track of their own writing process, empowering them to demonstrate their agency as writers if the provenance of their own writing is ever called into question.

By transparently communicating our approach to AI tools in our syllabi, our assignment prompts, and in other spaces in our classrooms, we give students the information they need to make informed choices about whether and how to use these tools in the context of our classes.

Principle #2: Create Space for Students to Learn What These Tools Can and Can't Do

The prevalence of punitive, policing-based approaches to AI in the classroom context can leave students fearful of asking professors questions about AI, lest they open themselves up to accusations of misuse. But students are understandably curious about generative AI tools, and by lowering the stakes in our own classrooms, we can create a safe space to nurture that curiosity and develop critical literacy. Open conversation, informed by CAIL, also provides important opportunities to address potential misconceptions about how AI tools work and what they can and cannot do.

For example, many students imagine that when they ask ChatGPT a question, what they get in response is an answer that reflects the actual truth about the world, drawn from credible sources. However, tools like ChatGPT are designed to produce text that is a *linguistically plausible* continuation of the prompt given by the user; the goal is to "sound predictable"—not to give us accurate information. As such, these tools often generate very realistic-looking citations for sources that do not actually exist (causing nightmares for librarians who are being asked to locate these references) and will provide answers to questions that may or may not be rooted in the work of uncredited scholars (van Rooij, 2022). Bender and Shah (2022) offer an important and accessibly written correction to these mistaken ideas about generative AI as a kind of "search engine." But we would not be able to share that correction with students if students don't feel as though they can talk with us about the ways they use AI tools.

Table 2.1, while not an exhaustive list, presents some of the things that these tools can and can't do, and might provide a useful starting point for explorations with students.

TABLE 2.1 Affordances and limitations of generative AI tools

(Some) things these tools CAN do	*(Some) things these tools CAN'T reliably do*
• Summarize/shorten complex texts (potentially helping with reading) • Generate examples of writing to fit different genre/style expectations or other constraints (e.g., "a literary analysis" vs. "a business letter") • Identify some overall strengths and areas for improvement in a student-generated piece of writing	• Provide accurate and up-to-date information • Know where the information comes from • Incorporate marginalized or underrepresented perspectives and languages • Do your analysis, thinking, and reflection for you

Strategy #2: Promote Curiosity and Experimentation Through Play

Research in applied linguistics shows us that *play* can be an important part of language and literacy development in the writing classroom (Shapiro & Leopold, 2012; Tardy, 2021). People love to play with language, and language play invites curious exploration and experimentation that can teach a number of important concepts in writing and linguistics (Gegg-Harrison, 2021). In other words, we can (and do!) have fun while developing CLA.

We can adopt the same playful approach to CAIL, inviting students to experiment with the tools (or in the words of beloved fictional teacher Ms. Frizzle, to "take chances, make mistakes, and get messy!"). If students trust that their classroom is a safe space for exploration, they can try out various ways of interacting with AI tools and reflect on what they learn from those experiments. In fact, one frequent outcome of in-class experimentation is that many students begin to realize the limitations of the tools and recognize what only human writers can do (Howell, 2023).

A favorite resource for playful approaches to critiquing AI tools is the website "AI Weirdness,"[1] where Janelle Shane delights in sharing her experiments with asking AI tools to generate pick-up lines, Halloween costume ideas, designs for baby onesies, and many other things. The results are often quite funny, but they also help students better understand what these tools are actually doing when they generate text and think more critically about potential uses and limitations.

Creating space for students to explore AI tools does require that we be willing to invite these tools into our classroom. We recognize that this may be a non-starter for instructors who have deep concerns about ethics, security, privacy, or other issues that CAIL helps us to understand. One possible solution is to partner with *another instructor* who already uses the tools and ask them to generate materials for your class to explore. Another is to invite those students in your classes who already use these tools to share their experiments with the rest of the class—something that will be much easier to convince them to do if you've created a safe, playful, curious space.

Principle #3: Help Students to Approach These Tools Critically

As we have discussed throughout this chapter, CLA and CAIL invite us to ask critical questions about AI in writing, informed by an understanding of social and linguistic contexts for these emergent tools, as well as an understanding of power and equity disparities that shape and are shaped by these tools. Students are often eager to engage in these issues but need opportunities and scaffolding to do so. Below are some questions we have enjoyed exploring with students, both in class discussions and at times in writing/research projects and other assignments.

- *What values have been built into the design of these tools, and what values are de-emphasized by these tools?*
- *How does privilege/power play into who might be inclined to try out these tools?*
- *What are the benefits and downsides of using an AI text-generator in writing? Who might stand to gain or lose the most from these tools?*
- *Which languages/language varieties do these tools recognize and use? Why might those languages/varieties be privileged? Who might be excluded?*
- *What beliefs about "good writing" (or "good language use") inform the work that these tools produce? What beliefs inform their work on the writing we ask them to "improve"?*
- *What are the potential economic, social, political, environmental, and other impacts of these tools, should their use become widespread?*

A critical approach also invites us to complicate some of the dominant narratives about these tools—for example, stories in the news or on social media about "how to cheat with AI!" or over-hyped claims of extremely high accuracy and low false positive rates from the producers of "AI-detection" tools. We can help our students understand that these issues are much more nuanced than what appears in the media. (A critical orientation to media is in fact a key component of both CLA and CAIL in general!) One of our favorite resources that helps students recognize inaccurate or incomplete narratives about AI is the list of "18 Pitfalls" on the AI Snake Oil website.[2] Students also need opportunities to think about these tools on a more micro level, so that they have a sense of their own individual relationship to them, including thinking deeply about the potential for over-reliance on these tools.

Strategy #3: Let Students Take the Lead on Investigating These Critical Issues

There are a number of activities and assignments we can use to help students engage in these critical explorations. First are reflective assignments in which students explore their own relationship to technology use (or another related theme) in writing. For example, one of the in-class writing prompts Whitney has used on the first day of class is: *"What's the point of learning how to write now that ChatGPT exists? What would be lost if we let ChatGPT write for us? What might be gained? What's the value of human writing?"* She has found student responses to this prompt to be thoughtful and nuanced.

AI can also be a focus for student research. For example, in some of Shawna's classes, students have the opportunity to conduct peer-to-peer interviews or surveys or to write a synthesis of secondary sources on a topic related to the course theme. A few of her students have chosen to address technology-related questions such as:

- How do students learn different styles of writing, including the difference between "textese" and academic English? (student interview project)
- Do Middlebury students think they are over-reliant on spelling and grammar checkers? (student survey project)
- How can high school teachers help students learn to use technology effectively as part of the writing process? (literature review/synthesis project)

Shawna expects more students to tailor their research to questions related to generative AI in the years to come.

A final assignment that can allow students to engage critically with generative AI is a public piece of writing or other media. The final assignment for Shawna's "Narrative in the News Media" course is a multimedia project in which students teach something they have learned to an audience of their peers. In the past few iterations of the course, a number of students have focused their projects on themes related to information literacy, including AI. For example, James Camp, a student in a Spring 2023 section of the course created a website entitled "AI in Misinformation Detection,"[3] in which he described how AI operates in general and how it is being used to root out misinformation online. The website includes a subpage on "Progress and Perils," where he expresses optimism about the future of this technology as well as some concerns that have been identified by experts in the field. James was proud to draw on his learning about linguistics and writing, as well as his past coursework in computer science, for this project.

Some instructors may wish to develop a new course or unit around AI text generation. At the time we were writing this chapter, Whitney was designing a new class entitled "Writing about and with AI." Three of the assignments that students complete in the course are:

1 An analysis of a piece of media about AI, using Kapoor and Narayanan's (2023) "18 Pitfalls to Be Aware of in AI Journalism" as a conceptual lens/framework.
2 A revision of #1 using AI tools, along with a reflection on that revision process (i.e., *How were the tools helpful? What were their weaknesses? How did sharing the writing process with an AI tool affect you?*)
3 A capstone project for which students choose one of two options: a) Investigate and report on an ethical issue related to AI and writing; b) Present a specific case study of AI use, using that case to illustrate and/or complicate concepts from class.

We hope we have demonstrated here the range of possibilities that exist for student-led exploration of AI text generation—either as one of many options or as a learning goal for the entire course. For more suggestions, check out Anna Mills's fabulous slideshow "Generative AI Activities for the Writing & Language Classroom," which she shares openly via a Creative Commons License.[4]

Principle #4: You Don't Have to Go Back to Square One

One of the dangers with the "crisis" rhetoric around AI text-generators is that instructors might mistakenly think that this "game-changing" technology means we need to abandon everything we're already doing in our courses. While some of us may decide to build new units and courses, as noted above, many of us will be infusing brief conversations and small but meaningful learning opportunities into our existing curricula. In her book, *Cultivating Critical Language Awareness in the Writing Classroom*, Shawna emphasizes that CLA "builds on best practices for writing/literacy instruction" (Shapiro, 2022, Chapter 3); these include teaching writing as shaped by context, helping students develop effective writing processes, and providing growth-centered feedback, all practices that can be enriched with CLA. Likewise, CAIL invites us to infuse awareness about AI into our existing curricula and pedagogical approaches without having to go back to square one.

In fact, some of the pedagogical guidance we have found most useful is from James Lang, whose 2013 book *Cheating Lessons*, written nearly a decade before the public release of ChatGPT, reminds us that student engagement is the best deterrent to academic dishonesty. As such, if we are worried about students using AI tools instead of doing their own work, we don't need to adopt a policing mindset! We can instead approach the issue with the goal of improving student engagement and learning since the pedagogical practices that reduce the likelihood of this kind of cheating are the same ones that produce better, deeper learning. At the heart of all of these practices is a focus on understanding students as individuals who seek meaning in their work and who want to grow as thinkers and communicators.

Strategy #4: Keep Doing What Works

Some of the best practices that Lang (2013) highlights as conducive to learning *and* to academic honesty include the use of low-stakes assignments and assessments, student-led projects, community-connected learning, and other "hands-on" writing for real audiences, as well as "flipped classroom" approaches, in which students work during class with instructor coaching on the content they have already engaged with via asynchronous instruction (video-recorded lectures, accessible readings, etc.). The good news is that these practices are already central to good writing pedagogy! While the exact implementation may vary from class to class, we can and should use what we already know works to keep students engaged in learning.

Importantly, all the practices described by Lang have the side-effect of making it less appealing for students to simply replace their own work with that of an AI text-generator. Lowering the stakes takes the pressure off students who might otherwise turn to AI text-generators because they feel their work needs to be "perfect." And when the work is student-led, personally relevant, and aimed at a genuine audience and purpose, this makes the work meaningful to students, which in turn increases their motivation to do the work themselves, while also requiring a level of specificity to their own experiences and community that an AI text-generator cannot easily replicate.

Dumin (2023) argues that when it comes to navigating the changes that AI has brought to the classroom, the pedagogical past can and should inform the present. She points to many of the familiar pedagogical approaches described by Lang, but also to Mezirow's (1991) concept of "transformative learning." In this approach, students are given a disorienting dilemma and supported as they explore and reflect on it as a class and individually. As we've already discussed (particularly in Principle 3), there are numerous potential "disorienting dilemmas" that generative AI tools present to us as educators and as learners, and any one of them would be valuable to explore with students in this way.

Conclusion: A Pedagogical Opportunity Rather Than a Threat

We hope that our application of CLA and CAIL insights and strategies to the knotty question of how to address AI text-generation tools in writing classrooms helps instructors understand why policing the use of these tools disproportionately harms already marginalized students. But more importantly, we hope this chapter allows instructors to see how these technologies, if approached with a critical lens, provide opportunities for learning and empowerment—not just for our students, but for us as professionals.

We realize that the questions before us related to AI text generation can be overwhelming at times. For instructors feeling a bit daunted by all the pedagogical possibilities, we offer the following as possible first/next steps:

- Let your own curiosity lead you—What do YOU find fascinating/confusing/concerning about AI text generation?
- Create space for students' own curious questions: What do *they* know and want to know about these technologies?
- Explore existing resources before you create something new (NOTE: we've put a list of some of our favorites here: https://tinyurl.com/CLACAIL!)
- Start small: Perhaps pick one principle or strategy from the list above and play around with it pedagogically.
- Keep student agency as the touchstone: How can we help students make informed, confident choices regarding whether and how they use these technologies?

Determining our approach to AI text generation in our classrooms forces us to "lean into" our pedagogical goals and values—sharpening our sense of what we do in our writing classes and why and helping us think through the balance of pragmatist and progressive orientations toward writing, toward language, and toward emergent technologies that generate language. We can teach students how to operate in the world as it is (with all its faults) while equipping them to critique that world and work to build a better one. And that sort of learning can be truly transformative.

Notes

1 https://www.aiweirdness.com/.
2 https://www.aisnakeoil.com/p/eighteen-pitfalls-to-beware-of-in.
3 https://jamescampnnmfinal.weebly.com/.
4 https://docs.google.com/presentation/d/1IbEBckhoOPKRWKQovCVL43-552rF4tlK.

References

Anderman, E. M., & Xie, K. (2023, June 6). 3 ways to use ChatGPT to help students learn—And not cheat. *The Conversation*. http://theconversation.com/3-ways-to-use-chatgpt-to-help-students-learn-and-not-cheat-205000

Aull, L. (2020). *How students write: A linguistic analysis*. Modern Language Association of America.

Bali, M. (2023, April 1). What I mean when I say Critical AI Literacy. *Reflecting Allowed*. https://blog.mahabali.me/educational-technology-2/what-i-mean-when-i-say-critical-ai-literacy/

Bender, E. M., & Shah, C. (2022, December 13). *All-knowing machines are a fantasy*. https://iai.tv/articles/all-knowing-machines-are-a-fantasy-auid-2334

Bjork-James, C. (2023, August 23). Why I'm banning AI-generated text from my indigenous rights course. *Carwil without Borders*. https://woborders.blog/2023/08/23/why-im-banning-ai/

Butler, W. D., Sargent, A., & Smith, K. (2021). Algorithmic bias. In *Introduction to college research* (pp. 17–19). Pressbooks. https://pressbooks.pub/introtocollegeresearch/chapter/algorithmic-bias/

Carter, R. (1997). *Investigating English discourse: Language, literacy, and literature*. Routledge.

Casal, J. E., & Kessler, M. (2023). Can linguists distinguish between ChatGPT/AI and human writing?: A study of research ethics and academic publishing. *Research Methods in Applied Linguistics*, *2*(3), 100068. https://doi.org/10.1016/j.rmal.2023.100068

Castillo, E. (2023, March 27). *These schools have banned ChatGPT and similar AI tools*. BestColleges. https://www.bestcolleges.com/news/schools-colleges-banned-chat-gpt-similar-ai-tools/

Choi, J. H., Hickman, K. E., Monahan, A., & Schwarcz, D. (2023). *ChatGPT goes to law school* (SSRN Scholarly Paper 4335905). https://doi.org/10.2139/ssrn.4335905

CNN Business. (2023, August 9). This is how college professors know you're cheating with AI. *CNN Business*. [video]. https://www.cnn.com/videos/business/2023/08/09/college-detection-chat-gpt-jo-contd-biz-orig.cnn-business

Conrad, K. (2023, July 17). Sneak preview: A blueprint for an AI bill of rights for education. *Critical AI*. https://criticalai.org/2023/07/17/a-blueprint-for-an-ai-bill-of-rights-for-education-kathryn-conrad/

Content @ Scale. (2023). AI content detector checks GPT-4, ChatGPT, bard, & more. *Content @ Scale*. https://contentatscale.ai/ai-content-detector/

Dell'Acqua, F., McFowland, E., Mollick, E. R., Lifshitz-Assaf, H., Kellogg, K., Rajendran, S., Krayer, L., Candelon, F., & Lakhani, K. R. (2023). *Navigating the jagged technological Frontier: Field experimental evidence of the effects of AI on knowledge worker productivity and quality* (SSRN Scholarly Paper 4573321). https://doi.org/10.2139/ssrn.4573321

Dumin, L. (2023, October 13). AI in Higher Ed: Using What We Already Know About Good Teaching Practices – EdSurge News. *EdSurge*. https://www.edsurge.com/news/2023-10-13-ai-in-higher-ed-using-what-we-already-know-about-good-teaching-practices

Edwards, B. (2023a, July 14). Why AI detectors think the US Constitution was written by AI. *Ars Technica*. https://arstechnica.com/information-technology/2023/07/why-ai-detectors-think-the-us-constitution-was-written-by-ai/

Edwards, B. (2023b, July 26). OpenAI discontinues its AI writing detector due to "low rate of accuracy". *Ars Technica*. https://arstechnica.com/information-technology/2023/07/openai-discontinues-its-ai-writing-detector-due-to-low-rate-of-accuracy/

Fowler, G. A. (2023, June 2). Analysis | Detecting AI may be impossible. That's a big problem for teachers. *Washington Post*. https://www.washingtonpost.com/technology/2023/06/02/turnitin-ai-cheating-detector-accuracy/

Gegg-Harrison, W. (2021). Encouraging playful, productive curiosity about language in the writing classroom. *Journal of Teaching Writing*, 36(1), 159–195.

Harwell, D. (2022). Cheating-detection companies made millions during the pandemic. Now students are fighting back. In Kirsten Martin (Ed.), *Ethics of data and analytics*. Auerbach Publications.

Howell, C. W. (2023). Don't want students to rely on ChatGPT? Have them use it. *Wired*. https://www.wired.com/story/dont-want-students-to-rely-on-chatgpt-have-them-use-it/

Jimenez, K. (2023, April 12). Professors are using ChatGPT detector tools to accuse students of cheating. But what if the software is wrong? *USA Today*. https://www.usatoday.com/story/news/education/2023/04/12/how-ai-detection-tool-spawned-false-cheating-case-uc-davis/11600777002/

Kapoor, S., & Narayanan, A. (2023, March 20). Eighteen pitfalls to beware of in AI journalism. *AI Snake Oil*. https://www.aisnakeoil.com/p/eighteen-pitfalls-to-beware-of-in

Klein, A. (2023, October 6). Teachers turn to pen and paper amid AI cheating fears, survey finds. *Education Week*. https://www.edweek.org/technology/teachers-turn-to-pen-and-paper-amid-ai-cheating-fears-survey-finds/2023/10

Lang, J. (2013). *Cheating lessons: Learning from academic dishonesty*. Harvard University Press.

Leffer, L. (2023). ChatGPT can get good grades. What should educators do about it? *Scientific American*. https://www.scientificamerican.com/article/chatgpt-can-get-good-grades-what-should-educators-do-about-it/

Liang, W., Yuksekgonul, M., Mao, Y., Wu, E., & Zou, J. (2023). GPT detectors are biased against non-native English writers. *Patterns*, 4(7). https://doi.org/10.1016/j.patter.2023.100779

Marche, S. (2022, December 6). The college essay is dead. *The Atlantic*. https://www.theatlantic.com/technology/archive/2022/12/chatgpt-ai-writing-college-student-essays/672371/

Martin, C. D., Branzi, F. M., & Bar, M. (2018). Prediction is production: The missing link between language production and comprehension. *Scientific Reports*, 8(1), Article 1. https://doi.org/10.1038/s41598-018-19499-4

Meaker, M. (2023, April 5). This student is taking on 'biased' exam software. *Wired*. https://www.wired.com/story/student-exam-software-bias-proctorio/

Metz, M. (2019). Accommodating linguistic prejudice? Examining English teachers' language ideologies. *English Teaching: Practice & Critique*, 18(1), 18–35.

Mezirow, J. (1991). *Transformative dimensions of adult learning*. Jossey-Bass.

Mills, A., & Goodlad, L. M. E. (2023, January 17). Guest forum: Adapting college writing for the age of large language models such as ChatGPT: Some next steps for educators. *Critical AI.* https://criticalai.org/2023/01/17/critical-ai-adapting-college-writing-for-the-age-of-large-language-models-such-as-chatgpt-some-next-steps-for-educators/

Mollick, E., & Mollick, L. (2023, September 25). *Student use cases for AI.* Harvard Business Publishing. https://hbsp.harvard.edu/inspiring-minds/student-use-cases-for-ai/?icid=top_nav

Moody, J. (2023, January 31). The DeSantis takeover begins. *Inside Higher Ed.* https://www.insidehighered.com/news/2023/02/01/desantis-puts-action-his-plan-end-woke-activism

Pennycook, A. (1997). Vulgar pragmatism, critical pragmatism, and EAP. *English for Specific Purposes, 16*(4), 253–269. https://doi.org/10.1016/S0889-4906(97)00019-7

Pollina, R. (2023, July 21). Autistic Purdue professor accused of being AI for lacking "warmth" in email. *New York Post.* https://nypost.com/2023/07/21/autistic-purdue-professor-accused-of-being-ai-for-lacking-warmth-in-email/

Ruecker, T., & Shapiro, S. (2020). Critical pragmatism as a middle ground in discussions of linguistic diversity. In Tony Silva and Zhaozhe Wang (Eds.), *Reconciling translingualism and second language writing.* Routledge.

Shapiro, S. (2022). *Cultivating critical language awareness in the writing classroom.* Routledge.

Shapiro, S., & Leopold, L. (2012). A critical role for role-playing pedagogy. *TESL Canada Journal, 29*(2), 120.

Stanger-Hall, K. F., & Hall, D. W. (2011). Abstinence-only education and teen pregnancy rates: Why we need comprehensive sex education in the U.S. *PLoS One, 6*(10), e24658. https://doi.org/10.1371/journal.pone.0024658

Tardy, C. M. (2021). The potential power of play in second language academic writing. *Journal of Second Language Writing, 53,* 100833. https://doi.org/10.1016/j.jslw.2021.100833

Terwiesch, C. (2023). Would Chat GPT3 Get a Wharton MBA? A prediction based on its performance in the operations management course. *Mack Institute for Innovation Management at the Wharton School, University of Pennsylvania.* https://mackinstitute.wharton.upenn.edu/wp-content/uploads/2023/01/Christian-Terwiesch-Chat-GTP.pdf

van Rooij, I. (2022, December 29). Against automated plagiarism. *Iris van Rooij.* https://irisvanrooijcogsci.com/2022/12/29/against-automated-plagiarism/

Warschauer, M., Tseng, W., Yim, S., Webster, T., Jacob, S., Du, Q., & Tate, T. (2023). The affordances and contradictions of AI-generated text for writers of English as a second or foreign language. *Journal of Second Language Writing, 64.* https://doi.org/10.2139/ssrn.4404380

Watson, M., & Shapiro, R. (2018). Clarifying the multiple dimensions of monolingualism: Keeping our sights on language politics. *Composition Forum, 38.*

Weaver, M. M. (2019). "I still think there's a need for proper, academic, standard English": Examining a teacher's negotiation of multiple language ideologies. *Linguistics and Education, 49,* 41–51.

White, J., Fu, Q., Hays, S., Sandborn, M., Olea, C., Gilbert, H., Elnashar, A., Spencer-Smith, J., & Schmidt, D. C. (2023). A prompt pattern catalog to enhance prompt engineering with ChatGPT (arXiv:2302.11382). arXiv. https://doi.org/10.48550/arXiv.2302.11382

Williams, R. M. (@FractalEcho@kolektiva. social). (2023, July 29). I shared "the email" because it was interesting to me that this happened to me when it's actually something I write about academically ... [Mastodon post]. *Mastodon.* https://kolektiva.social/@FractalEcho/110800085168655662

Yang, M. (2023, January 6). New York City schools ban AI chatbot that writes essays and answers prompts. *The Guardian.* https://www.theguardian.com/us-news/2023/jan/06/new-york-city-schools-ban-ai-chatbot-chatgpt

3

A GENERATIVE AI (GAI) WRITING PEDAGOGY

How Composition Pedagogy Can Inform the GAI Turn*

Brenta Blevins

Introduction

Toward the end of 2022, the latest innovations in Generative Artificial Intelligence (GAI) became widely accessible to the public. Most notable among these tools was ChatGPT, OpenAI's large language model tool that generated text by answering user-entered questions or directions called "prompts." Educators across disciplines from pre- and post-secondary levels raised numerous questions about how these technologies impacted teaching. Some instructors wondered whether GAI technologies meant the end of writing assignments (Marche, 2022; Rudolph et al., 2023), of writing assignments completed outside class time (Schatt, 2022; Yeadon et al., 2023), and of English classes (Herman, 2022). Some instructors revised assignments and curricula, whether to support GAI literacy or to assess learning outside GAI composing. Many educators expressed uncertainty about how to create effective and ethical integration of GAI within writing assignments.

This chapter contends that not only should writing education continue across the curriculum (McLeod & Miraglia, 2001), but that educators can approach GAI tools within existing composition pedagogy theory (broadly, the teaching of writing) adapted through a framework of writing and technology as inextricably linked (Baron, 2000; Haas, 1996; Kruse et al., 2023; Selfe, 1999) and writing-as-technology (Ong, 1982). While composition pedagogy might be best known among rhetoric and composition scholars and seems applicable primarily in writing classrooms, Kelly Ritter and Paul Kei Matsuda (2012) note that composition studies take place in multiple locations—a concept likewise noted in the Writing Across the Curriculum (WAC) approach (McLeod & Miraglia, 2001). Thus, even in a time when

---

* Multiple theorists contribute to different pedagogical approaches. As new emphases arise, these changes are termed "turns." For example, after the current-traditional rhetoric pedagogy focused on the final written product and formal features of writing, other theorists developed an approach focusing on the social and contextual aspects of writing, including discourse communities, power relations, identity, and culture. This change was deemed "the social turn," found discussed in such projects as *Social Issues in the English Classroom* (Hurlbert & Totten, 1992), *Pedagogy in the Age of Politics* (Sullivan & Qualley, 1994), and *Teaching Composition as a Social Process* (McComiskey, 2000).

DOI: 10.4324/9781003426936-5

GAI has introduced new literacy-impacting technology, educators across the curriculum can benefit from longstanding composition pedagogy, which has a longstanding tradition of viewing writing as a technology, as they explore GAI and writing education within their disciplines. Doing so supports literacy acquisition in an environment of ongoing technological change.

To develop this argument, this chapter begins by discussing some implications for GAI within writing instruction and assignments, then provides a composition pedagogy overview—positioned within a disciplinary understanding of the inseparable link between writing and technology, and, with this grounding in writing as a technology that is inseparable from technology, next identifies how different composition pedagogical implementations can align with the effective use of GAI. The chapter concludes by considering how some composition pedagogies may be less compatible with GAI and identifying opportunities for future research in an era of changing technologies.

To be clear, while this chapter discusses the possible inclusion of GAI in writing classes and assignments, it is not an argument for incorporating GAI into *every* writing occasion or mandating its use. Indeed, this chapter notes some writing situations in which GAI might not be appropriate for fulfilling writing or education aims. It will be worth discussing with students when GAI is appropriate for use, when it might not be, and why. Composition pedagogies offer perspectives that can frame such discussions, as well as course designs and writing assignments to prepare student writers for present and future occasions in which they may write and be expected to work and compose alongside AI.

An Overview of Generative AI Tools

As the editors note in their introduction, GAI technologies are software tools capable of generating text content, whether alphabetic, image, audio, or video, basically on statistically derived frequency. While ChatGPT is probably the most widely recognized GAI tool, numerous others exist in the text generation ecology, and more arrive routinely. The range of GAI tools includes those focused on producing alphabetic text (ChatGPT, Gemini, Copilot, Meta AI), visual imagery (DALL-E 2, Midjourney), and other media, including sound—from music (Meta's AudioCraft) to speech (Meta's VoiceBox), and video (YouTube's Dream Screen, Vimeo, Synesthesia).[1] Many other AI tools exist, including those to produce meeting notes (Read AI), summarize text input (ExplainPaper), provide transcription (Otter.ai), and query large texts (Adobe Acrobat AI Assistant).

All these tools work similarly: they survey large amounts of text—whether alphabetic, audio, or visual—and identify patterns. When users interact with GAI tools by inputting a prompt—a question or a command, the tool produces textual output by predicting statistically likely content. User prompts might be: "how can I organize a paper on time management in nursing," "create a recipe using these ingredients," and "generate an explanation suitable for an elementary school student, a high school student, and a college student." Applying inferences drawn from large databases of source material, GAI produces text responding to those requests rapidly—often within seconds.

Writers already interact with GAI, if nothing else, on a small scale within text message apps that offer predictive responses and email programs suggesting autocompletion strategies. Other writers use grammar and style tools that rely on GAI. In other words, GAI appears in writers' day-to-day lives and thus GAI needs to be addressed in writing education.

Generative AI Writing in Education

To support GAI literacy, some instructors have intentionally integrated GAI writing tools and assignments throughout the curriculum (Fyfe, 2022). The *TextGenEd* collection (Vee et al., 2023) presents various assignments focusing on AI literacy, creative exploration, professional writing, and rhetorical engagement, as well as ethical considerations. Southworth et al. (2023) argue for AI integration across the curriculum to support AI literacy and emphasize AI skills will be a differentiator in the workplace. Such AI literacy includes knowing not only the basics of AI but also the morals and ethics of AI, as well as issues around biases and reliability. Likewise, Bowen and Watson (2024) contend that AI will likely change every job given its wide use and that, while AI has led to inequities, educators should consider equity in ensuring students are prepared for using AI in any circumstance.

Laquintano et al. (2023) note that other forces, such as secondary schools and workplaces, may impact higher education's uptake of GAI. Students may arrive in higher education already habituated to using GAI in their composing while workplaces may expect them to arrive with GAI literacy. During an era of personal computers and educational technology software, Cynthia Selfe (1999) advocated for composition studies to consider the impact of computing technologies on writing. Given the latest digital development, Selfe's admonition to "pay attention" to technology bears renewed relevance, demonstrating that GAI is well within the purview of composition studies. As Kathy Mills (2010) notes, New Literacy Studies—a focus aligned with composition studies—took a "digital turn" with an increase in research to address how digital communication led to transformed literacy practices. The expansion of GAI accessibility has given way to a similar turn of attention.

This chapter aims to pay attention to technology by exploring the question "What can inform writing instruction in the GAI turn?" through existing composition pedagogy theory. In doing so, I contend that there are *multiple* potential approaches that can be applied, either singly or in concert. The multiplicity of models not only supports different instructors' pedagogical identities and local needs but also offers adaptability in ongoing adjustments in a rapidly evolving context.

Applicability of Composition Pedagogy in the GAI Era

Rhetoric and composition specialists have long considered the impacts of technology on writing (Selfe, 1999; Baron, 2000) and writing-as-technology (Ong, 1982). Dennis Baron has defined literacy as developing through different stages around various literacy technologies. To support his argument, Baron identifies various technologies that writing relies on, starting with writing itself—noting Plato's objections—and exploring tools such as the pencil. Baron positions the computer as "simply the latest step in a long line of writing technologies." From this perspective, GAI is now the most recent step in literacy technologies. More recently, rhetoricians and compositionists such as William Hart-Davidson (2018), Ann Hill Duin and Isabel Pedersen (2021), Chris Anson (2022), and Heidi McKee and James Porter (2022), among others, anticipated the growing significance of GAI prior to OpenAI's launch of ChatGPT. These recent scholarly contributions, however, are not the only resources that can help educators approach writing instruction.

Long-established composition pedagogy presents theoretical frameworks that can guide the design of curricula and strategies for discussing GAI and writing with students. Taggart et al. (2014) offer a definition of composition pedagogy as "a body of knowledge consisting of theories of and research on teaching, learning, literacy, writing, and rhetoric, and the related practices that emerge" (p. 3). Composition pedagogy has historically taken up ethical issues relevant to writing with GAI tools, including source usage, citation, and information literacy (Artman et al., 2010; Veach, 2018), and plagiarism (Howard, 1992, 1995), continuing rhetoric's concern with ethos. These topics pertain in the GAI era as professional organizations determine what GAI use is acceptable, how to cite such usage, whether to use technological checkers for AI-generated writing and what counts as plagiarism when GAI produces content frequently unique on a sentence level but often drawn from immense corpora of unattributed written work.

Composition pedagogy's concern with the ethics of plagiarism checkers (Amidon et al., 2019) bears relevance in an era when writing submitted to GAI may have no guarantee of privacy, meaning GAI tools may not guarantee the privacy of student writing.[2] In a related ethical concern, in 2023, authors sued OpenAI, alleging the company scanned their books into AI training databases without permission, an infringement of the authors' copyrights (Alter, 2023). Further, composition has also productively attended to ecological, environmental, and climate issues (Owens, 2001; Weisser & Dobrin, 2012). Such work bears renewed relevance given GAI's current environmental impact (Saenko, 2023).

Prior to recent composition scholarship on GAI, composition pedagogy theorists have attended to the material tools impacting writing processes and production. In 1999, Cynthia Selfe called on composition studies professionals "to understand and make sense of, *to pay attention to*, how technology is now inextricably linked to literacy and literacy education" (p. 413; *her emphasis*). Dennis Baron (2000) offered a historical rationale for this paying attention to technology:

> The computer, the latest development in writing technology, promises, or threatens, to change literacy practices for better or worse, depending on your point of view. For many of us, the computer revolution came long ago, and it has left its mark on the way we do things with words. We take word processing as a given. We don't have typewriters in our offices anymore, or pencil sharpeners.

Much as Baron wrote of computers at the turn of the 21st century, GAI presents as the newest step in a long line of writing technologies. Thus, Baron's historicizing perspective and Selfe's call remain relevant as GAI presents yet another link between technology, literacy, and literacy education.[3]

The next sections in this chapter present overviews of various composition pedagogies and how those pedagogies might exist alongside the use of GAI. Each of these pedagogical emphases lends perspective on GAI, whether in considering the technology or using it in learning contexts. Although it may be unexpected, the next sections do not address digital pedagogy, per se. As Baron notes, computers are a given in our contemporary composing processes, thus various composition pedagogies have already been used with computers in the digital era and can likewise lend productive application to GAI composing.

These different pedagogical discussions identify multiple assignment applications, as well as how different pedagogical stances might further inform GAI instruction. To be clear, the following sections do not present a comprehensive list of *all* possible pedagogies that could support writing instruction during the GAI turn, nor an exhaustive consideration of how these particular pedagogies can support writing instruction that accounts for GAI. This overview of composition pedagogies should be seen as a starting point for consideration and future research.

Regardless of the composition pedagogical strategy employed, this chapter posits that writing instruction and human instructors delivering purposeful teaching remain irreplaceable in higher education. As the MLA-CCCC joint task force notes (2023), writing helps students develop critical thinking, composing, process knowledge, and metacognition. Content knowledge—the subject matter studied and assessed for learning—is necessary to determine whether the GAI is outputting facts and content with accuracy or simply statistically likely phrases, which may offer no bearing upon truth or reality (a phenomenon AI researchers call a "hallucination") (Mollick & Mollick, 2023). For that reason, GAI users should review and revise GAI output as needed, an intervention that instructors should address.

Process and Post-Process Pedagogy

Process pedagogy emphasizes the composing processes—including critical thinking, research, drafting, revising, and metacognition—over the creation of a final product of polished prose, although there is considerable variation in process pedagogy (Anson, 2014). Process pedagogy emerged as a reaction to teaching methods that focused on students being presented with model writing, lectures on prescriptive grammar, mechanics, and style, and assignment prompts that students drafted outside class time. In 1972, Donald Murray clearly articulated a pedagogical recommendation in his article, "Teach Writing as a Process, Not Product." He wrote, "When we teach composition, we are not teaching a product, we are teaching a process" (p. 11). Murray emphasized a stage model for writing involving prewriting (where 85% of a writer's time should be spent), writing, and rewriting.

Researchers including Nancy Sommers (1980), Sondra Perl (1979), and Muriel Harris (1978, 1989) complicated this linear stage model of the writing process by noting the ways in which writers do not actually move neatly through stages. Instead, writers often combine invention, drafting, and revising. Receiving feedback can send writers into sustained engagement with invention and drafting. Thus, process pedagogy responded by rejecting a single canonical view of writing processes and supporting non-linear and recursive composing processes and became known as post-process pedagogy. From the initial and subsequent revised approaches, classes designed using this pedagogy have supported significant attention dedicated to exploring different writing strategies, time for iteration, workshops, peer review, responding to frequent feedback, and revision.

It is this pedagogical iteration that can inform course approaches in an era of GAI when ChatGPT and other LLMs can generate the kinds of technically correct written products that conform to the expectations that preceded process pedagogy. For example, human composers might iterate on different prompts at different stages of the composing process (Lingard, 2023). Students might begin by querying GAI to perform brainstorming to generate topic ideas and overcome the blank page syndrome. Once they identify a topic, students could issue a command to prompt the GAI to generate questions the writer would answer to develop student-generated content. Other strategies might be prompting the GAI to identify arrangement strategies of models, to ask the GAI to identify organization strategies based on the student-generated content or *several* different reorganizations of the content. Students can additionally ask for feedback on this content throughout, for example, by inputting content and requesting the GAI make writing more concise, suggest alternate phrasing, new topic sentences, or linking sentences, or add transitions. These iterative steps of refinement align with writing process pedagogy.

Given the rise of GAI, S. Scott Graham (2023) has proposed a revised writing process model. Instead of steps like "draft," "organize," "(peer) review," and "revise," Graham *adds* to this model a mirrored set of steps accounting for AI: "prompt," "curate," "fact check," and "revise" in a "multidimensional recursive AI-assisted writing process" (p. 167). Graham notes that this model accounts for the kinds of research, fact-checking, and continued revision necessitated by rapidly produced GAI text.

Further elaborations to Graham's model would emphasize the importance of reflection and metacognitive commentary to support student engagement with process-oriented learning. Kathleen Blake Yancey (1998) defines reflection as an activity in which writers revise and refine, identify future applications, and incorporate specific texts in demonstration of their learning. Students could perform this step after GAI use by writing reflection essays and by using word processors to annotate specific sections of the writing.

Other GAI process strategies include having students revise a rudimentary GAI-generated draft by adding detail, verifying GAI-produced content and adding additional sources, merging multiple versions, and adjusting the style to better reflect the composer's voice. An alternate strategy would be for the writer to develop the first draft, then have GAI revise the work and provide explanations for each revision. Yet another strategy for engaging with process pedagogy and GAI would be for students to learn about and practice the writing process in non-GAI contexts and then perform a similar writing activity using GAI. Students could then compare the results. Such activities support GAI process engagement.

Using these or similar GAI integrations, instructors can guide students to deepen their writing process strategies at all levels by using the rapid generative capacity of GAI. Instructors might suggest, for example, that students direct a GAI to create 10 titles or 20 titles for a topic, then the student chooses the best title. Students might similarly generate five different outlines for a project so they can explore the variety of ways in which writing might be organized. With GAI, students could create five different introductions and five different conclusions, then choose the elements that the student deems most effective. The students could then perform a kind of "cut-and-paste" revision previously implemented in the paper composing era.

To support and enable students to reflect on their GAI composing processes, instructors can request students submit their revised drafts, chat histories, and other documentation of their drafting processes. Instructors can direct students to comment on and annotate their personal revisions and additionally reflect on their composing processes, noting what text the GAI suggested that they kept and what they rejected and why.

In these ways and more, this GAI process pedagogy can support students' deepened knowledge of the writing process in the GAI era.

Collaborative Pedagogy

Collaborative writing pedagogies focus on how writing is produced by more than a single, isolated author. This pedagogical approach acknowledges how multiple individuals contribute to a written product, whether through collaborative learning (Bruffee, 1984), authorship (Ede & Lunsford, 2001), or within team authorship (Lunsford & Ede, 1986; Wolfe, 2010). Sheryl Fontaine and Susan Hunter (2006) acknowledge all writing is not collaborative but contend that "collaboration is at the heart of all writing" (p. 11). Collaborative pedagogy operates from a focus on how language and knowledge-making are social and that writers are influenced by others—whether as sources, audiences, reviewers, and more.

In some ways, collaborative pedagogy incorporates aspects of process pedagogy in getting feedback, such as through peer review or to aid invention and revision, although many of these activities focus on an individual writer *receiving* collaborative support. Lowry et al. (2004) recognize a variety of collaborative composing models: single author writing group-determined content; sequential single authoring of different sections in a document; parallel writing involving either individuals contributing different sections of a document or serving in different roles (author, editor, or reviewer), and reactive writing, in which writers perform various tasks in response to other team members' writing.

GAI may similarly participate in this digital collaboration ecology. As suggested by the name "ChatGPT," many GAI tools generate content by responding to user prompts issued either as questions or commands and thus are deemed "chatbots." Instructors and writers might approach GAI through a cooperative stance, by treating GAI as a "collaborator" (Laquintano et al., 2023). Such interactions might fit parallel team writing models in which the GAI acts alternately as author, editor, and/or reviewer in Lowry et al.'s model. As previously noted, GAI, which creates statistically likely strings of text, may produce seemingly factual content but may be misleading or even inaccurate. For that reason, GAI users should review and revise the written output as needed. Such review practices support a kind of information literacy crucial when working with content—whether human- or GAI-created.

Instructors who wish to retain more traditional collaborative assignments while working with GAI might have students individually or jointly create content using AI, then verify and revise that content, and reflect on what they learned and how they might apply, alter, or avoid these strategies in the future. Although not all GAI tools offer a shared environment supporting multiple individuals accessing the same session, writers might work in groups through these various processes using author, editor, and/or reviewer roles.

Another collaborative assignment could explore how GAI can help writers collaboratively author. Students would begin by developing a writing style guide to speak for the whole group, then each student could individually create various documents by creating prompts specifying the style guide's settings on voice, tone, style, and organization. Subsequently, students could compare the documents that they've individually created to consider how best to create writing style guidelines and prompts that could enable GAI to generate content on behalf of an organization, business, or other group.

In a GAI collaborative pedagogy model, assignments involve collaborating with a digital interlocutor who helps hone ideas, offers organizational and stylistic strategies, provides and implements feedback at directed levels, and iteratively refines content. Additionally, collaborative pedagogy might guide instructor-led conversations about how Large Language Models have been created using a compilation of texts from many authors, raising questions about whether GAI-produced texts qualify as collaboratively authored and the ethical implications of this. While collaborative pedagogy traditionally focused on co-creation among people, various human-GAI collaborations might reflect how writers could be asked to co-write material in the future, such as in the workplace.

Genre

Genre pedagogies draw from Carolyn Miller's (1984) definition of rhetorical genres as "typified rhetorical actions based in recurrent situations" (p. 159), meaning that genres arise and become reified because writers make similar choices in response to those made by other writers in comparable situations. These genre expectations aid both writers and readers, who come to recognize the situations and outcomes the writing endeavors to achieve.

Amy J. Devitt (2014) identifies three different genre pedagogies: teaching specific genres, teaching awareness of genres, and teaching genre criticism. The first approach articulates the formal qualities of genres, less as rules and more as understanding recurrent patterns in particular settings, ideally within meaningful settings. Genre awareness instruction focuses on identifying not just common textual characteristics but social contexts and ideological impacts. Finally, genre criticism enables students to acquire genre knowledge and to understand how they can apply genre knowledge and modify genres to respond to new situations in the future. Devitt recommends genre pedagogy implementations incorporate all three approaches: teaching specific genres, awareness, and criticism.

GAI genre pedagogy can leverage rapid GAI textual output to explore accelerated genre experimentation. Students might begin by directing GAI to produce multiple examples of genres. For example, in a business or professional communication course, students might generate various workplace letters: sales, offers, acknowledgments, fundraising, introduction, etc. Because GAI can rapidly produce numerous samples for students to work with, students can experiment with generating examples adopting different tones and styles. Students might explore how businesses and others (Swales, 1990) often use common moves and templates and consider how they might be expected to compose similarly for the workplace, and how workplace values, which differ from academic ethics, for textual production might, or might not, align with GAI (Anson, 2011, 2022).

Other genre class activities might be to generate an initial AI draft, and then have students revise the piece for different genres, audiences, and purposes. Students might repurpose researched content not just for different audiences but also for different genres. For example, they might explore the GAI-informed creation of an article, a children's storybook, a blog post, a video script, and/or a pamphlet. Students can then critically analyze these various products and reflect on the composing process.

Many GAI tools, like ChatGPT, emulate conversational interactions with users asking questions or issuing commands and the GAI responding not just with content but also content presented in a conversational tone. Thus, these GAI tools implicitly demonstrate the genre of a conversation. Class discussion could engage in exploration of why GAIs use that format. In another GAI genre criticism assignment, students might examine genre models and compare them with the output produced by GAI to analyze the GAI's formulaic assumptions.

As with other approaches, GAI genre pedagogy can incorporate aspects of other pedagogies. Similar to collaborative pedagogy, GAI genre pedagogy can attend to writing processes and process pedagogy, particularly attending to experimenting, altering, and innovating upon GAI genre content. Much as all GAI pedagogy should, GAI genre pedagogy can direct critical attention to GAI-produced text and the need for humans with sufficient knowledge and proficiency to review content before its publication. All these strategies can support GAI genre critical literacy.

Second Language and Multilingual Writing

Second language and multilingual pedagogy focuses on supporting writers who are writing in languages other than their first to support all writers in developing greater composing and linguistic knowledge, written proficiency, and academic literacy. Second language (L2) writers have become an "integral part of writing courses and programs" (CCCC, 2020). Given this population, Paul Kei Matsuda and Matthew J. Hammill (2014) recommend incorporating L2 approaches into *all* classes. Although this overview cannot encapsulate the richness of this pedagogical approach, briefly L2 pedagogy focuses on linguistic and cultural resources multilingual speakers possess, different cultural practices around text incorporation, how assignment designs should acknowledge that not all students have similar cultural experiences to apply, the potential need for explicit grammar instruction, and the recognition of the complexity and incremental nature of language acquisition, among other considerations.

As with previously discussed pedagogies, this pedagogy can incorporate elements of other teaching approaches. Not only might classes foster writing processes, but these classes might also attend to particular genres (Hyland, 2004). Much as collaboration pedagogy can inform GAI writing process discussions, L2/multilingual pedagogy might attend to larger conversations about social and cultural expectations. For example, classes might discuss how much academic publishing requires English publication and how GAI may help academic writers whose first language is not English share their research (*Nature*, 2023). Not only might that support greater equity, but knowledge may advance because more researchers can share their findings. Classes might draw on L2 students' L1 expertise by critiquing how AI tools translate documents and create text summaries.

A concern, however, is that a GAI may have embedded biases, depending on the tool's data sources (Laquintano et al., 2023). Many GAI tools are less fluent in non-English languages. Additionally, those tools orient toward particular kinds of English usage, which may compel certain "norms" of "standard" English rather than support linguistic diversity. Supposed GAI detectors, which allegedly identify text that has been produced by GAI tools, are unreliable, particularly when an author does not speak English as a first language, meaning that those who use these detectors may be reproducing bias. Compounding these concerns are the ways in which many commercial, proprietary GAI tools are "black-box" systems that lack transparency. Second language and multilingual pedagogy can lend to critiquing the assumptions in GAI and their causes.

Beyond class conversations to develop a kind of critical awareness of GAI usage, instructors can explore GAI from an L2/multilingual pedagogy standpoint. For example, instructors might encourage L2 writers to explore writing in both English and their first language, then to use a translation tool like DeepL to translate into English. Writers can then compare the two different versions and perhaps develop a synthesized third version. Other assignments can critique and reflect on bilingual text production (Xu, 2024).

Instructors can also help all students, L2 and L1, develop effective prompts to guide a GAI into providing real-time writing feedback. For example, instructors might guide students who are willing to share their writing with ChatGPT to create prompts to ask, for example, ChatGPT to analyze their writing for the most common usage or style issues and then to ask ChatGPT to provide five examples demonstrating correct usage and to link to resources related to the usage. As with previous pedagogy examples, instructors will need to emphasize the importance of validating GAI-created information. Given the process-oriented nature of this example, this illustration demonstrates how instructors may apply multiple pedagogical approaches in support of GAI composing literacy for academic and workplace purposes.

Disability Studies

Disability studies pedagogy focuses on creating inclusive learning environments for students and to accommodate diverse learning needs. Critiquing cultural focus on disability in terms of deficit or medical models, disability pedagogy aims to promote accessibility, equity, and social justice in higher education by challenging ableist assumptions and practices. In their introduction to *Disability and the Teaching of Writing*, Cynthia Lewiecki-Wilson and Brenda Jo Brueggemann (2008) explain that disability studies approaches involve

> thinking carefully about language and its effects, to understand the role of the body in learning and writing, to view bodies and minds as inherently and wonderfully divergent, to consider issues of access and exclusion in policies and in the environment, and to reengage with theories of difference and diversity.
>
> *(p. 1)*

Disability studies-informed classes are designed inclusively with attention to accessibility, may include disability-themed content, and larger considerations of disability, ableism, stigma, equality, culture, and more, particularly in combination with intersectional approaches, and involve continued teaching reflection.

A GAI disability studies pedagogy might adopt reflective considerations such as those raised by Ella Browning (2014) for composition classes prior to the contemporary GAI era. For example, do technologies exclude or make assumptions about users' abilities? Do classroom activities privilege ablebodiedness or attend to multiple bodies and ways of learning? Disability studies-informed class conversations around the bodily diversity and embodied nature of composing can apply helpful perspectives to the way GAI machines seem to compose without humans. Addressing GAI in composition studies, Courtney Stanton (2023) applies a disability studies perspective to critique how GAI "carry the potential to oversimplify writing to a mere mechanical task, an impediment to be addressed." Stanton uses this approach to center composition and to invite consideration between "what AI can/will and cannot/will not accomplish."

Disability studies further invite students to consider and investigate GAI accessibility. As Christina V. Cedillo (2018) notes, recognizing and foregrounding intersectional engagement with bodily diversity means that "students learn to compose for accessibility and inclusivity." Class conversation can provide opportunities for students to learn about accessibility and to critique the accessibility of different GAI tools and their output. Class activities might guide students to explore whether AI-generated content includes accessible design features, such as text headings, and whether visuals include alt text. Students might critique the quality of that accessibility and also practice using the tools to compose their own accessible content. Additional activities might include explorations of how GAI tools are accessible—or inaccessible—to assistive technologies, such as screen readers or voice interfaces. Such work expands students' accessibility proficiency, whether for human- or GAI-composed content.

Adopting disability studies pedagogy might also mean incorporating content that supports investigating how GAI could support broader accessibility. For example, the Be My Eyes tool uses OpenAI's visual recognition to point a camera at a scene, such as a refrigerator, building, sign, or street, and get information interpreting the camera's visual input.[4] If the user points the camera inside a refrigerator's interior, the app might name the refrigerator's contents, then the user could ask the tool for a recipe using the identified contents (OpenAI, 2023). Another disability studies discussion could engage the under-representation of individuals with disabilities in visual images, television, and other media, and therefore may not be present in the datasets used to train GAI models. These strategies are just a few ways that disability studies pedagogy can inform processes and discussions of GAI composing.

Other Composition Pedagogies

As noted at the beginning of this chapter, the teaching overviews and applications provided here are just a few of the ways different composition pedagogies may inform the GAI era. Other pedagogical theories can certainly respond to GAI composition. For example, multi-modal pedagogy focuses on understanding how communication uses multiple modes: linguistic, audio, visual, spatial, gestural, and multimodal, which is the combination of modes (New London Group, 1996). As noted in this chapter's introduction, GAI can compose for each of those modes, even to make websites (Eyman, 2023). While multimodality existed prior to digital technology, digital composing led to new ways of thinking about multimodality. GAI may likewise bring fresh perspectives on composing and literacy, including composing with and for code (Vee, 2013). Other pedagogies may yield additional approaches for GAI.

However, while many pedagogies may support GAI, this chapter is not intended to be an argument for either mandating the use of GAI in all writing situations or all writing instruction. While multiple composition pedagogies may prove compatible, GAI may not fit as easily with certain approaches to composition pedagogy. Expressive pedagogy, which aims to "foster a writer's aesthetic, cognitive, and moral development," including to the point of insisting upon "a sense of writer presence" even in research-based writing (Burnham, 2001, p. 19), may not align as comfortably with GAI.

Similarly, WAC pedagogy integrates writing instruction beyond introductory, general education composition courses and departments of English and writing. WAC models involve writing instruction integrated into all courses across the curriculum using the genres appropriate to the discipline. Within WAC, the writing to learn (WTL) model de-emphasizes writing as a transactional task and emphasizes writing as an opportunity to learn or confirm learning. Syrene Forsman (1985) described this approach as "Writing to Learn Means Learning to Think." McLeod and Miraglia (2001) similarly emphasize WAC as developing not just communication skills, but critical thinking and problem-solving. Forsman provides a WTL example of a journal assignment, in which students use writing to work out new concepts and connections related to their learning.

In 2023, the Association for Writing across the Curriculum (AWAC) Executive Committee issued a statement indicating that the intellectual activity of WTL is crucial to "cognitive and social development of learners and writers. This vital activity cannot be replaced by AI language generators." OpenAI researchers have noted that GAI may be able to automate programming and writing tasks, but not critical thinking (Eloundou et al., 2023). The AWAC statement also poses questions about future research. Researchers might investigate whether students could prompt GAI to ask them questions that they could respond to in order to direct and record their learning in a GAI log, not dissimilar to Forsman's journal assignment. More research is needed.

This chapter advocates that instructors and writers will need to negotiate their own approaches and identities to best suit their purposes and contexts. Research will need to investigate how best to support composing processes in the GAI turn. That research will need to account for the ways in which each GAI tool is different, how GAI continues to change, the way GAIs produce unpredictable results, how GAI may be customizable, and more.

Conclusion

This chapter has aimed to demonstrate how various composition pedagogy theories may support writing curricula and assignment design in the GAI era by recognizing writing as inseparable from technology and adjusting each pedagogical approach to account for GAI. The ability to adapt these different pedagogies demonstrates that GAI should not be an end to writing instruction or assignments. Writing instruction has persisted and adapted to such technological innovations as computers and word processors, spelling and grammar checkers, Wikipedia, the Internet, and even erasers. As previously noted, this exploration has not been an exhaustive exploration of all possible composition theories and strategies for integrating or responding to GAI writing. Instead, this chapter suggests possible assignment interventions and how they can align with existing pedagogies.

Again, this chapter does not seek to demonstrate that any specific pedagogy, whether named in this chapter or not, is better suited for teaching in this era. Instead, instructors should develop authentic approaches for their teacherly identities and local contexts, perhaps employing overlapping pedagogical approaches. To be clear: There is no one right composition pedagogy for all instructors for all occasions. Even the suggested considerations in this chapter need to be modified for different instructors, classes, and settings. Nevertheless, these options may provide a starting point for teaching writing during the GAI era.

While these final paragraphs appear under a heading labeled "Conclusion," GAI will continue to change and therefore pedagogies will continue to respond, taking into account future teaching, learning, and writing research and changing technologies. Given the rapid rate of change in generative text tools—which are relatively new technologies, research will need to continue to examine how writers effectively adjust their approaches and how instructors can best support students in writing and learning composing strategies during ongoing technological change. This chapter has claimed that such research need not start from a vacuum but can instead draw on the long history of scholarship and research into writing practices and education.

Notes

1 All names were current as of the writing of this chapter, although it is worth noting that new tools are constantly arising, and some tools may change names. Please note that although this chapter mentions various GAI tools, it does not endorse any specific product.
2 For example, in the United States the November 4, 2024 Privacy Policy of ChatGPT notes collection of user's usage, device, and potentially location data and that the contents of any messages may be collected (OpenAI, 2024).
3 Composition studies-related professional organizations, such as the CCCC, MLA, and AWAC, have issued statements about GAI.
4 I am grateful to my student Andrea Darmawan for sharing with me her knowledge of Be My Eyes.

References

Alter, A. (2023, September 20). Franzen, Grisham and other prominent authors sue OpenAI. *The New York Times.* https://www.nytimes.com/2023/09/20/books/authors-openai-lawsuit-chatgpt-copyright.html

Amidon, T. R., Hutchinson, L., Herrington, T. K., & Reyman, J. (2019). Copyright, content, & control: Student authorship across educational technology platforms. *Kairos: A Journal of Rhetoric, Technology, and Pedagogy, 24*(1). https://kairos.technorhetoric.net/24.1/topoi/amidon-et-al/turnitin.html

Anson, C. M. (2011). Fraudulent practices: Academic misrepresentations of plagiarism in the name of good pedagogy. *Composition Studies, 39*(2), 29–43.

Anson, C. M. (2014). Process pedagogy and its legacy. In G. Tate, A. T. Rupiper, K. Schick, & H. B. Hessler (Eds.), *A guide to composition pedagogies,* 2nd ed. (pp. 212–230). Oxford University Press.

Anson, C. M. (2022). AI-based text generation and the social construction of "fraudulent authorship": A revisitation. *Composition Studies, 50*(1), 37–179.

Artman, M., Frisicaro-Pawlowski, E. & Monge, R. (2010). Not just one shot: Extending the dialogue about information literacy in composition classes. *Composition Studies, 38*(2), 93–110.

AWAC Executive Committee. (2023, January 30). Statement on artificial intelligence writing tools in writing across the curriculum settings. https://wacassociation.org/resource/statement-on-ai-writing-tools-in-wac/

Baron, D. (2000). From pencils to pixels: The stages of literacy technology. https://debaron.web.illinois.edu/essays/pencils.htm

Bowen, J. A., & Watson, C. E. (2024). *Teaching with AI: A practical guide to a new era of human learning.* Johns Hopkins University Press.

Browning, E. R. (2014). Disability studies in the composition classroom. *Composition Studies, 42*(2), 96–117.

Bruffee, K. A. (1984). Collaborative learning and the "conversation of mankind". *College English, 46*(7), 635–652.

Burnham, C. (2001). Expressive pedagogy: Practice/theory, theory/practice. In G. Tate, A. Rupiper, & K. Schick (Eds.), *A guide to composition pedagogies*, 1st ed. (pp. 19–35). Oxford University Press.

Cedillo, C. V. (2018). What does it mean to move?: Race, disability, and critical embodiment pedagogy. *Composition Forum, 39*. https://compositionforum.com/issue/39/to-move.php

Conference on College Composition and Communication. (2020, May). CCCC statement on second language writing and multilingual writers. https://cccc.ncte.org/cccc/resources/positions/secondlangwriting

Devitt, A. J. (2014). Genre. In G. Tate, A. T. Rupiper, K. Schick, & H. B. Hessler (Eds.), *A guide to composition pedagogies*, 2nd ed. (pp. 146–162). Oxford University Press.

Duin, A. H., & Pedersen, I. (2021). *Writing futures: Collaborative, algorithmic, autonomous.* Springer.

Ede, L., & Lunsford, A. A. (2001). Collaboration and concepts of authorship. *PMLA, 116*(2), 354–369.

Eloundou, T., Manning, S., Mishkin, P., & Rock, D. (2023, August 22). GPTs are GPTs: An early look at the labor market impact potential of large language models. https://arxiv.org/pdf/2303.10130.pdf

Eyman, D., & ChatGPT. (2023). Making a webtext with ChatGPT. *Kairos: A Journal of Rhetoric, Technology, and Pedagogy, 28*(1). https://kairos.technorhetoric.net/28.1/disputatio/eyman-chatgpt/index.html

Fontaine, S. I., & Hunter, S. M. (2006). *Collaborative writing in composition studies.* Thomson Higher Education.

Forsman, S. (1985). Writing to learn means learning to think. In A. R. Gere (Ed.), *Roots in the sawdust: Writing to learn across the disciplines* (pp. 162–174). National Council of Teachers of English.

Fyfe, P. (2022). How to cheat on your final paper: Assigning AI for student writing. *AI & Society, 38*(4), 1395–1405.

Graham, S. S. (2023). Post-process but not post-writing: Large language models and a future for composition pedagogy. *Composition Studies, 51*(1), 162–168.

Haas, C. (1996). *Writing technology: Studies on the materiality of literacy.* Routledge.

Harris, M. (1978). Evaluation: The process for revision. *Journal of Basic Writing, 1*(4), 82–90.

Harris, M. (1989). Composing behaviors of one-and multi-draft writers. *College English, 51*(2), 174–191.

Hart-Davidson, W. (2018). Writing with robots and other curiosities of the age of machine rhetorics. In J. Alexander, & J. Rhodes (Eds.), *The Routledge handbook of digital writing and rhetoric* (pp. 248–255). Routledge.

Herman, D. (2022, December 9). The end of high-school English. *The Atlantic.* https://www.theatlantic.com/technology/archive/2022/12/openai-chatgpt-writing-high-school-english-essay/672412

Howard, R. M. (1992). A plagiarism pentimento. *Journal of Teaching Writing, 11*(2), 233–45.

Howard, R. M. (1995). Plagiarisms, authorships, and the academic death penalty. *College English, 57*(7), 788–806.

Hurlbert, C. M., & Totten, S. (Eds.). (1992). *Social issues in the English classroom.* National Council of Teachers of English.

Hyland, K. (2004). *Genre and second language writing.* University of Michigan Press.

Kruse, O., Rapp, C., Anson, C. M., Benetos, K., Cotos, E., Devitt, A., & Shibani, A. (2023). *Digital writing technologies in higher education: Theory, research, and practice.* Springer Nature.

Laquintano, T., Schnitzler, C. & Vee, A. (2023). Introduction to teaching with text generation technologies. In A. Vee, T. Laquintano, & C. Schnitzler (Eds.), *TextGenEd: Teaching with text generation technologies*. The WAC Clearinghouse. https://doi.org/10.37514/TWR-J.2023.1.1.02

Lewiecki-Wilson, C., & Brueggemann, B. J. (Eds.) (2008). *Disability and the teaching of writing*. Bedford/St. Martin's.

Lingard, L. (2023). Writing with ChatGPT: An illustration of its capacity, limitations & implications for academic writers. *Perspectives on Medical Education, 12*(1), 261–270. https://doi.org/10.5334/pme.1072

Lowry, P. B., Curtis, A., & Lowry, M. R. (2004). Building a taxonomy and nomenclature of collaborative writing to improve interdisciplinary research and practice. *The Journal of Business Communication, 41*(1), 66–99.

Lunsford, A., & Ede, L. (1986). Why write… together: A research update. *Rhetoric Review, 5*(1), 71–81.

Marche, S. (2022, December 6). The college essay is dead. *The Atlantic*. www.the-atlantic.com/technology/archive/2022/12/chatgpt-ai-writing-college-student-essays/672371/

Matsuda, P. K. & Hammill, M. J. (2014). Second language writing. In G. Tate, A. T. Rupiper, K. Schick, & H. B. Hessler (Eds.), *A guide to composition pedagogies*, 2nd ed. (pp. 266–282). Oxford University Press.

McComiskey, B. (2000). *Teaching composition as a social process*. Utah State University Press.

McKee, H. A., & Porter, J. E. (2022, July). Team roles & rhetorical intelligence in human-machine writing. In *2022 IEEE international professional communication conference (ProComm)* (pp. 384–391). IEEE.

McLeod, S. H. & Miraglia, E. (2001). Writing across the curriculum in a time of change. In S. H. McLeod, E. Miraglia, M. Soven, & C. Thaiss (Eds.), *WAC for the new millennium: Strategies for continuing Writing-Across-the-Curriculum programs* (pp. 1–27). National Council of Teachers of English.

Miller, C. R. (1984). Genre as social action. *Quarterly Journal of Speech, 70*(2), 151–167.

Mills, K. (2010). A review of the "digital turn" in the New Literacy Studies. *Review of Educational Research, 80*(2), 246–271

MLA-CCCC Joint Task Force on Writing and AI. (2023, July). Working paper 1: Overview of the issues, statement of principles, and recommendations. https://hcommons.org/app/uploads/sites/1003160/2023/07/MLA-CCCC-Joint-Task-Force-on-Writing-and-AI-Working-Paper-1.pdf

Mollick, E. R. & Mollick, L. (2023, March 17). Using AI to implement effective teaching strategies in classrooms: Five strategies, including prompts. The Wharton School Research Paper. https://doi.org/10.2139/ssrn.4391243

Murray, D. (1972, November). Teach writing as a process not product. *The Leaflet, 71*, 11–14.

Nature. (2023, September 27). AI will transform science—now researchers must tame it. https://www.nature.com/articles/d41586-023-02988-6

New London Group. (1996). A pedagogy of multiliteracies: Designing social futures. *Harvard Educational Review, 66*(1), 60–92.

Ong, Walter J. (1982). *Orality and literacy*. Methuen.

OpenAI. (2023, March 14). OpenAI customer story: Be My Eyes. https://openai.com/customer-stories/be-my-eyes

OpenAI. (2024, November 4). Privacy policy. https://openai.com/policies/row-privacy-policy/

Owens, D. (2001). *Composition and sustainability: Teaching for a threatened generation*. National Council of Teachers of English.

Perl, S. (1979). The composing processes of unskilled college writers. *Research in the Teaching of English, 13*(4), 317–336.

Ritter, K. & Matsuda, P. K. (2012). Introduction: How did we get here? In K. Ritter & P. K. Matsuda (Eds.), *Exploring composition studies: Sites, issues, perspectives* (pp. 1–10). University Press of Colorado.

Rudolph, J., Tan, S., & Tan, S. (2023). ChatGPT: Bullshit spewer or the end of traditional assessments in higher education? *Journal of Applied Learning and Teaching, 6*(1), 342–363.

Saenko, K. (2023, May 25). A computer scientist breaks down generative AI's hefty carbon footprint. *Scientific American*. https://www.scientificamerican.com/article/a-computer-scientist-breaks-down-generative-ais-hefty-carbon-footprint/

Schatt, J. (2022, September 14). Will artificial intelligence kill college writing? *The Chronicle of Higher Education*. https://www.chronicle.com/article/will-artificial-intelligence-kill-college-writing

Selfe, C. L. (1999). Technology and literacy: A story about the perils of not paying attention. *College Composition and Communication, 50*(3), 411–436.

Sommers, N. (1980). Revision strategies of student writers and experienced adult writers. *College Composition and Communication, 31*(4), 378–388.

Southworth, J., Migliaccio, K., Glover, J., Reed, D., McCarty, C., Brendemuhl, J., & Thomas, A. (2023). Developing a model for AI Across the curriculum: Transforming the higher education landscape via innovation in AI literacy. *Computers and Education: Artificial Intelligence, 4,* 100127.

Stanton, C. (2023). A dis-facilitated call for more writing studies in the new AI landscape; or, finding our place among the chatbots. *Composition Studies, 51*(1), 182–220.

Sullivan, P. A. & Qualley, D. J. (Eds.). (1994). *Pedagogy in the age of politics: Writing and reading (In) the academy.* National Council of Teachers of English.

Swales, John. (1990). *Genre analysis: English in academic and research settings.* Cambridge University Press.

Taggart, A. R., Schick, K., & Hessler, H. B. (2014). What is composition pedagogy? An introduction. In G. Tate, A. R. Taggart, K. Schick, & H. B. Hessler (Eds.), *A guide to composition pedagogies,* 2nd ed. Oxford University Press.

Veach, G. (Ed.). (2018). *Teaching information literacy and writing studies: Volume 1, first-year composition courses.* Purdue University Press. https://doi.org/10.2307/j.ctv15wxpj8

Vee, A. (2013). Understanding computer programming as a literacy. *Literacy in Composition Studies, 1*(2), 42–64.

Vee, A., Laquintano, T., & Schnitzler, C. (Eds.). (2023). *TextGenEd: Teaching with text generation technologies.* The WAC Clearinghouse. https://doi.org/10.37514/TWR-J.2023.1.1.02

Weisser, C. R., & Dobrin, S. I. (Eds.). (2012). *Ecocomposition: Theoretical and pedagogical approaches.* SUNY Press.

Wolfe, J. (2010). *Team writing.* Bedford/St. Martin's.

Xu, W. (2024). Bilingual genre redesign with AI. In A. Vee, T. Laquintano, & C. Schnitzler (Eds.), *TextGenEd: Teaching with text generation technologies.* The WAC Clearinghouse. https://doi.org/10.37514/TWR-J.2023.1.1.02

Yancey, K. B. (1998). *Reflection in the writing classroom.* Utah State University Press.

Yeadon, W., Inyang, O. O., Mizouri, A., Peach, A., & Testrow, C. P. (2023). The death of the short-form physics essay in the coming AI revolution. *Physics Education, 58*(3), 035027.

4

WHOSE WORDS ARE THEY?

Authorship in the Age of Artificial Intelligence

Kimberly Vinall and Emily Hellmich

Introduction

It was about eight years ago that Kimberly found herself in what is, to many language instructors, a familiar situation: she encountered the use of a rather noteworthy construction in an assignment written by a first-semester Spanish learner: "se nos uniría" (it would unite us). Convinced of the learner's inability to accurately produce a reflexive conditional verb with an object pronoun and reflecting on the academic honesty statement in the syllabus that equated machine translation (MT) use to plagiarism, Kimberly invited the learner to her office. In order to deemphasize questions of morality and punitive measures in favor of creating a learning opportunity, Kimberly pointed out that, at a novice proficiency level, it was impossible for her to have produced these words. Furthermore, Kimberly added, using MT in this way would not help her to actually learn the language.

In response, the learner freely admitted to having used Google Translate, explaining that she had input her English words and copied and pasted the translation; however, the learner's reply to the insinuation that she had done something wrong was one of disbelief, insisting "but, these are my words." Furthermore, the learner continued, how could she have done something wrong if she had learned what she considered to be a "sophisticated" vocabulary word?

At the heart of this idea that words and texts can be owned is the concept of authorship. Once tied to notions of an individual's originality, i.e., the production of a text imbued with the subject's creativity and imagination, the concept of authorship's codification into law and later industrialization at the turn of the 20th century as a mass-produced commodity (Latham, 2019) has given rise to conflicting historical constructions, whose faultlines have been further exacerbated in the digital age. Indeed, Kimberly was confronted with new manifestations of these faultlines in her conversation with this learner in the context of the use of machine translation to produce a text in a Spanish classroom: Were they the learners' words or not? Is it true of all translation that words cease being one's own once translated or is it, in this case, attributable to the medium and/or to the specific context of an assignment written for a

DOI: 10.4324/9781003426936-6

language classroom? If they were not the learners' words, did Google Translate "own" them? Why is the ownership of words so intricately tied to beliefs about language learning? How are responses to these questions being challenged anew in an age of AI?

Artificial Intelligence, Machine Translation, and This Chapter

AI technologies that are built on and "produce" language bring into sharp relief questions of authorship. For instance, since its debut in late 2022, generative AI tools such as ChatGPT have spurred similar and new questions related to the ownership of not only words but also ideas themselves. Recent debates around questions of educational integrity, attribution, and intellectual property rights have led to calls to more closely examine and even transform academic practices themselves (see, for example, Bozkurt, 2024; Wise et al., 2024).

The same is true for MT, tools that translate text from one language to another using machine or computer software (Liu & Zhang, 2015). While MT has always been considered a form of AI, this moniker has developed new meaning with the increased performance capabilities of neural network-based MT systems (Poibeau, 2017; Wu et al., 2016). Indeed, MT tools have raised concerns in language education for over a decade, providing a relevant foundation for examining similar authorship issues and changes brought about by today's generative AI.

Early research on MT in language learning focused on perceptions of its acceptability and ethicality. For example, a 2013 study conducted by Clifford and colleagues demonstrated that 77% of instructors disapproved of student use of MT in writing, and of these 42% considered it cheating. Reflecting these beliefs, many instructors, as demonstrated in the opening anecdote, have instituted complete or partial bans on its use, advocating for a policy of using one's "own words," as this is considered the best way to support authentic learning (Hellmich & Vinall, 2021). While concerns about ethicality remain, as do many of these bans, more recent research has demonstrated shifting perspectives, including calls for the integration of MT tools with the belief that they may be able to support L2 learning (Hellmich & Vinall, 2021; Jolley & Maimone, 2015; Vinall & Hellmich, 2021) in addition to helping learners produce better quality writing (Fredholm, 2019; Kol et al., 2018) and develop metalinguistic awareness (Thue Vold, 2018). Yet, despite the calls to explore these potentials of MT tools, many of the tensions that undergird beliefs about MT use in relationship to authorship remain unexamined.

In this chapter, we center the question "whose words are they?" in these broader conversations around the use of MT in language learning. We do so to explore and identify how faultlines between historically conflicting understandings of authorship are challenged or reinforced by MT platforms and their use in language classrooms. First, we explore the construction of the author, from birth to death, from two predominant Western theoretical perspectives: the modern and the postmodern. We then trace these conflicting notions of textual ownership and authorship and their relevance across three interconnected domains – translation studies, MT, and language learning – in order to identify if and how these faultlines emerge in these contexts and/or if new ones arise. The potential benefits of identifying these faultlines and understanding their implications extend beyond MT to encompass generative AI tools, and other emerging technologies, to fully explore their potential and navigate their critical use.

While this chapter is primarily a conceptual exploration, we draw on our long-term research project on language learning and MT to illustrate these faultlines as they are currently playing out in language education today. More specifically, we reference data from two phases of this project. The first phase explored university-level language instructors' perceptions of MT in relation to acceptability, student use and motivation, and its impact on the language teaching profession through a large-scale qualitative survey (n = 165) and follow-up focal interviews (n = 11) (Vinall & Hellmich, 2021; Hellmich & Vinall, 2021). Closed-ended survey questions were analyzed using descriptive statistics; open-ended questions and interviews were analyzed using open, inductive coding. The second phase examined how university language learners use MT and other online resources when completing writing tasks in the L2 (Hellmich, 2021; Hellmich & Vinall, 2023; Vinall et al., 2023). For this phase, 74 university-level learners of French, Spanish, and Mandarin in the United States completed a short writing task in the target language while their screens were observed and recorded, which was followed by a stimulated recall (Bowles, 2018; Gass & Mackey, 2016) and post-interviews to triangulate the data (Patton, 1990; Spradley, 1979). Data analysis relied on iterative and inductive coding (Saldaña, 2009); code categories focused on the actions that participants made as well as the different factors that influenced those actions.

Our aim in exploring these faultlines is to contribute to larger discussions about how to develop critical uses of MT and generative AI tools to support language learning, which we consider in the implications. Overall, the exploration reveals the limits of modernist assumptions of authorship and the potential contributions of a postmodern perspective to the development of critical approaches to AI tools to support language learning.

Theoretical Framing: How Is the Author Constructed?

This theoretical framing draws from Pennycook's (1996) exploration of the development of Western views of textual ownership, which he, in turn, draws from Kearney's (1988) genealogy of Western imagination. Whereas Pennycook applied these understandings to textbook plagiarism in university-level academic writing, we seek to expand this exploration into the digital domain, using MT and language learning as a use case in order to expand the work into generative AI technologies. Specifically, we highlight two dominant Western paradigms in relationship to the construction of the author: the modern and the postmodern.

The birth of the author can be traced to the Enlightenment when imagination ceased being the result of divine inspiration that relied on images to reproduce reality, a premodern perspective, and instead, imagination came to be viewed as a productive force that resides in the human subject (Kearney, 1988). This modernist notion of authorship is thus based on a humanist subject who engages in individual acts of creativity and meaning making that result in individual works of literature, history, or autobiography (Foucault, 1977/1984), or as Kearney (1988) elaborates: "the coming into being of the notion of 'author' constitutes the privileged moment of individualization in the history of ideas, knowledge, literature, philosophy, and the sciences" (p. 101). The development of printing technology extended this process of individualization to language, it "created a new sense of ownership of words" (Ong, 1982, p. 131). With this individualization of ideas and ownership of language came the development of legal notions of copyright and intellectual property rights because there is now an originating author, "an actual body that gave life to words" (Willinsky, 1990, p. 77). Plagiarism as it is understood today can be situated in this tradition: borrowing the words of others requires attribution, and the penalties for not doing so include not just the weight of a moral judgment but potential legal consequences.

The postmodern challenged the location of meaning as residing in the individual by proclaiming the death of the subject and, by extension, according to Barthes (1977), the death of the author. There is no longer an "I" but multiple subjectivities; meaning is no longer attached to authorial intent but resides in the interactions between text and context as discursive formations; subjects do not create language but are created by and in it; and words do not belong to us but are "filled with others' words" (Bakhtin, 1986/1936, p. 89). This perspective simultaneously breaks the link between an individual author and the notion of originality as expressed in text:

> A text is not a line of words releasing a single "theological" meaning (the "message of the Author-God") but a multi-dimensional space in which a variety of writings, none of them original, blend and clash. The text is a tissue of quotations drawn from the innumerable centres of culture.
>
> *(Barthes, 1977, p. 146)*

Defining plagiarism from this perspective is much more complicated: what does it mean to borrow the words of others if those words are themselves already borrowed?

From these modern and postmodern understandings of authorship, we highlight three faultlines that emerge across the domains of translation studies, MT, and language learning – domains that are directly implicated in understandings of authorship in L2 contexts today and have contributed uniquely and collectively to these faultlines.

The first faultline is where meaning(s) reside(s): is it in the author, as the originator of the singular act of the creative production of a text, or is it multiplied in each reader's interaction with the text? The second faultline is the location of the original text: is each text wholly original or are all texts intertextual, shaped by the influences of other words in other texts? The third faultline is the question that began this chapter, that of the ownership of words: do they belong to the speaker as an originator of meaning or does all language use always already contain traces of other meanings (Derrida, 1967/1997)?

New and Old Faultlines: Exploring Theorizations of Authorship

Translation: Where Does Meaning Reside?

The modern and postmodern perspectives have influenced understandings of the role of the translator and the act of translation itself, which together bring to the fore the larger question of where meaning resides: in the "original" text or in the interaction with the text.

A modernist perspective on translation posits the translator as a conduit who transfers meaning wholly contained in one language and, in a sense, re-languages it into another with the goal of providing a faithful reproduction. The end result, the translated text, is judged acceptable when

> it reads fluently, when the absence of any linguistic or stylistic peculiarities makes it seem transparent, giving the appearance that it reflects the foreign writer's personality or intention or the essential meaning of the foreign text – the appearance, in other words, that the translation is not in fact a translation, but the "original."
>
> *(Venuti, 2017, p. 1)*

The process of translation is thus understood as a transfer of meaning that assumes that there is an original text, that meaning wholly resides in this original text and is transparent, and the act of translation itself is based on the identification of equivalences, of words and structures, to render this meaning perfectly intact in another language.

From a postmodern perspective, the translator is not a conduit but a mediator. Admittedly, mediation has been variably understood from within translation studies (see Liddicoat, 2016 for an overview); however, throughout these varied understandings there is an element – albeit to differing degrees – of meaning making in the act of translation (Katan, 2004): it is an interpretive activity that creates something new and different in another language (Venuti, 2013). Meaning, in this case, does not reside in the text, but in the interaction with the text, and the text itself is not a stable source, there is no "original." As Emmerich (2017) explained:

> when it comes to translation we often resort to rhetoric that suggests that the changes wrought by translation are inflicted upon an otherwise stable source… But the "source," the presumed object of translation, is not a stable ideal, not an inert gas but a volatile compound that experiences continual textual reconfigurations.
>
> *(p. 2)*

As a mediator, the translator interacts with all of these reconfigurations, while creating yet more, in the act of translation itself.

Stepping back for a moment, we acknowledge the broader (re)emerging debates in SLA and world language education about whether language teaching broadly speaking, and the teaching of writing more specifically should involve translation at all as a pedagogical tool (see Cook, 2010; Vinall & Hellmich, 2022). While these differing perspectives are certainly present in our research, engaging them goes beyond the scope of the current chapter. Instead, we mention them because attached to these debates, or perhaps alongside them, are fears that MT perpetuates modernist assumptions undergirding translation, or, as one instructor expressed it: "our job should not be to teach translation. MT perpetuates the idea that languages are on [sic] a one-to-one correspondence" (Instructor, survey response). In other words, attached to the teaching of translation are concerns that MT reinforces the modernist belief that meaning from one language can be faithfully and transparently rendered into another language. It is worth noting parenthetically that this concern does not always manifest consistently across language learning materials. For example, textbooks commonly present lists of target vocabulary words alongside their English equivalents with no additional glossing of meanings or cultural nuances; however, this textbook practice does not seem to produce the same fear of perpetuating the idea that languages have a one-to-one correspondence as does the use of MT.

These instructor fears are validated in some student perceptions of translation through MT use, particularly those who imbue the technology with the power to produce the "answer," or the equivalent word they are seeking (e.g., "Google Translate gives you the answer," Anne, a student of French). In this case, while translation is still understood as a search for equivalences, MT itself is the conduit, the translator, while the student assumes a passive role in the process.

However, not all instructors share the same fear and not all learners engage with MT in the same way. In the survey, one instructor highlighted the potentialities of translation, specifically MT, to disrupt this belief in equivalences: "they learn about translation, its limits, its inaccuracies but also the difference in conveyed meaning across languages. I think MT is helpful to understand, evaluate and appreciate the intricacies of translation" (Instructor, survey response).

This process of coming to appreciate these intricacies unfolds in the student data. In one example, Maggie, a student of Spanish, looked up <hike> in Google Translate and received the word <caminata.> She rejected this equivalence and by extension the role of MT as conduit. Instead, Maggie consulted Word Reference and found a different word <excursión>, which, based on the provided example sentence, she determined represented "exactly the type of feeling I wanted in the sentence." This "feeling," she highlighted, was based on her knowledge of Flagstaff, the city she was writing about, and the experiences she had had of what hiking felt and looked like in that context.

This example suggests that there is a possibility that translation, and specifically translation through any online tools, can help learners to understand their roles as mediators between languages and cultures as they also explore the limits of this notion of equivalence and engage in meaning-making processes themselves, which represents a more postmodern perspective.

Machine Translation: Where Is the Original Text?

The question of authors and authorship in relation to MT will be broached at two levels – that of the technology and that of the user. In both cases, what emerges as a central tension is the (im)possibility of identifying the location of the original text.

In terms of technology, current iterations of MT tools use advances in neural networks to draw out patterns in raw data sets. In other words, deep learning MT software constructs (or learns) rules from linguistic input (Lewis-Kraus, 2016; Poibeau, 2017). But where does this linguistic input come from? Where are the original texts? And who are the authors?

MT tools update continuously: new training data is crowdsourced to users who provide valid feedback and new texts in translation are continuously available. In both cases, these contributors remain mostly anonymous. In terms of the original training data sets, there are two primary sources of parallel corpora. The first included publicly available structured sets of translated texts. One example is the Europarl Corpus, which contains the proceedings of the European Parliament from 1996 to 2012 in what is now 11 languages (Koehn, 2005).

The second is translation memories. These began to accumulate in the 1990s when companies that required vast amounts of translations realized that there was repetition in the texts being translated. Rather than approaching each sentence as if it had never been translated before, they started creating translation memories, or electronically stored translations, that human translators could search by fragments or sentences in the creation of future translations. These translation memories came to contain millions of translation units, which became a significant source of training data for MT algorithms (Kenny, 2022).

In both cases, any translated text may have had multiple translators, but most, if not all of them, are unidentifiable. For example, translation memories were created, or authored, by human translators; however, all electronic metadata that includes identifiable information about them is removed when they are transferred to the company or organization that contracted the translation service (Moorkens, 2022). It is this company who "owns" them, simultaneously giving them the freedom to reuse them and even to sell them, and individual translators themselves have no means of claiming attribution or royalties for their labor as having contributed these raw materials to MT tools.

Thus, at the level of the technological tool, the question of authorship is largely ignored as there are seemingly no concerns on the part of companies or users about original text or authorship, except when it comes to use. Hence in some ways, these raw materials are quite postmodern – these tools are literally built on the words of others (and the same can be said of generative AI tools, like ChatGPT). More holistically, however, in the process, these platforms largely strip texts of the context of their production as well as their use and by extension their meanings. To further highlight this decontextualization process, it is important to note that "context" in the case of MT algorithms is understood not in relation to current or past uses but to the proximity of the target word in the large databases that drive MT processes (Poibeau, 2017).

These issues of authorship in relation to MT platforms are not lost on the users of these platforms, including the instructors we interviewed. As one explained:

> If they look up anything more than like a word, they won't have an authentic text example because it is generated by the AI or whatever it is and so it sort of deculturalizes, decontextualizes whatever words that are coming there. So that's why I tell them to look at these other things that will take actual authentic texts. It searches for these texts and then it shows you like 16 different ones where you can see that same word embedded, and that way you can pick really the right one. And it's like authentic, it's not created by a machine. It's just found by a machine.
>
> *(Raquel, instructor, interview)*

MT is imbued with the power to "create" words because they have already been stripped of all prior meanings through the decontextualization process that Raquel extends to include deculturalization, perhaps here understood as also stripping words and texts of their cultural meanings. Thus, these words become "original" words, unlike those that are embedded in "authentic" texts that a machine finds, which have the potential to retain all their past meanings.

Shifting perspectives from the anonymous creators to that of the users, it is frequently assumed that MT users simply input texts, for example, into Google Translate, and then copy and paste the output that is "created." In our student use data, we did observe this kind of usage, copying and pasting MT outputs. However, we also discovered that the reality is much more complex in that the majority of learners analyzed MT outputs, they actively participated – to differing degrees – in the process of recontextualizing or, borrowing Raquel's words, even "reculturalizing" words and texts. More precisely, across learners of French and Spanish, 52% of MT use in our data involved analysis. Looking across students, 65% could be categorized as analysts, defined as analyzing MT output 50% of the time or more. In terms of time spent, students of French and Spanish spent on average 12 seconds looking at MT output. Across languages, these queries were predominantly at the word level, so this analysis focused on single words or phrases.

Learner analysis involved employing multiple strategies such as double-checking, rephrasing, changing the input, and seeking examples of language in use that also included multiple tools as well as textbook use. For example, Carlana, a student of French, looked up "a dish" in Google Translate. Not completely satisfied with the results, because she wanted to find "something in context," she changed the input to "a food dish," before shifting to the English/French Cambridge Dictionary to look up "dish" where she sought examples of the options used in sentences before making her final selection. In a sense, throughout this process, Carlana engages in the meaning-making process herself; she may not be the creator of the word, but she does recontextualize the word based on her own story.

Through their analysis of MT outputs, new meanings and ideas emerge in their writing in interaction with all these tools, in addition to other semiotic resources. Of note, educators who propose integrating generative AI into the writing process using a Socratic approach – in which ideas are shaped and developed in dialogue with the tools – point to the same process of discovery (Berg, 2023). Indeed, in the end, we can ask the same unanswerable questions about these learner-generated texts that we ask about the linguistic input used to train MT tools (and, by extension, that of generative AI tools): Where does the linguistic input ultimately come from? Where is the original text? And, ultimately, who are the authors?

Language Learning: Whose Words Are They?

As shown in the aforementioned discussions, the use cases of MT demonstrate how employing technologies to translate and create texts in the language classroom further complicates questions of authorship because it brings to the fore the question of whose words they are. Pennycook has complicated answers to this question with his own: "because all language learning is, to some extent, a practice of memorization of the words of others, on what grounds do we see certain acts of textual borrowing as acceptable and others as unacceptable?" (Pennycook, 1996, p. 202).

As we have already highlighted, questions of acceptability and ethicality are perhaps the most common area of research inquiry at the intersection of MT and language learning (e.g., Correa, 2011; Clifford et al., 2013; Jolley & Maimone, 2015; Case, 2015), with many considering MT use to be plagiarism and, therefore, a violation of academic honesty. This belief was reflected in our study, as mirrored in the words of an instructor, who stated: "relying on MT is a violation of Academic Honesty within my department, because you are trying to pass someone else's work off as your own" (Instructor, survey response).

There are factors that have been identified, such as text length and type of assignment (Hellmich & Vinall, 2021), that have complicated this picture. Overall, however, concerns around plagiarism generally center the question of whether or not the work "belongs" to the students (never about questions of whose words they really are), conjuring notions of the ownership of words. Even more prevalent with generative AI, there emerge additional questions of the ownership of ideas themselves, which have led to calls for learners to cite ChatGPT when it is used as an originator of ideas with others arguing that ChatGPT cannot be considered an author as it "lacks the fitting mental states like knowledge, belief, or intention, and cannot take responsibility for the texts it produces" (Woudenbert et al., 2024, p. 224). Central to these debates are modernist assumptions about meaning and language residing in the individual brain and writing as an individual act of production. As one instructor expressed it, those instructors who are against its use "have this antiquated idea that any outside support to the language production that students do is cheating. If it's not coming from inside your own brain, if you have any outside support for that production, that's cheating" (Raquel, instructor, interview).

In reality, writing in a language classroom is rarely an individual act and rarely is it the "work" of the students in isolation, and plagiarism itself can and perhaps must be understood as a social construct (Anson, 2022). It would be fairly common at the beginning and even intermediate levels, for example, for a learner to copy sentences or sentence fragments from a textbook into a writing assignment or to request help from an instructor (how do you say a word or a phrase), with no attribution. Additionally, many reading comprehension exercises are designed so that students learn words and phrases and then incorporate them into their writing. At more advanced levels, writing literary analysis would most certainly include ideas generated from class discussions and notes, with no such concerns for the attribution of ideas. All these practices are not commonly considered plagiarism, but learning. On the other hand, if a learner copies and pastes a sentence generated by Google Translate with no attribution, this is considered, to some, plagiarism.

Perhaps a possible explanation for this contradiction can be found in underlying assumptions around intentionality:

> They tend to use it [MT tools] when they are running out of time or do not want to invest time and effort into the class.
>
> *(Instructor, survey response)*

> It's an easy way out and I'm sure most of them would rather have good grades than an actual understanding of the language.
>
> *(Instructor, survey response)*

Unlike asking their teachers or consulting their textbooks, these perspectives suggest that learners use MT with the intention to cheat because they are lazy, they don't want to do the work, or they are not interested in learning, which, in some cases, furthers the moral outrage around MT use. However, our previously mentioned data regarding the time spent by learners analyzing MT outputs suggest that its use might not be a time-saving mechanism at all and that such analysis suggests a desire to learn and to understand.

Students we interviewed have also taken up modernist views on authorship, most notably in the belief that they need to do the work as an individual act of producing words and meaning:

> Aside from academic integrity, I do want to do it on my own.
>
> *(Mae, student of Spanish, interview)*

> I'm still trying my best to come up with everything myself.
>
> *(Sasha, student of French, retrospective recall)*

Beyond fears of accusations of cheating, learners may avoid the use of online tools as much as possible in the apparent belief that doing it on "one's own" is supposed to be part of the learning process, or, its final phase, as indicated in the words of an instructor: "my biggest concern at this point is whether they [the students] will ever get to the point where they can create text on their own if they always have access to machine translation support" (instructor survey). In a sense, the question is not only ownership of words but ownership of the learning process itself, which also ultimately resides in the individual and not in dialogue with others or even with others' words. This perspective negates any exploration of the potential of MT or other digital tools to actually support the process of learning.

Learners themselves admit to not always understanding the distinctions drawn between acceptability and the use of different tools. For example, Bailey, who took French classes where the use of MT tools was strictly forbidden, admitted to using them anyway to complete writing assignments even though she reported that she had "gotten into trouble because perhaps there's been words in there that we haven't learned." However, Bailey explained that she does not really "understand the issue" since a dictionary also has words that she does not know. This contradiction, she concluded, is not only "confusing" but, for her, it complicated learning because "it's kind of hard just relying on like a textbook dictionary or lists of words." The acceptability of "borrowing" words perhaps depends on where they come from, lists that have been curated by instructors or output from MT tools.

When asked if she specifically learned anything from using Google Translate, Bailey responded that in addition to words she learned "versatility with different words." As she elaborated: "it also just made me think, okay, which one is acceptable because, as someone here in the States I don't know what they're saying in France when they use those different words." Her unsanctioned use of GT opened a space for her to contemplate the possibility that words mean differently when used by different speakers in different contexts, a more postmodern awareness of language in use.

Whereas Bailey was concerned with the correct usage of the words, MT's use also opened up the possibility to borrow words in order to play with language and with ideas. For example, one of the instructors interviewed, Lee, commented on a writing assignment in which learners had to describe the objects in their backpacks: "And I could see a few places where they had to look stuff up. Some of it was quite ironic. And it was grammatically all a mess. But it was all quite comprehensible" (Lee, instructor, interview). He concluded that this use of MT tools was "perfectly acceptable" because "they felt like they were doing the assignment. They were communicating. They were being funny" (Lee, instructor, interview).

Modernist perspectives on authorship may foreclose possibilities to explore how MT tools can be used to support learning and engaging with language in ways that include play, while also reifying assumptions that language learning itself can and should be "owned" by the student, as an individual, internalized process that happens in the mind, not in interaction with others. Postmodern perspectives embrace collective understandings of authorship as classroom texts emerge in dialogue with the instructor, fellow students, online tools, including MT, and other resources, such as textbooks, which together open multiple points of entry into the learning process.

Implications: Moving Forward

In this exploration, we have attempted to tease out the influences of modernist and postmodernist understandings of the author and authorship with a specific focus on MT use cases in order to consider their broader implications for the use of other AI tools, including generative AI, in language learning. In the process, numerous faultlines have emerged, bringing to the fore old questions in this new context: Is student writing in a language classroom an individual or collaborative act? Does meaning, and perhaps by extension learning, reside in the individual learner's mind or does it emerge as part of the interaction with the teacher, the textbook, and online resources?

Questions of authorship are deeply tied to questions of knowledge production. Therefore, independently of the tools used, MT or generative AI tools, and alongside concerns about who is the author of a text written for a Spanish or French class we perhaps also should ask broader questions about what knowledge(s) are we expecting students to produce in our language classrooms?:

1 Is it knowledge of how to use words (and language structures) to accurately express their individual ideas?
2 Is it knowledge of how to make meaning through, in, and across languages?
3 Is it knowledge of how to critically engage with learning tools?

A modernist perspective on AI tool use and language learning may support the attainment of the first goal; however, this form of knowledge production collapses the possibility of play, where accuracy is not privileged, as well as reinforces the centrality of the individual in language learning and use, calling into question the role of communication in communicative language teaching. A postmodern perspective would entail a different process of knowledge construction and production, as a dialogic process, while it opens space for learners to critically engage with the other two questions.

Doing so in the language classroom might involve re-engaging with the act of writing from a process-oriented approach that includes explorations of tool functionalities and responsible uses. This move would reverse current trends in classroom practices, particularly with the emergence of generative AI tools, that have shifted toward learners individually writing assignments by hand in the classroom to prevent unauthorized tool use. With respect to generative AI tools, Anson (2022) has proposed focusing on the situatedness of the act of writing as part of a complex system that has its own set of rules, assumptions, and values. In the classroom, co-constructing classroom policies with learners that include reflections on the assumptions and values that undergird tool use can facilitate their awareness of this situatedness and their understanding of what is at stake in relation to their own writing practices. Furthermore, the use of writing journals, in which learners document when and how they use digital tools in relation to the successful communication of their ideas, is a strategy that invites learners to document these decisions while they explore the dialogic nature of writing itself through all its iterative stages, from brainstorming through editing. Classroom time could then be spent discussing this process, focusing specifically on tool uses that were not successful either due to the functionality of the tools or the learners' own language knowledge, thereby building additional opportunities for learning. In this case, assessment practices would not focus solely on the final product, but the process itself and learner engagement in the process.

While researchers in CALL have argued that digital-era learners have increased agency and autonomy in their learning because of the available technological resources outside of the classroom (Godwin-Jones, 2015; Kern, 2021), the current reflection complicates this belief. From a modernist perspective, if MT is imbued with the power "to create" words because it produces equivalents as the mediator between languages, the role of learners remains passive. However, as the student use data reported here suggests, if learners analyze MT outputs, instead of imbuing the tools with the power of providing the answer, and if they are supported in their efforts to engage with MT critically, they also have the potential to explore the intricacies of translation and their own power to recontextualize words and to engage with their prior meanings and to play with language. From this postmodern perspective they are agents who have the potential to learn the language, but also to learn about meaning-making processes themselves.

In addition to exploring the act of writing as a complex system in the language classroom, a postmodern perspective reifies the importance of learners exploring their own roles as authors as they learn about and engage with meaning-making processes. The online writing journal as described above is one way for them to develop their own agency, as they explore the affordances and limitations of the online tools with respect to the decisions they make in the communication of their ideas. The domain of translation studies offers additional potential possibilities for the language classroom. For example, learners at all levels of language study can render their own translation of a short paragraph from a reading text into their L1, generate translations from an MT platform and a generative AI platform, such as ChatGPT, and analyze how meaning changes across and between languages and translation tools (see Klekovkina & Denié-Higney, 2022, for a concrete example). As a dialogic process with each other and with the texts, analyzing these outputs may also bring to the fore broader considerations of what it means to be an author, where meaning resides, and where learning takes place.

Together, the faultlines revealed in this analysis point to the limits of a modernist understanding of authorship. They also reveal the potential of a postmodern perspective to challenge not only whose words they are but certain tenants of language learning itself, such as where learning resides, and its ultimate goals. Indeed, as Lensmire and Beals (1994) point out:

> we are born and develop, learn to speak, read and write, awash in the words of others... Our words are always someone else's words first; and these words sound with the intonations and evaluations of others who have used them before, and from whom we have learned them.
>
> *(p. 411)*

Thus, this perspective opens new possibilities to explore the development of critical uses of MT and other online tools, such as generative AI tools, to support language learning. Moving forward, perhaps one of the most significant areas for future research involves the further development and elaboration of these pedagogical interventions, articulated across all levels of language instruction, as well as documentation that evaluates their impacts and potentials. The questions that emerge in these faultlines and the exploration of these critical uses take on new urgency and implications as new technologies continue to challenge understandings of the ownership of words.

Conclusion

Returning to the anecdote that began this chapter, we wonder how this exploration of notions of authorship might have altered this scenario. From a postmodern understanding, abandoning attachments to the ownership of words and the individualization of learning would have resulted in removing the ban on using MT in favor of co-constructing classroom policies. The result might have opened the possibility to guide reflections on the assumptions and values that undergird why she chose to use the tool in addition to training on how to critically do so. This training, in addition to the use of a writing journal, might have significantly altered how the learner interacted with the tools in the act of writing, specifically with regard to reflecting on the structure and lexical choices produced and how this output contributed to the expression of her ideas, or not, and what other alternatives might have been available. Follow-up classroom discussions might have also opened space to reflect on why she interpreted the word as a "sophisticated" one and what meaning she attached to using "sophisticated" language in her writing. Building classroom opportunities to collectively analyze MT outputs with instructor support or through triangulating outputs with other tools, such as ChatGPT, specifically structures or words that are not familiar, might have also created space to engage with this output. Introducing the concept of conditional verbs and reflexive constructions might build anticipation for the future study of these linguistic structures, and to think more broadly about how to express hypothetical situations through language. In the process, the learner would have the support to use AI language tools in ways that are agentive, as opposed to imbuing the tools themselves with this power. Perhaps the evaluation of the learner's production of knowledge would have taken into consideration not only the language, but the knowledge gained about how it is used to express meaning and how AI tools can be used to facilitate the process.

References

Anson, C. M. (2022). AI-based text generation and the social construction of 'Fraudulent authorship': A revisitation. *Composition Studies*, 50(1), 37–46.

Bakhtin, M. (1986/1936). *Speech genres and other late essays*. University of Texas Press.

Barthes, R. (1977). The death of the author. In S. Heath (Ed.), *Image, music, text* (pp. 142–148). (Translated by S. Heath). Fontana/Collins.

Berg, C. (2023). The case for generative AI in scholarly practice. https://doi.org/10.2139/ssrn.4407587

Bowles, M. A. (2018). Introspective verbal reports: Think-alouds and stimulated recalls. In A. Phakiti, P. de Costa, L. Plonsky, & S. Starfield (Eds.), *The Palgrave handbook of applied linguistics research methodology* (pp. 339–357). Palgrave Macmillan UK. https://doi.org/10.1057/978-1-137-59900-1

Bozkurt, A. (2024). GenAI et al.: Cocreation, authorship, ownership, academic ethics and integrity in a time of generative AI. *Open Praxis*, 16(1), 1–10. https://doi.org/10.55982/openpraxis.16.1.654

Case, M. (2015). Machine translation and the disruption of foreign language learning activities. *ELearning Papers*, 45, 4–16.

Clifford, J., Merschel, L., & Munné, J. (2013). Surveying the landscape: What is the role of machine translation in language learning? *@Tic. Revista D'Innovació Educativa*, 10, 108–121. https://doi.org/10.7203/attic.10.2228

Cook, G. (2010). *Translation in language teaching*. Oxford University Press.

Correa, M. (2011). Academic dishonesty in the second language classroom: Instructors' perspectives. *Modern Journal of Language Teaching Methods*, 1(1), 65–80.

Derrida, J. (1967/1997). *Of grammatology* (G. C. Spivak, Trans.) John Hopkins University Press.

Emmerich, K. (2017). *Literary translation and the making of originals*. Bloomsbury Academic.

Foucault, M. (1977/1984). What is an author? In D. F. Bouchard (Ed.), *Language, counter- memory, practise: Selected essays and interviews* (pp. 113–138). Cornell University Press. (Reprinted in The Foucault Reader (Paul Rabinow, Ed.), 1994, pp. 101–120).

Fredholm, K. (2019). Effects of Google translate on lexical diversity: Vocabulary development among learners of Spanish as a foreign language. *Revista Nebrija de Lingüística Aplicada a la Enseñanza de las Lenguas*, 13(26), 98–117.

Gass, S. M., & Mackey, A. (2016). *Stimulated recall methodology in applied linguistics and L2 research*. Routledge.

Godwin-Jones, R. (2015). Emerging technologies: Contributing, creating, curating: Digital literacies for language learners. *Language Learning & Technology*, 19(3), 8–20.

Hellmich, E. A. (2021). Machine translation in foreign language writing: Student use to guide pedagogical practice. *Alsic*, 24(1). https://doi.org/10.4000/alsic.5705

Hellmich, E. A., & Vinall, K. (2021). FL instructor beliefs about machine translation. *IJCALLT*, 11(4), 1–18.

Hellmich, E. A., & Vinall, K. (2023). Student use and instructor beliefs: Machine translation in language education. *Language Learning & Technology*, 27(1), 1–27. https://hdl.handle.net/10125/73525

Jolley, J. R., & Maimone, L. (2015). Free online machine translation: Use and perceptions by Spanish students and instructors. In A. Moeller (Ed.), *Learn language, explore cultures, transform lives* (pp. 181–200). Robert M. Terry.

Katan, D. (2004). *Translating cultures: An introduction for translators, interpreters, and mediators.* St. Jerome.

Kearney, R. (1988). *The wake of imagination.* University of Minnesota Press.

Kenny, D. (2022). Human and machine translation. In D. Kenny (Ed)., *Machine translation for everyone: Empowering users in the age of artificial intelligence* (pp. 23–50). Language Science Press.

Kern, R. (2021). Twenty-five years of digital literacies in CALL. *Language Learning & Technology, 25*(3), 132–150. http://hdl.handle.net/10125/73453

Klekovkina, V., & Denié-Higney, L. (2022). Machine translation: Friend or foe in the language classroom? *L2 Journal, 14*(1). https://doi.org/10.5070/L214151723 Retrieved from https://escholarship.org/uc/item/3c9161pw

Koehn, P. (2005). Europarl: A parallel corpus for Statistical Machine Translation. In *Proceedings of machine translation summit X* (pp. 79–86). https://aclanthology.org/2005.mtsummit-papers.11

Kol, S., Schcolnik, M. & Specter-Cohen, E. (2018). Google translate in academic writing courses? *The EuroCALL Review, 26*(2), 50–57.

Latham, S. (2019). Industrialized print: Modernism and authorship. In I. Berenshmeyer, G. Buelens, & M. Demoor (Eds.), *The Cambridge handbook of literary authorship* (pp. 165–182). Cambridge University Press.

Lensmire, T. J., & Beals, D. E. (1994). Appropriating others' words: Traces of literature and peer culture in a third-grader's writing. *Language in Society, 23*, 411–426.

Lewis-Kraus, G. (2016, December 14). The great AI awakening. *The New York Times Magazine.* Retrieved from: https://www.nytimes.com/2016/12/14/magazine/the-great-ai-awakening.html

Liddicoat, A. (2016). Translation as intercultural mediation: Setting the scene. *Perspectives, 24*(3), 347–353.

Liu, Q., & Zhang, X. (2015). Machine translation: General. In C. Sin-wai (Ed.), *The Routledge encyclopedia of translation technology* (pp. 105–19). Routledge. https://doi.org/10.5860/choice.188800

Moorkens, J. (2022). Ethics and machine translation. In D. Kenny (Ed)., *Machine translation for everyone: Empowering users in the age of artificial intelligence* (pp. 121–140). Language Science Press.

Ong, W. (1982). *Orality and literacy: The technologizing of the word.* Methuen.

Patton, M. Q. (1990). Qualitative interviewing. In *Qualitative evaluation and research methods* (2nd ed., pp. 277–368). Sage Publications.

Pennycook, A. (1996). Borrowing others' words: Text, ownership, memory, and plagiarism. *TESOL Quarterly, 39*(2), 201–230.

Poibeau, T. (2017). *Machine translation.* MIT Press.

Saldaña, J. (2009). *The coding manual for qualitative researchers* (2nd ed.). Sage Publications Ltd.

Spradley, J. P. (1979). *The ethnographic interview.* Wadsworth.

Thue Vold, E. (2018). Using machine-translated texts to generate L3 learners' metalinguistic talk. In Å. HaukÅs, C. Bjørke & M. Dypedahl (Eds.), *Metacognition in language learning and teaching* (pp. 67–97). Routledge.

Venuti, L. (2013). *Translation changes everything: Theory and practice.* Routledge.

Venuti, L. (2017). *The translator's invisibility: A history of translation.* Routledge.

Vinall, K., & Hellmich, E. A. (2021). Down the rabbit hole: Metaphor, machine translation, and instructor identity/agency. *Second Language Research and Practice, 2*(1), 99–118.

Vinall, K. & Hellmich, E. A. (2022). Do you speak translate?: Reflections on the nature and role of translation. *L2 Journal, 14*(1), 4–25.

Vinall, K., Wen, W., & Hellmich, E. A. (2023). Investigating L2 writers' uses of machine translation and other online tools. *Foreign Language Annals, 57*(2), 499–526.

Willinsky, J. (1990). Intellectual property rights and responsibilities: The state of the text. *The Journal of Educational Thought, 24*, 68–82.

Wise, B., Emerson, L., Van Luyn, A., Dyson, B., Bjork, C., & Thomas, S. E. (2024). A scholarly dialogue: Writing scholarship, authorship, academic integrity and the challenge of AI. *Higher Education Research & Development, 43*(3), 578–590.

Woudenbert, R., Ranalli, C., & Bracker, D. (2024). Authorship and ChatGPT: A conservative view. *Philosophy and Technology, 37*(34). https://doi.org/10.1007/s13347-024-00715-1

Wu, Y., Schuster, M., Chen, Z., Le, Q. V., Norouzi, M., Macherey, W., Krikun, M., et al. (2016). Google's neural machine translation system: Bridging the gap between human and machine translation. Retrieved from: https://arxiv.org/abs/1609.08144

5

BLESSING OR CURSING

Second language writing teachers' perceptions of using ChatGPT in classrooms

Wei Xu and Xiao Tan

Introduction

Artificial intelligence (AI), referred to as "applications of software algorithms and techniques that allow computers and machines to simulate human perception and decision-making processes to successfully complete tasks" (Murphy, 2019, p. 2), has impacted human life in multiple facets (Ng et al., 2021). In the winter of 2022, OpenAI's ChatGPT stormed campuses and garnered wide attention from professionals in second language (L2) education. With users feeding prompts, this AI-powered chatbot is able to interact with users in a turn-by-turn conversational way by providing responses to the prompts, conducting logical thinking, and admitting mistakes (OpenAI, 2022). These advanced functions ignited unprecedented discussions on how ChatGPT may serve as a viable tool for students' technology-enhanced language learning and writing development (e.g., Kasneci et al., 2023).

Within the intersection of language learning and writing instruction, the application of generative AI-powered tools in L2 writing, defined as writing in a different language other than the writer's first language (Hyland, 2019), has only been explored by few scholars before the age of ChatGPT. However, a survey of recently published works indicates that there is a growing interest in the application of generative AI tools in L2 writing classrooms (e.g., Barrot, 2023; Yan, 2023), which possibly were motivated by the whirlwind advancement of ChatGPT. Most of these studies draw on observation of students' learning behaviors and reflections, whereas less empirical data is collected in terms of teachers' perceptions, which might be attributed to an overall lack of teachers' experience and knowledge of incorporating AI tools in their classrooms (Kim & Kim, 2022). Understanding teachers' perceptions is important, as perceptions guide teaching actions in practice (Fives & Buehl, 2012). In addition, faced with possible disruptions that AI technologies may lead to, teachers should be involved in co-designing the AI-assisted learning with the learners (Godwin-Jones, 2022).

Perceptions from L2 writing teachers as an essential group of stakeholders will also contribute to our understanding of the nature of the relationship between the use of technology and human instructors, thereby offering implications for administrative policymaking. To bridge the gap, this study collects data from 122 L2 writing teachers working in diverse

DOI: 10.4324/9781003426936-7

educational contexts via an online survey and interviews with some of them. We hope to provide empirical evidence regarding how L2 writing teachers respond to the emerging AI tool (i.e., ChatGPT), their current experience with it, and their attitudes toward its possible intervention in classrooms, based on which possible suggestions for AI-assisted pedagogical practices and regulations that involve the use of AI-powered text generation tools are produced.

Literature review

AI technologies in writing classrooms

How to leverage AI technologies, such as chatbots, machine translation tools, and grammar-checking tools in writing instruction, predates the advent of ChatGPT. Research indicates that chatbots help expand writers' repertoire of vocabulary in use (Nagata et al., 2019), provide meaningful instructions to facilitate their writing process (Bailey, 2019), improve learners' syntactic complexity in writing (Gayed et al., 2022), offer interactive feedback (Guo et al., 2022), and facilitate students to improve their writing quality through AI-supported paraphrasing tools (Kurniati & Fithriani, 2022). Hwang et al. (2023) also developed an AI-based app to create authentic writing contexts for EFL writers to produce meaningful content and provide sample sentences. In addition, popular machine translation tools (e.g., Google translate) and grammar-checking applications (e.g., Grammarly) prove to assert a positive influence on students' writing performance (Dizon & Gayed, 2021), improving their writing accuracy and overall length (Cancino & Panes, 2021; Tsai, 2019). Wang's (2024) study on students' AI-assisted writing processes verifies the positive influence that AI wields on students' writing experience. In addition, beyond text-based writing, AI technology also assists students in voice expression in multimodal composition (Tan et al., 2024). Together, these studies emphasize the pedagogical potential of applying AI-based tools in developing learners' writing performance and skills through classroom-based empirical evidence. Research that highlights learners' perceptions of incorporating these technology-enhanced tools into writing classrooms also indicates a generally positive user experience and attitude (e.g., Hostetter et al., 2023; Sumakul et al., 2022; Yan, 2023).

The release of ChatGPT in November 2022 attracted researchers to extend the previous quest of how to capitalize on the power of the new generation of chatbots in writing pedagogy, the year after which witnessed a growing number of studies on the use of ChatGPT in writing. Specifically, ChatGPT has been experimented with to produce various academic genres. For example, one of the experiments returns promising performance of ChatGPT generating literature reviews (Aydın & Karaarslan, 2022). Gao et al. (2023) conducted another experiment using ChatGPT to produce abstracts of journal articles in medical studies and identify the difficulty for human reviewers to distinguish between ChatGPT-generated and human-generated texts. A similar experiment conducted by Casal and Kessler (2023) corroborates linguists' unsuccessful attempts to identify AI and human writing, which alludes to the high quality of ChatGPT-generated texts while begetting ethical concerns for further discussion. These studies suggest that ChatGPT is powerful in producing high-quality texts that sometimes cannot be distinguished from human-generated texts.

In pedagogical settings, multiple benefits of incorporating ChatGPT in L2 writing classrooms are reported and reviewed, such as helping students improve text quality by encouraging individual exploration and group discussion (Yan, 2023), providing linguistic input, decreasing writing anxiety, facilitating topic generation, and offering written feedback on various levels (Barrot, 2023). Meanwhile, scholars have pointed out concerns regarding the use of ChatGPT in an academic context, including the risks of negatively impacting academic honesty and educational equity, impeding learning goals in writing classrooms, compromising students' critical thinking and voice expression, causing linguistic injustice and devaluing writing (Barrot, 2023; MLA-CCCC Joint Task Force on Writing and AI, 2023; Yan, 2023). Vetter et al. (2024) also propose a framework for local interrogation of ethics in AI-assisted writing. Despite the varying perspectives on the potential risks and benefits of ChatGPT used as a pedagogical tool in writing instruction, we are still in a paucity of knowledge and empirical evidence that can be used as a foundation for generating guidelines and developing curricula for using ChatGPT in writing instruction.

Teachers' perceptions of using AI for pedagogical purposes

Perception could be understood as "tacit, often unconsciously held assumptions about students, classrooms, and the academic materials to be taught" (Kagan, 1992, p. 65). Teacher perception refers to the subjective perspectives held by educators in three dimensions – cognitive, emotional, and attitudinal – about their teaching roles, process, and environment (Demirdağ & Efe, 2023). Examining teachers' perceptions is of vital importance because it influences not only teachers' instructional decisions (Hoy et al., 2009) and students' learning outcomes (Rubie-Davies et al., 2012) but also the interactions with their students and colleagues (Demirdağ & Efe, 2023). In technology-enhanced teaching, teachers' perceptions could impact the success of implementing new technologies in classrooms (Fernández-Batanero et al., 2021). Related to teachers' perceptions are their experiences and knowledge. Tan and Matsuda (2020) clarify that the difference between perception and knowledge is that perception comprises stronger affective and evaluative components than knowledge (Nespor, 1987). Rock (1985) explains that knowledge, which comprises representations of past experiences, can affect one's perception in multiple ways. As shown by previous research, teacher perceptions, experiences, and knowledge are intertwined constructs that collectively exert an impact on teaching practices.

A survey of the literature indicates that there is a lacuna of research on teachers' perceptions of generative AI implementation in classrooms. Such scarce literature is possibly due to teachers' insufficient experience of incorporating AI tools in their classrooms (Kim & Kim, 2022). The lack of experience may be caused by affective factors such as teacher anxiety about new technologies (Zimmerman, 2006) and their viewing of AI as an occupational threat (Luckin et al., 2016). Two key studies in this strand are Hostetter et al.'s (2023) survey study that collects responses from 82 faculty in regard to their perceptions of using AI in writing instruction and Kim & Kim's (2022) research that delves into K-12 teachers' perceptions of AI-based tools as scaffolding for scientific writing. Kim and Kim's (2022) study suggests that K-12 teacher participants hold an overall positive attitude toward ChatGPT as a scaffolding tool, whereas both studies (Hostetter et al., 2023; Kim & Kim, 2022) indicate that common ethical concerns were expressed by teachers regarding the shifting teachers' role and ChatGPT's potential effects on pedagogical practices. Zimotti et al.'s (2024) mixed-method study suggests that L2 educators' attitude toward the use of ChatGPT in language education is statistically correlated with their previous personal experience with ChatGPT, and a large percentage of their participants indicate the confidence in identifying students' uses of ChatGPT in their works. Xu and Tan (2024) adopt visualizations to explore the metaphors of the role of AI in writing classrooms and conclude that L2 writing teachers metaphorize AI as a tool, a resource, a threat, and an unknown entity. These studies point to education practitioners' nuanced mixed attitudes toward the increasing salience of AI tools in their classrooms.

Considering the significance of exploring teachers' perception systems, investigating L2 writing teachers' perceptions of using ChatGPT as a pedagogical tool in writing instruction may offer multiple insights. Firstly, it may open a window for us to envision how L2 writing teachers respond to the potential and uncertainty brought by the developing AI tools; secondly, it offers a chance for instructors to revisit learning goals in L2 writing classrooms; and thirdly, it could provide empirical foundations for institutions to generate guidelines and relevant pedagogical support. Given the importance of understanding L2 writing teachers' perceptions of using ChatGPT in classrooms and the reported issues and affordances of it in the extant literature, specifically, this study examines:

1 What knowledge and experience do L2 writing teachers have about ChatGPT?
2 How do L2 writing teachers perceive the ethical issues involved in using ChatGPT?
3 How do L2 writing teachers perceive the pedagogical affordances and potential risks of using ChatGPT in writing classrooms?

Method

Research design

Based on our research aim, the research tools of this study consist of two parts: a qualitative survey and follow-up interviews with some survey respondents. A qualitative survey offers multiple advantages, such as providing rich and deep data when viewed in its entirety, circumventing the risk of having a small sample of data from participants who speak in a dominant social position as in an interview study, and being affordable and unobtrusive (Braun et al., 2021). In addition to those benefits, we particularly value that it serves to capture "a diversity of perspectives, experiences, or sense-making" (Braun et al., 2021, p. 643) and that it is the most appropriate research tool when "a population is dispersed, hard to engage or access and/or diverse" and "a wide range of perspectives or positionings is sought" or "the topic suits a 'wide-angle lens'" (ibid., p. 651). Our survey was launched to multiple email listservs and a public social media group of L2 writing teachers, which includes a heterogeneous population. Therefore, the highlighted benefits of a qualitative survey proposed by Braun et al. (2021) are well aligned with our research context and goal. Our survey adopts a design of multiple sections, which means it provides a cross-sectional portrait of one group's opinions (Fink, 2003). Informed by Braun et al. (2021) and the theoretical framing of the interconnected relations between teachers' perceptions, knowledge, and experience, as previously explicated, apart from the section on demographic information, topic-based survey questions cover six categories (see Appendix A): teachers' observation of students' use of ChatGPT, ethical issues, pedagogical affordances, potential risks, teacher knowledge and experience with ChatGPT, and institutional and professional support. Each category comprises two to three questions that tap into the topic of the category. Questions are mainly designed in three types: multiple choice, matrix table, and text entry. Most questions end with an open-text entry item that invites respondents to share anything else that they think is essential to mention. Survey respondents could also choose to enter their contact information for further participation in the follow-up interviews. The survey was available via Qualtrics, a well-known professional online survey software, from mid-April to mid-May 2023. The follow-up semi-structured interviews (see Appendix B), which were conducted one month after the survey, were designed based on our research questions. Roulston (2010) proposes that interviews may be efficient in collecting data for the research questions under the theoretical perspectives of phenomenology and hermeneutics. As our research questions delve into L2 writing teachers' perceptions, knowledge, and experience, we see interview transcripts as a strong complementary data source to provide possible explanations for the survey result. The nine main questions cover the same topic domains in the survey. With the participants' consent, the interviews were conducted and audio-recorded online by the first author via Zoom. Following Roulston's (2010) constructionist perspective of interviews, the interviewer reacted to interviewees' responses to the interview questions rather than being the passive vessel of their input. Where necessary, probing questions were asked following the original questions on the protocol.

Participants and setting

The survey was shared through L2 writing instructors' email listservs and an open social media group of L2 writing teachers that the researchers have access to in April 2023. The participation was strictly voluntary, and no financial compensation was provided for the participants. Though our original intention was to extend the reach as much as possible, we adopted the nonprobability sampling method for participant selection, as the participant selection procedure is based on availability, convenience, and self-selection, which works for the study where no statistical representative data is needed and the purpose of which is explanatory in nature (Daniel, 2012). Consequently, the channels through which the survey was launched led to the result that the major participants are L2 writing instructors who work in higher education in the US. The data of survey respondents' demographic information indicates that more than 80% of 122 survey respondents work at four-year universities. 13 of them who attended the follow-up interviews all work in the US four-year universities having two to more than ten years experience of teaching L2 writing (Table 5.1).

Data analysis

Survey

Situated in our research questions and related literature on incorporating AI-based tools in writing classrooms, we adopted a holistic content analysis method to reveal underlying patterns based on themes. We adopted a holistic approach as Braun et al. (2021) warn researchers that it can be counterproductive to summarize responses based on each question in a qualitative survey. Drawing on the approach used in Karakoyun & Lindberg (2020), we reported frequencies and percentages in the first round of interpretation of data. Then, given the guidance that materials contributing to understanding an issue may not be confined

TABLE 5.1 Demographic Information of Interviewees

Name (Pseudonym)	Gender	L1	Teaching Context/Position	Yrs. Teaching L2 Writing
Mary	F	Spanish	Four-year university, US/Graduate Teaching Associate	Less than 2 yrs
John	M	English	Four-year university, US/Associate Professor	More than 15 yrs
Alice	F	English	Four-year university, US/Lecturer	More than 5 yrs
Jack	M	English	Four-year university, US/Assistant Professor	15 yrs
Cecile	F	Mandarin	Four-year university, US/Assistant Professor	8 yrs
Amy	F	English	Four-year university, US/Lecturer	12 yrs
Emma	F	Mandarin	Four-year university, US/Graduate Teaching Associate	4 yrs
Kate	F	English	Four-year university, US/Lecturer	20 yrs
Lily	F	English	Community College, US/Lecturer	18 yrs
Katherine	F	English	Four-year university, US/ESL Specialist	10 yrs
Daisy	F	Turkish	Four-year university, US/Graduate Teaching Associate	3 yrs
Norton	M	English	Four-year university, US/Lecturer	More than 15 yrs
Mina	F	Ukrainian	Four-year university, US/Lecturer	More than 5 yrs

to participants' responses to a single question (Terry & Braun, 2017), we combined quotes from the interviews to reach a more reflective interpretation of patterns generated from the survey data.

Interviews

Interview audio recordings underwent full transcribing and were de-identified. Full transcriptions were generated to avoid missing co-constructed details between the interviewer and interviewee. Next, the two researchers conducted bottom-up thematic coding independently (Braun & Clarke, 2012). The initial coding resulted in a high rate of agreement (95%). The remaining discrepancies were solved after an in-depth discussion.

Findings

This study seeks to understand how knowledgeable and familiar L2 writing teachers are with ChatGPT and what they think about this technology in writing education. The following sections are organized in response to the three research questions that tap into L2 writing teachers' knowledge of and experience with ChatGPT, their perceptions of ethical issues involved in using ChatGPT in teaching, and their perceptions of its pedagogical affordances and risks.

L2 writing teachers' knowledge of and experience with ChatGPT

The first research question seeks to understand how knowledgeable and experienced L2 writing teachers are with ChatGPT. As Figure 5.1 shows, the survey suggests that the majority of respondents (80%) self-identified as having some experience with ChatGPT. Among these respondents, 43% indicated that they used ChatGPT primarily to understand its capacity and limitations, while 19% employed ChatGPT to assist with writing for different purposes. Other common reasons for using ChatGPT include information search (16%) and lesson planning (13%).

The interviews with the 13 participants, while largely corresponding to the survey results, generate a more complicated picture of how ChatGPT is used for various reasons. Curiosity acts as an important motivation for using ChatGPT, which may not involve any real purpose other than exploring the capacity of the chatbot. Emma's interview response illustrates the playness of such an attempt: "I get on there and mess around with things, and if I type in a potential prompt, I see what it comes up with because I want to know what I'm dealing with." On the contrary, some of the participants have leveraged the power of ChatGPT for their personal usage in both academic and nonacademic contexts. For example, both Amy and Mina used ChatGPT to assist with dissertation. Amy asked ChatGPT questions about dissertation defense, while Mina inquired about proposal writing. In particular, educated in a non-English background, Mina commented positively on how ChatGPT helped her navigate the difficult genre. Other personal uses of ChatGPT include helping the elderly to learn a new language (Emma), searching for information about gardening (Mina), and writing personal emails (Cecile).

The survey and interviews also tap into L2 writing teachers' knowledge regarding the use of ChatGPT in educational settings. When asked to rate their familiarity with the capacities and limitations of ChatGPT (see Figure 5.2), 63% indicated that they were either familiar or very familiar with this aspect. In comparison, the confidence level drops significantly when it comes to understanding students' views of using ChatGPT in writing, as only 23% selected

Q10 - I used ChatGPT in order to

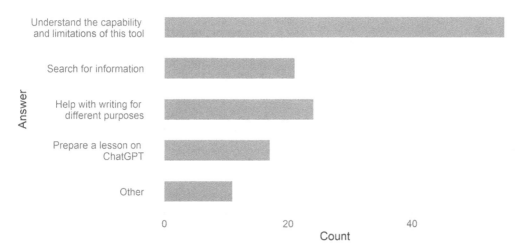

FIGURE 5.1   Result of the Question about Teacher Experience (Count).

Q11 - Indicate how famillar you are with the following aspects

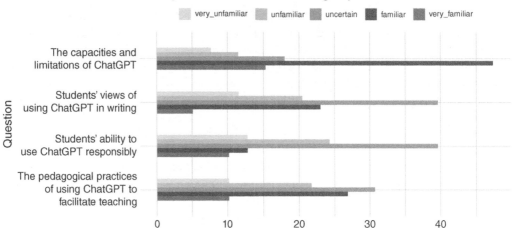

FIGURE 5.2   Result of the Question about Teachers' Familiarity with ChatGPT (%).

"familiar" or "very familiar," while 40% indicated that they were uncertain. A similar pattern is observed in the question about students' ability to use ChatGPT responsibly. Lastly, a slightly more positive light is shed on the last question about the pedagogical practices of using ChatGPT to facilitate teaching, as 37% indicated "familiar" or "very familiar," and 31% selected "uncertain."

The interview data further shed light on participants' uncertainty about using ChatGPT in educational settings. With regard to ChatGPT's capacities and limitations, our interviewees discussed extensively the textual features of texts generated by ChatGPT, identifying them as "generic" (Jack, Norton), "fabricated" and "detached" (Emma), and "limited" (Mina). But the participants also acknowledged ChatGPT's ability to summarize articles (Emma), create poems (Norton; Mina), and write emails for different audiences (Daisy). However, interviewees hold different views about students' attitudes toward this technology and their ability to use it. Lily, Mary, and Katherine hypothesized that the use of ChatGPT among L2 students was driven by the pressure to produce correct, acceptable academic English, which could compensate for their limited linguistic repertoires. On the contrary, Norton reasoned that most of his L2 graduate students were reluctant to use ChatGPT due to the concerns of their original ideas being entered into the database. With regard to students' ability to use this tool, Norton is confident that his graduate students "definitely know what they need," while Emma doubts that students have yet mastered digital literacy with ChatGPT. Moreover, while interviewees generally agreed that teacher intervention with ChatGPT is important, they held different views as to what type of intervention is needed. Cecile, Emma, and Norton highlighted teaching the skills of prompting ChatGPT to accomplish certain tasks (e.g., giving personalized feedback), while Katherine emphasized critical awareness against fake information. Two participants, Lily and Mary, acknowledged their lack of knowledge about this technology and its pedagogical implications.

Finally, the study seeks to locate where teacher knowledge about ChatGPT comes from. As Figure 5.3 presents, a common source of information, selected by 20% of the survey

Q12 - My knowledge of ChatGPT comes from

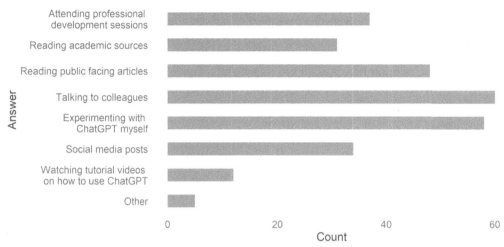

FIGURE 5.3   Result of the Question about Source of Teachers' Knowledge (Count).

respondents, is the casual conversation with colleagues. In addition, 28% of survey respondents received information from scholarly, as well as nonacademic, publications. 13% indicated that they attended professional development devoted to discussing this issue, while 12% also acquired information from social media. In the "other" category, sources of information also include talking to students and previous computational knowledge.

The interviews also highlight the professional and scholarly conversations about ChatGPT. Such conversions could take place with colleagues either in the same field (Emma) or in a different discipline (John). Professional journals, newsletters, listservs, online discussion forums, and webinars are also crucial venues for knowledge exchange (Lily; Katherine; Alice; Emma). Most importantly, these academic conservations seem to shape teachers' attitude, as John recounted his experience:

> When I first heard about it, I think, of course, my gut reaction was something…. the English teacher was "oh, crap! Now I have to fight this too because plagiarism is bad enough without having a generator. It's the end of the world, as we know it. My god!" But as I attended webinars and read articles, and so forth, I was slowly persuaded of many of the things.

In sum, the data suggest that L2 writing teachers have had some first-hand experiences using ChatGPT for various purposes; they also gained knowledge by participating in academic conversations and professional development sessions. But at the same time, the survey and interviews also reveal varying degrees of knowledge about the use of ChatGPT in educational contexts.

Ethical issues

The second research question asks how L2 writing teachers perceive the ethical issues involved in using ChatGPT in teaching and learning. Survey respondents and interview participants have shared with us various ethical concerns, suggesting that the use of ChatGPT in the educational realm remains an ethically contested issue. The survey results (see Figures 5.4 and 5.5) show that more than 60% of the respondents agree or strongly agree that it is ethical to use ChatGPT to brainstorm ideas, search for information, and generate language for teaching resources. On the other hand, respondents were less certain about using ChatGPT to generate feedback and assess students' work. Responses were split rather equally between those who agree/strongly agree (37%) and those who disagree/strongly disagree (38%) with the use of ChatGPT in providing feedback. In terms of using ChatGPT to grade students'

Q4 - To what extent do you agree with the following statements?

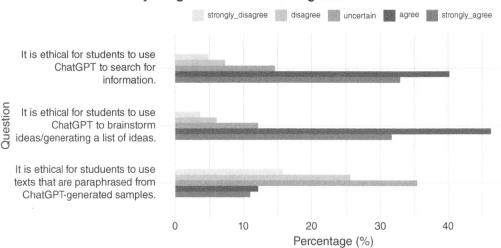

FIGURE 5.4   Result of the Question about Ethnicity of Students' Use of ChatGPT (%).

Q5 - To what extent do you agree with the following statements?

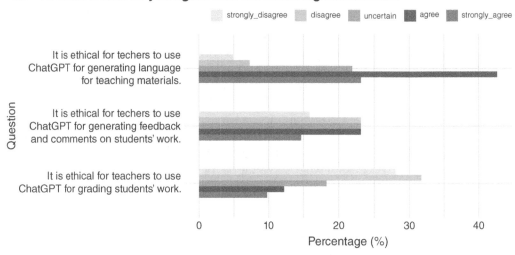

FIGURE 5.5   Result of the Question about Ethnicity of Teachers' Use of ChatGPT (%).

work, the majority (60%) showed a negative attitude, with only 22% indicating agree or strongly agree and 18% selecting uncertain.

The interview participants also seem to express a varying degree of acceptance toward the use of ChatGPT in various tasks. Nevertheless, participants seem to be uniform that passing ChatGPT-generated texts as one's own could violate academic integrity, as 9 out of 13 participants have explicitly said so. Less consensus is achieved in other categories. Daisy, for example, believes that it is not ethical for teachers to use ChatGPT to generate feedback or grading, as she reasoned:

> Either the student or the teacher, if they are using ChatGPT to kind of ask it to do their responsibility, then this is not ethical, and the teacher's main responsibility is to give feedback and to grade student work.

Along the same line, Daisy also red-flagged the use of ChatGPT to summarize readings, as such tasks are essentially part of the student's responsibility. However, it is important to note that the ethical concerns might succumb to external constraints such as a heavy workload. John, Lily, and Norton pointed out that a heavy teaching load might "lure" writing teachers into using ChatGPT as an assisting tool. Norton's response depicts such a moral dilemma:

> I'm afraid that when I was a composition teacher and I had 50 students, and you know, in the middle of the semester I got 50 papers to read, you know. I'm afraid it could be too tempting just to kind of cut and paste what ChatGPT said. I don't think that's ethical, but definitely, it's a tool. Why not use it? Why not? It can focus on problems immediately.

> Lastly, despite the different opinions, we have identified some principles underlying the "ethical" use of ChatGPT in teaching and learning that are described in multiple interviews.

Cecile, Emma, and Katherine believe that the use of ChatGPT should be made transparent for both teachers and students. Eight participants argued that ChatGPT should be positioned as a supporting tool, with enough human effort devoted to generating the desirable outcome. For example, Mary explained why she believes that using ChatGPT to brainstorm is ethical:

> It was fine for me because sometimes you don't know what to write, so it could be like a suggestion if it gives you just ideas and you develop your ideas and your own perspectives from those ideas. I think you're putting enough of yourself rather than, like, copying everything from the AI tool.

Pedagogical affordances and potential risks

The third question investigates L2 writing teachers' views about the pedagogical affordances and potential risks of using ChatGPT in teaching. The top three selected pedagogical affordances (see Figure 5.6) include "helping students brainstorm ideas for the planning of writing" (14.95%), "providing students with more linguistic input" (14.46%), and "demonstrating the critical use of technology" (14.22%). Acknowledging ChatGPT as a useful tool for

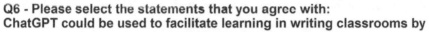

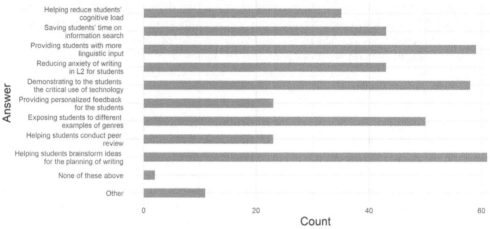

FIGURE 5.6 Result of the Question about Pedagogical Affordances of ChatGPT (Count).

brainstorming aligns with the previous finding that most survey respondents accepted the use of ChatGPT in generating ideas as an ethical practice.

The interview data adds nuances to our understanding of the perceived benefits of using ChatGPT in teaching and learning. Opinions diverge on whether ChatGPT could be used to help with searching for information and reducing students' cognitive load. Norton, for example, cautioned the use of ChatGPT in information searches because he believes that "if there's not a lot of data there, it just makes stuff up." Equally contentious is whether ChatGPT could be leveraged to help students process complex information. Katherine challenged the idea of reducing cognitive load for students, explaining that a heavy cognitive load is a necessity in college education. On the other hand, Jack, Emma, and Mina spoke in favor of this point. Jack gave a hypothetical scenario in which ChatGPT could be applied to help with reading comprehension:

> You're given some complex text like technical texts, it's way outside your league. You can put that in ChatGPT, get like it and say, ChatGPT, convert this to plain language. You can get the plain language summary. Use that as a roadmap to read that, or understand that technical text for reading comprehension.

In terms of the risks with the use of ChatGPT, as Figure 5.7 suggests, 27.52% of the survey respondents fear that ChatGPT might make copy and pasting machine-generated texts too easy for students. 24.03% selected the reduction of critical engagement with information as a potential risk, and 22.09% cautioned that the use of ChatGPT might negatively influence students' attitudes toward writing. 21.71% worried that the use of ChatGPT could perpetuate the misconception that writing is a formulaic and mechanical performance.

Besides these potential risks, our study has also assembled several other potential risks that concern L2 writing teachers. Norton and Lily raised the issue of losing one's own voice

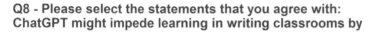

**Q8 - Please select the statements that you agree with:
ChatGPT might impede learning in writing classrooms by**

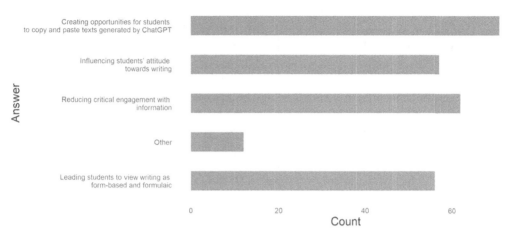

FIGURE 5.7   Result of the Question about Risks of ChatGPT (Count).

in writing if ChatGPT is used to assist with the writing process. Cecile envisioned an enlarging intellectual gap between students who always engage critically with information and those who try to get away with writing assignments. Daisy pointed out that the use of ChatGPT could impede learning by curtailing the kind of social interaction that usually happens in in-person teaching. In the face of the potential problems, interviewees also duly noted that some problems are not necessarily caused by the emergence of ChatGPT. For example, the uncritical use of information, according to Cecile, has always been a concern in her class.

Lastly, the fact that ChatGPT is able to generate texts with certain linguistic and textual features is perceived both as a risk and as a potential. Two survey respondents, through text entry, pointed out that the use of ChatGPT could normalize white upper-class English and reinforce the standards that are associated with a particular social group. However, in the interview, Norton provided a counterargument by highlighting the possible impact of ChatGPT on academic publications. He argued that non-native English-speaking scholars with a "written accent" could be spared of spending dollars on "nativizing" their articles and thus have an equal footing in publication:

> I've heard people, colleagues say the problem with the ChatGPT is that it's now normalizing white middle upper-class English, but you can counter that. You can say now it takes that privilege away. You don't have to be a native speaker to have a native accent...and suddenly this tool is available, to make your accent very clear in North American academic English, that's enormous power. Definitely use it.

In conclusion, our participants share to a certain extent the consensus about using chatbot in teaching. However, it's important to note that wide rifts exist in some areas among the participants, calling for more empirical research that validates or repudiates the speculations.

Discussion

Our finding indicates a relatively high level of L2 writing teachers' self-identified first-hand experience of experimenting with ChatGPT, which accords with Kim & Kim's (2022) observation that "teachers personally interacted with the AI-based educational tool before its implementation in schools" (p. 9). Such hands-on experience may raise the teachers' awareness of what these technological tools can do and increase their level of comfort in exploring them for pedagogical purposes (Kim & Kim, 2022). This also explains that more than half of our survey respondents self-perceived as being familiar with the capacities and limitations of ChatGPT.

Despite the L2 writing teachers' overall confidence in their knowledge of ChatGPT, they expressed their uncertainty about their students using ChatGPT in L2 writing. Specifically, for our L2 writing teachers, these caveats are mainly related to the characteristics of ChatGPT-generated texts, which were described as "generic," "limited," "detached," "fabricated," etc. Remarkably, the features perceived by the L2 writing teachers do not coincide with empirical evidence provided by research, as current research proves that ChatGPT is able to produce texts that are not distinguishable from human-written texts (Casal & Kessler, 2023; Gao et al., 2023). This could mean that the evaluation of ChatGPT-generated texts may be influenced by dynamic contextual factors, such as the purpose of the use of GPT-generated texts, the different evaluation criteria systems adopted by the referees, and the way how specific prompts are produced for ChatGPT to generate texts.

In addition, in our study, though representing the minority, we indeed capture the aversion toward ChatGPT held by some survey respondents. For example, one of our survey respondents points out in a text entry that "interesting how many of these you phrase as doing something FOR students." One possible reason for such negative perceptions of ChatGPT-generated texts is that people are disturbed by the changes brought by ChatGPT and may be generally aversive to AI-generated writing (Hostetter et al., 2023). Nevertheless, the positive perceptions held by the majority of our participants suggest L2 writing teachers' open mindset of introducing ChatGPT in their classrooms.

What is equally important is the interviewees' reported understanding of students' use of ChatGPT. Wang's (2024) study on how six students from a first-year writing class in US higher education practice AI-assisted writing reveals that undergraduate students use AI for brainstorming and addressing both global and local issues in writing. Our findings from the interviews indicate that L2 writing teachers who teach students of different levels hold diversified viewpoints of students' practices. Teachers who teach L2 undergraduate writing courses believed that students use ChatGPT out of pressure of limited linguistic and grammatical repertoire, while teachers who observed L2 graduate students pointed out that L2 graduate students were reluctant to use ChatGPT out of fear of their data leaking. The divergent students' views identified by some L2 writing teachers, together with the overall low level of survey respondents' familiarity with students' view of using ChatGPT, point to future research needs of conducting in-depth investigations of different groups of students' attitudes toward using ChatGPT in L2 writing.

Another theme identified in our interview findings in response to the first research question is the advocacy for AI critical literacy in both teachers and students. In our study, the interviewees propose that AI critical literacy is of vital significance for teachers to determine the type of intervention needed and for students to critically evaluate the information fed by

ChatGPT and other generative AI tools. This complements the recommendations proposed in the working paper produced by MLA-CCCC Joint Task Force on Writing and AI (2023), that AI critical literacy is needed for faculty leaders, administrators, and publishers and editors. In addition, corresponding with calls for pedagogical professional development of technology use (e.g., Froemming and Cifuentes, 2020), our findings imply a similarly important role of having open dialogues among teacher peers, evidenced by a high percentage of respondents indicating the source of their relevant knowledge coming from peer conversations of professional development.

The findings regarding ethical issues of using ChatGPT in writing suggest a similar pattern to the survey results in Hostetter et al. (2023), in which most respondents rated it unethical for students to use technology to write part or entire paper by copying and pasting. The solutions to tackling ethical issues proposed by our interviewees overlap with the recommendations in MLA-CCCC Joint Task Force on Writing and AI (2023) and Vetter et al.'s (2024) framework responsible uses of AI in writing classrooms, which include the ethical elements of pedagogy, criticality, agency, reliability, and accessibility. Our interviewees unanimously suggest that AI should be positioned as tools, and human efforts are essential for a desirable outcome in writing, which shares the same value that writing is valuable in developing thinking (MLA-CCCC Joint Task Force on Writing and AI, 2023). Despite the prevalent positioning of AI as *tool*, a caveat lies in Anderson's (2023) critiques of the metaphor of ChatGPT as *tool*, as she believes that we are so used to crediting any contributors in our process of writing as coauthors, we may blur the boundaries between tools and coauthors and gradually forget about the human components embedded within the use of machines. Secondly, most of our interviewees call for making the use of ChatGPT transparent, a remaining issue of which is how teachers should react to students' disclosure of their use of ChatGPT. This question may be more complicated for L2 writing teachers than general composition teachers and implies the need for further research on how plagiarism should be defined in the new era. In the six tenets of the post-plagiarism era proposed by Eaton (2021), it is pointed out that hybrid human-AI writing will gain prevalence and humans may relinquish control but not responsibility. How instructors and students perceive plagiarism in the post-plagiarism era, therefore, is another direction for future research.

The findings for the last research question share interesting similarities and nuances in terms of the affordances and risks of using ChatGPT in writing classrooms as reported in extant literature. Most of our respondents and interviewees agree that ChatGPT reduces students' cognitive workload and helps with information search, which corresponds with Barrot's (2023) claim that two of the outstanding affordances of using ChatGPT in L2 writing are to make students feel less stressed and to provide extensive corpus as strong resources of information. Nevertheless, these agreed-upon opinions are not without contentions in our findings, as some of our interviewees challenge the reliability of information offered by ChatGPT, and others point out that pursuing reduced cognitive load for college students may not always be good. These contentious voices point to potential pedagogical implications for L2 writing teachers. For example, in addition to training students in conducting information searches with the assistance of ChatGPT, teachers may need to equip students with the skills to identify reliable information. Moreover, L2 writing teachers need to balance how certain intellectual activities may serve the development of students' L2 writing competence, bearing in mind the caveat that ChatGPT may result in over-reduction of students' cognitive load and cause laziness.

A recognized potential risk of using ChatGPT in L2 writing is that writers may lose their voice in writing. In response to this concern, Barrot (2023) suggests that L2 writing teachers may encourage students to incorporate their personal experiences in writing. This presents opportunities for L2 writing teachers to design pedagogical materials that may assign more weight to writer's voice and identity. Albeit multiple potential risks identified, one implication of our findings is that teachers may need to ponder over if ChatGPT is the only cause of these potential risks, some of which may have existed long before the era of technology. Pedagogically, the question of whether ChatGPT creates the risks or reinforces them may serve as a starting point for students to critically reflect upon. Moreover, given the teachers' lack of knowledge of students' views in our findings, students as key stakeholders should not be prescribed how to use ChatGPT but encouraged to form their own critical thinking about it. Such instructional interrogation may increase students' critical digital literacy (Anderson, 2023).

Finally, the nature of double-sidedness of using ChatGPT in writing does not escape the issue of equity. ChatGPT may hurt marginalized populations, as it requires access to cutting-edge technology and applauds standardized English (MLA-CCCC Joint Task Force on Writing and AI, 2023). However, a counterargument emerged from our findings indicating that ChatGPT may empower non-native English scholars by equipping them with tools to nativize their articles, thereby contributing to equity in academia, echoing Eaton's (2021) claim that one's L1 may matter less with the facilitation of AI tools. Thus far, scant empirical evidence can be referred to in the correlation between equity and AI. Especially given the emergence of the paid version of ChatGPT, which may exacerbate the already existing equity issues, the question calls for future research on the relationship between the application of ChatGPT and the equity issue for underprivileged populations.

Conclusion

To conclude, this study reveals varying levels of knowledge and attitudes reported by our L2 writing teachers. It also explores ethical issues along with perceived affordances and risks of incorporating ChatGPT in L2 writing classrooms. Based on the discussion, we also suggest pedagogical implications for L2 writing teachers who may consider further exploring the role of ChatGPT in their classrooms and propose future research avenues. One caveat of this study is that our L2 writing teacher participants' perceptions may develop as time goes by and with accumulating pedagogical experience of incorporating ChatGPT in writing classrooms, as quite a few of our interviewees expressed their intent of continuously exploring this topic in future semesters. Additionally, with the unpredictably rapid advancement of ChatGPT and increasing professional support offered by academia and other related fields, the findings and implications of this study should not be viewed as prescriptive and static but as heuristic and evolving.

Appendix A

Sample Survey Questions

[1] Students' use of ChatGPT

1 Have you observed student(s) using ChatGPT on their own?
2 From your observation, how did your student(s) use ChatGPT on their own to complete their writing tasks?
3 Among all the students you teach, **approximately** how many students have used ChatGPT on their own in your writing class(es), from your observation?

[2] Ethical issues

To what extent do you agree with the following statements (Likert scale)

4 It is ethical for students to use ChatGPT for the purpose of

  i   Searching for information
  ii Brainstorming ideas/generating a list of ideas
  iii Producing example texts in one's writing by using ChatGPT-generated texts
  iv Others_____

5 It is ethical for teachers to use ChatGPT in the following situations

  i   Generating language for teaching materials
  ii Generating feedback and comments on students' work
  iii Grading students' work
  iv Others_____

[3] Pedagogical affordances

Select the statement(s) you agree with:

6 ChatGPT could be used to facilitate learning in writing classrooms by_____

  Helping reduce students' cognitive load
  Saving students' time on information search
  Providing students with more linguistic input
  Reducing anxiety about writing in L2 for students
  Demonstrating to the students the critical use of technology
  Providing personalized feedback for the students
  Exposing students to different examples of genres
  Helping students conduct peer review
  Helping students brainstorm ideas for the planning of writing
  None of the above
  others_____

7 ChatGPT could be used to facilitate teaching by_____

  Generating teaching materials
  Generating teaching ideas

Helping with generating assessing rubric
Helping with massive labor-required grading
Others_____

[4] Risks

8 ChatGPT might impede learning in writing classrooms by

   a Creating opportunities for students to copy and paste texts generated by ChatGPT
   b Influencing students' attitudes toward writing
   c Reducing critical engagement with information

[5] Teacher knowledge of and experience with ChatGPT

9 I have some experience with using ChatGPT

   a Yes
   b No → continue with 11

10 I used ChatGPT in order to

   a Understand the capability and limitations of this tool
   b Search for information
   c Help with writing for different purposes
   d Prepare a lesson on ChatGPT
   e other _____

11 Indicate how familiar you are with the following aspects (likert scale)

   a The capacities and limitations of ChatGPT
   b Students' views of using ChatGPT in writing
   c Students' ability to use ChatGPT responsibly
   d The pedagogical practices of using ChatGPT to facilitate teaching

12 My knowledge of ChatGPT comes from:

   a Attending professional development sessions
   b Reading academic sources
   c Reading public facing articles
   d Talking to colleagues
   e Experimenting with ChatGPT myself
   f Social media posts
   g Watching tutorial videos on how to use ChatGPT
   h others_____

[6] Institutional & professional support

13 What institutional and professional support have you received so far?

   a Policies and guidelines from your institution that address the use of ChatGPT in writing classrooms
   b Professional development opportunities from your institution
   c Professional development opportunities from academic organizations

d Paid training opportunities provided by profitable organizations
e None of these above
f Others____

14 What institutional and professional support do you hope to receive in the future?

a Policies and guidelines from your institution that address the use of ChatGPT in writing classrooms
b Professional development opportunities from your institution
c Professional development opportunities from academic organizations
d Paid training opportunities provided by profitable organizations
e All of the above apply
f Others_____

Demographic info

1 What is your institutional context?
2 What are the courses that you are currently teaching or have taught?
3 What are your student groups?
4 How many years have you taught L2 writing?
5 What is your age range?
6 Are you willing to participate in a short follow-up interview?

Appendix B

Semi-Structured Interview Protocol

[1] Teacher demographic information
Could you please briefly introduce yourself and your teaching context?

[2] Teacher's observations of/encounter with the phenomenon
Could you please tell me a little bit about how you first came to realize that ChatGPT was used by your students? If you select "not sure," could you please explain what makes you feel uncertain?

[3] Ethical issues
ChatGPT can do a number of things. When used in the pedagogical context, what use of ChatGPT is ethical and what is not? Where do you draw the line?

Do you think the ethical principles that you just discussed also apply to teachers using ChatGPT to assist in teaching?

[4] Pedagogical affordances
Now we are going to show the list of choices in the survey. You select the ones that are most outstanding to you, which means the ones you strongly agree with or disagree with. Can you envision some scenarios where ChatGPT supports students' learning of L2 writing?

[5] Risks
What do you envision as the challenges of using ChatGPT in L2 writing classrooms?

[6] Teaching practices
Have you talked about ChatGPT with the students? If yes. How did you address this topic in your class? Have you purposefully incorporated the use of ChatGPT in your class? If no. Why not?

[7] How do teachers conceptualize ChatGPT?
If you were to choose three adjectives that are associated with ChatGPT, what would those be? What caused you to select these three words? Is there anything that you want to add to explain your choice of words?

[8] Teacher development support
What kind of support do you think writing teachers need in order to better address the use of ChatGPT in teaching?

Optional: Please draw/visualize the role of ChatGPT in L2 writing pedagogy.

References

Anderson, S. S. (2023). "Places to stand": Multiple metaphors for framing ChatGPT's corpus. *Computers and Composition, 68*, 102778. https://doi.org/10.1016/j.compcom.2023.102778

Aydın, Ö., & Karaarslan, E. (2022). OpenAI ChatGPT generated literature review: Digital twin in healthcare. *SSRN Electronic Journal.* https://doi.org/10.2139/ssrn.4308687

Bailey, D. (2019). Chatbots as conversational agents in the context of language learning. In *Proceedings of the fourth industrial revolution and education* (pp. 32–41).

Barrot, J. S. (2023). Using ChatGPT for second language writing: Pitfalls and potentials. *Assessing Writing, 57*, 100745. https://doi.org/10.1016/j.asw.2023.100745

Braun, V., & Clarke, V. (2012). *Thematic analysis.* American Psychological Association.

Braun, V., Clarke, V., Boulton, E., Davey, L., & McEvoy, C. (2021). The online survey as a *qualitative research tool*. *International Journal of Social Research Methodology*, *24*(6), 641–654. https://doi.org/10.1080/13645579.2020.1805550

Cancino, M., & Panes, J. (2021). The impact of Google translate on L2 writing quality measures: Evidence from Chilean EFL high school learners. *System*, *98*, 102464. https://doi.org/10.1016/j.system. 2021.102464

Casal, J. E., & Kessler, M. (2023). Can linguists distinguish between ChatGPT/AI and human writing?: A study of research ethics and academic publishing. *Research Methods in Applied Linguistics*, *2*(3), 100068. https://doi.org/10.1016/j.rmal.2023.100068

Daniel, J. (2012). Choosing between nonprobability sampling and probability sampling. In *Sampling essentials: Practical guidelines for making sampling choices* (pp. 66–80). SAGE Publications. https://doi.org/10.4135/9781452272047

Demirdağ, S., & Efe, A. K. (2023). Exploring communication skills, transformational leadership, and intergenerational climate in educational institutions. In Soner Polat, & Çaglar Çelik (Eds.), *Perspectives on empowering intergenerational relations in educational organizations* (pp. 278–304). IGI Global.

Dizon, G., & Gayed, J. M. (2021). Examining the impact of Grammarly on the quality of mobile L2 writing. *JALT CALL Journal*, *17*(2), 74–92. https://doi.org/10.29140/jaltcall.v17n2.336

Eaton, S. E. E. (2021). *6 tenets of postplagiarism: Writing in the age of artificial intelligence* [Infographic]. https://doi.org/10.11575/PRISM/40770

Fernández-Batanero, J. M., Román-Graván, P., Reyes-Rebollo, M. M., & Montenegro-Rueda, M. (2021). Impact of educational technology on teacher stress and anxiety: A literature review. *International journal of environmental research and public health*, *18*(2), 548.

Fink, A. (2003). *How to manage, analyze, and interpret survey data* (No. 9). Sage.

Fives, Helenrose, & Buehl, Michelle M. (2012). Spring cleaning for the "messy" construct of teachers' beliefs: What are they? Which have been examined? What can they tell us? In K. R. Harris, S. Graham, T. Urdan, S. Graham, J. M. Royer, & M. Zeidner (Eds.), *APA educational psychology handbook*, Vol 2: Individual differences and cultural and contextual factors (pp. 471–499). American Psychological Association. https://doi.org/10.1037/13274-019

Froemming, C., & Cifuentes, L. (2020). Professional development for technology integration in the early elementary grades. In *Society for information technology & teacher education international conference, (Waynesville: Association for the Advancement of Computing in Education (AACE))* (pp. 444–450).

Gao, C. A., Howard, F. M., Markov, N. S., Dyer, E. C., Ramesh, S., Luo, Y., & Pearson, A. T. (2023). Comparing scientific abstracts generated by ChatGPT to real abstracts with detectors and blinded human reviewers. *Npj Digital Medicine*, *6*(1), 75. https://doi.org/10.1038/s41746-023-00819-6

Gayed, J. M., Carlon, M. K. J., Oriola, A. M., & Cross, J. S. (2022). Exploring an AI-based writing Assistant's impact on English language learners. *Computers and Education: Artificial Intelligence*, *3*, 100055. https://doi.org/10.1016/j.caeai.2022.100055

Godwin-Jones, R. (2022). *Partnering with AI: Intelligent writing assistance and instructed language learning*. Language Learning.

Guo, K., Wang, J., & Chu, S. K. W. (2022). Using chatbots to scaffold EFL students' argumentative writing. *Assessing Writing*, *54*, 100666. https://doi.org/10.1016/j.asw.2022.100666

Hostetter, A., Call, N., Frazier, G., James, T., Linnertz, C., Nestle, E., & Tucci, M. (2023). Student and faculty perceptions of artificial intelligence in student writing [Preprint]. PsyArXiv. https://doi.org/10.31234/osf.io/7dnk9

Hoy, A. W., Hoy, W. K., & Davis, H. A. (2009). Teachers' self-efficacy beliefs. In Kathryn R. Wentzel, & David B. Miele (Eds.), *Handbook of motivation at school* (pp. 641–668). Routledge.

Hwang, W.-Y., Nurtantyana, R., Purba, S. W. D., Hariyanti, U., Indrihapsari, Y., & Surjono, H. D. (2023). AI and recognition technologies to facilitate English as foreign language writing for supporting personalization and contextualization in authentic contexts. *Journal of Educational Computing Research*, 073563312211372. https://doi.org/10.1177/07356331221137253

Hyland, K. (2019). *Second language writing*. Cambridge University Press.

Kagan, Dona M. (1992). Implications of research of teacher belief. *Educational Psychologist*, *27*(1), 65–90. https://doi.org/10.1207/s15326985ep27016

Karakoyun, F., & Lindberg, O. J. (2020). Preservice teachers' views about the twenty-first century skills: A qualitative survey study in Turkey and Sweden. *Education and Information Technologies*, *25*(4), 2353–2369. https://doi.org/10.1007/s10639-020-10148-w

Kasneci, E., Seßler, K., Küchemann, S., Bannert, M., Dementieva, D., Fischer, F., ... & Kasneci, G. (2023). ChatGPT for good? On opportunities and challenges of large language models for education. *Learning and Individual Differences*, 103, 102274.

Kim, N. J., & Kim, M. K. (2022). Teacher's perceptions of using an artificial intelligence-based educational tool for scientific writing. *Frontiers in Education*, 7, 755914. https://doi.org/10.3389/feduc.2022.755914

Kurniati, E. Y., & Fithriani, R. (2022). Post-graduate students' perceptions of Quillbot utilization in English academic writing class. *Journal of English Language Teaching and Linguistics*, 7(3), 437–451.

Luckin, R., Holmes, W., Griffiths, M., and Forcier, L. B. (2016). *Intelligence unleashed: An argument for AI in education.* Pearson Education.

MLA-CCCC Joint Task Force on Writing and AI. (2023, July). MLA-CCCC joint task force on writing and AI working paper: Overview of the issues, statement of principles, and recommendations. *2023 modern language association of America and conference on college composition and communication.*

Murphy, R. F. (2019). Artificial intelligence applications to support K-12 teachers and teaching: A review of promising applications, challenges, and risks. *Perspective*, 10, 1–20. https://doi.org/10.7249/PE315

Nagata, R., Hashiguchi, T., & Sadoun, D. (2019). Is the simplest chatbot effective in English writing learning assistance? In *International conference of the pacific association for computational linguistics* (pp. 245–256). Springer. https://10.1007/978-981-15-6168-9_21

Nespor, J. (1987). The role of beliefs in the practice of teaching. *Journal of Curriculum Studies*, 19(4), 317–328. https://doi.org/10.1080/0022027870190403

Ng, D. T. K., Leung, J. K. L., Chu, S. K. W., & Qiao, M. S. (2021). Conceptualizing AI literacy: An exploratory review. *Computers and Education: Artificial Intelligence*, 2, 100041. https://doi.org/10.1016/j.caeai.2021.100041

OpenAI. (2022, November 30). ChatGPT: Optimizing language models for dialogue. *OpenAI*. https://openai.com/blog/chatgpt/

Rock, I. (1985). *Perception and knowledge. Acta Psychologica*, 59(1), 3–22.

Roulston, K. (2010). Considering quality in qualitative interviewing. *Qualitative Research*, 10(2), 199–228. https://doi.org/10.1177/1468794109356739

Rubie-Davies, C. M., Flint, A., & McDonald, L. G. (2012). Teacher beliefs, teacher characteristics, and school contextual factors: What are the relationships?: Teacher efficacy, expectations, and goal orientation. *British Journal of Educational Psychology*, 82(2), 270–288. https://doi.org/10.1111/j.2044-8279.2011.02025.x

Sumakul, D. T. Y. G., Hamied, F. A., & Sukyadi, D. (2022). Students' perceptions of the use of AI in a writing class. *67th TEFLIN international virtual conference & the 9th ICOELT 2021 (TEFLIN ICOELT 2021)*, Padang, Indonesia. https://doi.org/10.2991/asschr.k.220201.009

Tan, X., & Matsuda, P. K. (2020). Teacher beliefs and pedagogical practices of integrating multimodality into first-year composition. *Computers and Composition*, 58, 102614. https://doi.org/10.1016/j.compcom.2020.102614

Tan, X., Xu, W., & Wang, C. (2024). Purposeful remixing with generative AI: Constructing designer voice in multimodal composing. *arXiv preprint*. https://arxiv.org/abs/2403.19095

Terry, G., & Braun, V. (2017). Short but often sweet: The surprising potential of qualitative survey methods. In V. Braun, V. Clarke, & D. Gray (Eds.), *Collecting qualitative data: A practical guide to textual, media and virtual techniques* (pp. 15–44). Cambridge University Press.

Tsai, S.-C. (2019). Using google translate in EFL drafts: A preliminary investigation. *Computer Assisted Language Learning*, 32(5–6), 510–526. https://doi.org/10.1080/09588221.2018.1527361

Vetter, M. A., Lucia, B., Jiang, J., & Othman, M. (2024). Towards a framework for local Interrogation of AI ethics: A case study on text generators, academic integrity, and composing with ChatGPT. *Computers and Composition*, 71, 102831. https://doi.org/10.1016/j.compcom.2024.102831

Wang, C. (2024). Exploring students' generative AI-assisted writing processes: Perceptions and experiences from native and nonnative English speakers. *Technology, Knowledge and Learning*, 1–22. https://doi.org/10.1007/s10758-024-09744-3

Xu, W., & Tan, X. (2024). Beyond words: L2 writing teachers' visual conceptualizations of ChatGPT in teaching and learning. *Journal of Second Language Writing*, 64, 101110. https://doi.org/10.1016/j.jslw.2024.101110

Yan, D. (2023). Impact of ChatGPT on learners in a L2 writing practicum: An exploratory investigation. *Education and Information Technologies.* https://doi.org/10.1007/s10639-023-11742-4

Zimmerman, J. (2006). Why some teachers resist change and what principals can do about it. *NASSP Bulletin, 90,* 238–249. https://doi.org/10.1177/0192636506291521

Zimotti, G., Frances, C., & Whitaker, L. (2024). The future of language education: Teachers' perceptions about the surge of AI writing tools. *Technology in Language Teaching & Learning,* 6(2), 1–24. doi.org/10.29140/tltl.v6n2.1136

PART II

Praxis in Context

6

"NEVER LET A GOOD [LITERACY] CRISIS GO TO WASTE"

Writing Across the Curriculum Administration Amid Artificial Intelligence Anxiety

Christopher Basgier

Since at least the 1840s, periodic literacy crises have signaled shifts in the political, ideological, and cultural landscape of the United States (Trimbur, 1991). Because literacy is not only a set of reading and writing skills but also a complex socio-political phenomenon, its meaning changes across time and context (see, e.g., Vieira et al., 2019, p. 36). Those new meanings can spur literacy crises and may lead to structural reforms in higher education. For example, *Newsweek*'s December 1975 cover story, "Why Johnny Can't Write," played a key role in launching the Writing Across the Curriculum (WAC) movement. Maimon (2006) recalled the day her former dean at Beaver College (now Arcadia University) called her to his office, tossed the *Newsweek* issue at her, and asked what she planned to do about that literacy crisis. In response, she secured a National Endowment for the Humanities grant, which allowed her to fund one of the first writing pedagogy workshops in the United States for faculty across disciplines (Maimon, 2006). Presciently, Maimon recognized "that curriculum change depends on scholarly exchange among faculty members," a principle that has remained essential to the WAC movement (Palmquist et al., 2020; see also "Statement of WAC Principles and Practices," 2014).

In the fall of 2022, when OpenAI released ChatGPT, higher education was on the cusp of yet another literacy crisis. Because of ChatGPT's ability to produce fluent-sounding prose quickly, alongside sensationalist headlines prophesying the end of college writing (e.g., Marche, 2022), many of us wondered how to assign, teach, and assess writing when students have tools that can generate sentences, paragraphs, and even entire documents.

While it may be too soon to understand how the artificial intelligence (AI) crisis will change conceptions of literacy and its attendant political and ideological implications, we have begun to see how it challenges some of the educational structures that arose during previous literacy crises, such as WAC. Indeed, as a full-time administrator for a campus-wide writing center and WAC program at Auburn University, a central part of my job is teaching teachers how to teach writing. WAC programs like mine provide professional development for faculty across disciplines, encouraging them to adopt pedagogical and curricular changes so students get ample opportunities to write, revise, reflect, and deepen their communication

DOI: 10.4324/9781003426936-9

skills and conceptual learning. When it was released, ChatGPT seemed poised to disrupt this entire premise.

Then, in winter 2022–23, my supervisor, Norman Godwin, Associate Provost for Academic Affairs, changed my perspective. He encouraged me to explore how I might use the technology to *further* our program's mission of supporting students as thinkers and communicators. He invoked an axiom that is attributed to Winston Churchill, but often repeated in politics and business: "Never let a good crisis go to waste." He asked how I might use the ChatGPT literacy crisis to engage colleagues across campus—especially those with whom I had had little contact—to think about the intersections between the technology and disciplinary writing pedagogy. In response, I devised ways of fostering nuanced, intellectually rich conversations about the new technology among faculty members. Could the panic surrounding generative AI—a literacy technology—become a means to grow, rather than eliminate, the use of evidenced-based writing pedagogies across the disciplines?

In this chapter, I will discuss how I answered that question. I will describe how I engaged colleagues across campus in stimulating conversations about generative AI as an emerging technology and led them to transformative learning about WAC pedagogy. To do so, I followed Sandra Tarabochia's (2017) relational ethic for cross-curricular literacy (CCL)[1] work: "commit to reflexive practice" (p. 146), "maintain a learner's stance" (p. 148), and "approach CCL conversations as a pedagogical performance" (p. 151). According to Tarabochia, these practices contribute to productive interpersonal conversations "where the possibility of embracing pedagogical potential"—and, I would add, curricular potential—"can be … strengthened" (p. 145). By taking on this relational ethic as praxis, I sought to move faculty and administrators toward a reflective and proactive, rather than reactive, stance toward generative AI.

In what follows, I first provide an overview of the institutional and programmatic context in which I have conducted workshops and discussions about writing and AI. Then, I define the elements of Tarabochia's (2017) relational ethic and illustrate how I used it as a praxis to guide my activities. As I reflect on my experiences, I also note ways in which I did and did not practice the relational ethic as successfully as I could have. Finally, I extend Tarabochia's relational ethic with additional principles attuned to the challenges of leading conversations about generative AI: acknowledging different values, centering intellectual commitments, and recognizing different comfort levels.

Institutional and Programmatic Context

Auburn University is a research-intensive land grant institution located in the Southeastern United States, enrolling approximately 30,000 students annually. Launched in 2010, the Office of University Writing (or just "University Writing," for short) is a comprehensive writing center and WAC program centrally located in the Office of the Provost. Our primary mission is to support students as thinkers and communicators by helping them become better writers, primarily through the Miller Writing Center (MWC) and graduate support services, and to extend our reach by supporting faculty who teach high-impact, writing-focused courses and curricula across the disciplines. We offer free one-on-one appointments with any student at any stage of the writing process in the MWC, multi-session programs tailored to the needs of graduate writers, and WAC workshops and workshop series that help faculty learn about effective, discipline-specific writing pedagogy. In addition to supervising two associate directors who run the MWC and graduate programs, my main responsibility in University Writing is to lead our WAC efforts. In that capacity, I developed or co-developed a slate of AI-focused programs, activities, and resources in late 2022 and into 2023, and I mobilized Tarabochia's (2017) relational ethic in the process.

Defining and Practicing a Relational Ethic

Tarabochia (2017) argued that CCL professionals need a relational ethic so they can "adjust communication strategies to foster productive conversations with faculty in other disciplines, build sustainable relationships, and revise writing curricula amid complicated, ever-changing dynamics" (p. 6). These needs apply as much to campus-wide discussions about generative AI as they do to more traditional WAC or writing center discussions. AI discussions require adjusting to others' relative comfort with the technology, sustaining engagement over time, and contemplating revisions to courses and curricula in response to rapid technological advancements. Such conversations are also fundamentally pedagogical and ethical. In what follows, I define the three pedagogical and three ethical dimensions of Tarabochia's (2017) framework and illustrate how I put them into practice with specific examples from my campus-wide work on AI in University Writing's WAC program.

Pedagogical Principles and AI Conversations

To build her relational ethic, Tarabochia (2017) first identified three main pedagogical practices used by CCL professionals in their interactions with colleagues across disciplines: negotiating expertise, transformative learning, and play.

Negotiating Expertise

For Tarabochia (2017), negotiating expertise involves "putting one's knowledge and experience in conversation with others' differently situated knowledge and experience" (p. 24). This pedagogical principle is especially important in CCL contexts where the kind of expert-novice relationships typical of classrooms do not apply. Instead, those of us who lead CCL programs like WAC often find ourselves sharing expertise about rhetoric, writing, or literacy with individuals who have expertise in a different domain—usually another academic discipline—with their own disciplinary and idiosyncratic writing processes and practices. We need to find ways to share our expert knowledge without discounting theirs.

With this principle in mind, I contacted department chairs in early spring 2023 with an offer to lead department-wide conversations about generative AI and writing. At the time of this writing, I have conducted more than 20 such conversations, usually lasting between 30 and 60 minutes, with departments like English; Mechanical Engineering; Nursing; and World Languages, Literatures, and Cultures. Early on, these conversations typically involved a hands-on demonstration of ChatGPT and a discussion of different modes of response to generative AI, which I discuss in detail below (see "Pedagogical Performance").

During these conversations, I sought "to recognize faculty members' existing expertise and productively shift or expand" our responses to this technology's limitations and affordances (Tarabochia, 2017, p. 146). To that end, I focused these conversations on hands-on experimentation with AI, typically by soliciting a prompt related to faculty members' discipline. For example, the Aerospace Engineering faculty asked me to prompt ChatGPT to explain how to calculate the aerodynamics of a frisbee. After they observed that the explanation included no math, I prompted it to rewrite the output with an equation. The faculty pointed out that ChatGPT's equation was incorrect and that the response had no references. I asked it to rewrite the response with references, and, unsurprisingly, the faculty quickly realized that it had fabricated references. I did not need to guide this conversation in any specific direction; instead, I invited the faculty to identify key places in which the ChatGPT output was doing the intellectual work of their discipline, and they proceeded to use their expertise to attend to conceptual accuracy, mathematics, and citations, all of which manifest in discipline-specific writing conventions.

My conversations with these faculty members thus helped me refine a technique I had learned from other WAC scholarship (e.g., Glotfelter et al., 2020): to center the intellectual work of the disciplines in my conversations about generative AI. As the above example illustrates, the disciplines' intellectual core can be a means for faculty to engage with the technology deliberately and critically, and we cannot negotiate expertise if our colleagues' ways of thinking and communicating are not central to the conversation. When we work to surface faculty members' intellectual commitments, we can better practice a relational ethic because our respective areas of expertise and their associated values are more transparent and therefore open to negotiation.

Transformative Learning

Negotiations of expertise helped me take up the second element of Tarabochia's (2017) pedagogical framework, transformative learning, which promotes iterative and recursive "change in [faculty] perspectives and practices" (p. 73).[2] I follow this approach to transformative learning in my signature program, the WAC Academy, a five-part workshop series that engages departmental teams in focused conversations about disciplinary threshold concepts (Meyer & Land, 2005; Adler-Kassner & Wardle, 2015; Adler-Kassner & Wardle, 2019), writing in the discipline, scaffolded writing instruction, and effective design for writing assignments and peer review experiences. The outcome of the WAC Academy is a plan for integrating writing across a departmental curriculum and sample classroom artifacts that can be used or adapted to facilitate implementation.

Frequently, I adjust the default sequence of WAC Academy activities to suit particular needs and desires (e.g., to focus on ePortfolios in Speech, Language, and Hearing Sciences or undergraduate research in Psychology). In fall 2023, I incorporated material on critical thinking and AI at the request of a team of political science faculty. These faculty members were understandably concerned that students might use ChatGPT to write for them. In response, I invited them to consider bringing the technology into the classroom explicitly and turning its output into an object of inquiry rather than simply a tool for composing. They seemed to find this idea provocative, and together we brainstormed several AI-engaged activities for multiple courses in the undergraduate political science major.

In one such activity, the faculty wanted students to learn how to apply and evaluate game theory, which they had identified as a persistently troublesome set of concepts in the major. They asked students to prompt ChatGPT to explain a recent political event using several different possible games, and then evaluate which explanation was most compelling and why. To me, this kind of assignment represented a transformation in the political science faculty's conception of teaching and writing pedagogy in the age of AI. They saw how it could be leveraged as a means of reinforcing students' learning in a way that is akin to writing-to-learn, with ChatGPT as a sounding board rather than a replacement for thinking and analysis.

Play

While most of my interactions with faculty about generative AI were based on academic inquiry—how it works and what it means for teaching—I also utilized play to encourage colleagues to learn about the technology. Tarabochia (2017) defines the pedagogical principle of play as the use of "metaphor, storytelling, and silliness" to "invigorate[] the epistemic, reflexive, and relational dimensions of pedagogical activity" (p. 108–109). For me, the relational aspect of play is especially valuable. I regularly use play in many of my interactions across campus because, like Tarabochia, I find that humor and storytelling help alleviate tensions and build meaningful relationships. Low stakes and highly relational engagement seemed especially beneficial amid fears over generative AI's disruptive potential, fears that coincide with pre-existing anxiety over the contraction of higher education (Basgier, 2023). Aware of these fears, my colleague Chesly Hooper (Auburn's Adobe expert) and I explicitly promoted play in an event we designed called the Generative AI Playground.

During the Generative AI Playground, we invited faculty and staff from across campus to experiment with ChatGPT and Adobe Firefly, an AI-powered image generator now part of Adobe's Creative Cloud. After introducing basic definitions of generative AI and the technology's ethical complications, we tasked participants with generating a children's book about their area of expertise using those two platforms. Chelsy and I demonstrated the process with our AI-generated children's books, one about rhetoric (one of my areas of expertise) and one about creativity (Chelsy's area of expertise).

When we first conceptualized the workshop, we wanted to give participants an immersive, low-stakes experience of using generative AI to compose so they could better understand what it could and could not do. We decided on the idea of a "playground" to make the event sound inviting and to avoid any expectation that we might be training participants in best practices. Instead, we wanted participants to take up the opportunity for playful experimentation. Tarabochia (2017) named storytelling as one possible playful technique that can be used in CCL conversations, and we saw firsthand how the events encouraged participants to create stories that mattered to them. For example, Carrie Hill, a research librarian, created a story about a child who convinces an adult community member to stop attempting to ban books from the library. The story she created is compelling and timely, and she and Chelsy continue to use it as an example in other workshops about AI.

Our choice of genre, too, centered play. Children's books can address serious subjects, like book bans, through humor and play. In doing so, they render the complexities of life approachable. By asking participants to create a children's book about their area of expertise, we hoped they could experience the often-challenging blend of the new and familiar that our students experience when writing in new curricular contexts. Additionally, we selected a multimodal genre for participants to familiarize themselves with text and image generators and explore their expertise in visual modes. Altogether, the low-stakes task provided participants with an opportunity for meaning-making, as they could compose with AI without fear of reprisal or pressure to publish.

Ethical Principles and AI Conversations

Based on her analysis of negotiating expertise, transformative learning, and play, Tarabochia (2017) also distilled three core ethical principles that she recommended CCL professionals pursue in their work: reflective practice, a learner's stance, and pedagogical performance.

Reflective Practice

Tarabochia's (2017) first ethical principle involves "reflecting systematically on one's own values and assumptions in relation to new, sometimes counterintuitive ideas" (p. 146). Reflective practice can be ethical when it supports connection and transparent negotiation of values with others who are often positioned differently in the institution.

Because generative AI can appear "new" and "counterintuitive," it can be a convenient starting point for reflective practice for CCL professionals ourselves. To me, ChatGPT looked like a challenge to one of my core values: collaboration. I attempt to bring a collaborative ethos to my teaching, faculty development, administration, and research, even as I recognize the uneven power dynamics that can arise in those situations (Trimbur, 1989). With ChatGPT, however, I could imagine a future with very little collaborative writing. It seemed to value speed over slower, more deliberate collaborative work. I did not, and still do not, see the technology as a collaborator because collaboration requires intentionality, the understanding that people bring multiple experiences and identities to bear on their work, and attention to power dynamics that can interrupt group functions and exclude individuals from meaningful labor. ChatGPT cannot access this information about me; it cannot analyze and respond to my unstated assumptions as a collaborator might.

After reflecting on my own values, I was in a better position to respond to others' reactions to generative AI. Most readers will probably be familiar with criticisms of ChatGPT as a direct affront to the values of novelty, textual ownership, and academic integrity that circulate in many Western academic contexts, including institutions and disciplines. How could we be sure that students' and scholars' words and ideas were "their own?" Gavin P. Johnson (2023) argued that such responses to generative AI amount to "paranoia and an impulse of surveillance" (p. 173). In some group discussions with faculty, I saw the paranoid impulse on full display, such as one faculty member who likened students' use of generative AI to copying from a roommate. Although I did not have the opportunity to talk with this individual at length, it occurred to me afterward that his response may not have been so different from mine. After all, what is "copying" but an illicit form of collaboration? Perhaps, like me, he simply did not see ChatGPT as a legitimate learning collaborator. In this way, reflective practice enabled me to build empathy for an individual I might otherwise dismiss as paranoid and destructive. I could also respond constructively, which I have done in subsequent workshops by discussing the circumstances that might lead students to cheat and ways of curbing academic misconduct via effective assignment design (e.g., Anderson et al., 2016; Winkelmes, 2013).

A Learner's Stance

These reflections also positioned me to occupy what Tarabochia (2017) called a learner's stance, "discursively acknowledging the knowledge and expertise others bring to CCL conversations and to teaching writing" (p. 149), a point that intersects with the pedagogical principle of negotiating expertise.

For example, while I was conducting departmental discussions, I learned that several faculty members had been investigating the extent to which ChatGPT could accomplish the intellectual work of their disciplines. David Marshall and David Naff (2024), experts in educational research methods, conducted a study about researchers' perceptions of the ethics of using generative AI in qualitative research. Based on a descriptive survey of 101 researchers, they found that study participants thought it was acceptable to use the technology for transcription and initial coding, but not for all coding, analysis, and manuscript writing. Similarly, James Long and his many colleagues in accountancy studied ChatGPT's performance on accounting assessment questions (Wood et al., 2023), finding that students generally outperformed ChatGPT at the time of the study, but not always. These interactions showed me how generative AI could be addressed in different disciplinary contexts, and they helped me develop a more nuanced understanding of the spectrum of faculty's responses to the technology, between the poles of complete rejection and uncritical embrace.

Sometimes, however, I let these discussions devolve into cautionary tales instead of deeper pedagogical opportunities. For example, when the English Department faculty asked if ChatGPT could cite and analyze poetry, I said, let's see. We quickly learned that it could, especially with well-known literature, but we also caught it fabricating lines that only sounded like a given poet. In response, I told faculty they could use this result to caution students about relying too readily on the technology. In retrospect, however, I do not think my response was satisfactory because, at that moment, I was not maintaining a learner's stance.

As Tarabochia (2017) put it, "[M]aintaining a learner's stance is a vital part of engaging in pedagogical activity because it promotes knowledge production and transformation within individual and collaborative meaning-making frameworks" (p. 148–149). To that end, I could have asked the English faculty to design activities that would utilize the problematic ChatGPT response to deepen students' learning of literary analysis. Perhaps students could use ChatGPT to fabricate a poem by a particular poet and then compare it to an authentic poem to identify matters of style, tone, and theme. Had I maintained a learner's stance, I could have refocused the conversation on disciplinary knowledge, thus inviting everyone in the room to consider a more nuanced understanding of the pedagogical potential of generative AI as an object of inquiry and advance our collective knowledge of what the technology could and could not do.

Pedagogical Performance

Tarabochia's (2017) final ethical principle, pedagogical performance, means recognizing "teacher behaviors not as the natural consequence of identity, style, or institutional structure, but as performance genres that can be strategically manipulated, juxtaposed, employed, etc., for particular pedagogical effects" (p. 151). In other words, teaching is always a performance that involves using the body, space, technologies, discourse, and instructional techniques to achieve various pedagogical goals.

In late spring 2023, I had my first opportunity to self-consciously engage in a pedagogical performance regarding generative AI that differed from what I might have done otherwise. Previously, I had positioned myself as a co-inquirer and co-critic. However, I had to perform a different stance when the Chair of the University Senate invited me to speak to Senators but asked me to remain neutral toward generative AI, neither embracing it nor rejecting it. Despite my conviction that collectively, faculty must use AI to understand it, but that they ought to do so with an appropriately skeptical, even critical, mindset, I had to leave room for colleagues to sidestep it or forbid it outright.

I decided to treat this request as an opportunity to practice a relational ethic. In her study, Tarabochia (2017) found, "Writing specialists … created opportunities for active learning, reflection, and cross-disciplinary connection-making *by temporarily withholding advice,*" resulting in transformative learning when faculty came to new or refined understandings of writing pedagogy for themselves (p. 146; emphasis mine). My aim was similar: even as I withheld any specific recommendation regarding responses to generative AI, I wanted faculty to see that their pedagogy could account for or even draw on the technology to enhance learning.

To help faculty make informed decisions that centered on learning, I developed four modes of pedagogical response to generative AI:

- Prohibition: requesting that students not use it in any way for any assignment, with the caution to faculty that AI detection services are flawed.
- Permission: allowing students to use it in approved ways, with appropriate attribution.
- Pedagogy: preventing dishonest use of it via practices such as scaffolded activities, peer and instructor feedback, or reflective writing, which can build students' self-efficacy and empower them to write, with or without generative AI as a tool.
- Engagement: either directly incorporating generative AI into assignments and activities such as critiques or indirectly addressing the technology through discipline-specific questions, such as ethics or environmental impact.

Across my discussion of these modes, I self-consciously performed agnosticism to highlight a more fundamental principle: I wanted listeners (and eventual readers of the document version) to understand that they should teach their disciplinary ways of thinking with writing more transparently, no matter their response to generative AI. Across my description of all four modes of response, I encouraged faculty to communicate with students why they were responding as they were, grounding their reasons in the ways of making and circulating knowledge germane to their disciplines. For example, in prohibiting the use of generative AI, art history professors might explain that they want students to hone their ability to identify and interpret visual details. In contrast, physics faculty might ask students to debate ChatGPT about the merits of Newtonian versus Lagrangian mechanics so they could learn when to use which approach.[3] In leaving these options open, I hoped to seed transformative learning by prompting faculty to understand how conceptual and rhetorical transparency can support students' learning and engagement, with or without generative AI in the mix.

A Relational Ethic for Leading Campus Conversations about Generative AI

In this final section, I elaborate on Tarabochia's (2017) relational ethic for CCL work, focusing on some additional practices for CCL professionals who lead campus conversations about generative AI. Although these practices are inspired by, and intersect with, Tarabochia's, I also see them as uniquely suited to address and disrupt the crisis narrative that has followed in the wake of ChatGPT. They are relational, in that, taken together, they remind us to see our colleagues, and ourselves, as whole people who bring a complex mix of values, intellectual commitments, and affective responses to generative AI. Similarly, they are ethical in that they require us to interrupt the impulse to impose our own views of emerging technologies on our colleagues who work in different curricular, institutional, and disciplinary spaces; instead, they place an ethical premium on transparency to guide change.

Acknowledge Different Values

Generative AI cuts to the core of many academic and personal values. CCL professionals are committed to a deep, critical understanding of the impact of literacy technologies on reading and writing for individuals and wider educational and social systems. However, even within those same systems, other values circulate. Most obviously, individuals across academia have expressed reservations about generative AI due to concerns about academic dishonesty. Simultaneously, many faculty treasure academic freedom, which may be threatened by institutional policies that prohibit any use of generative AI in student work. Faculty who value their research more than teaching may not feel compelled to commit to ongoing, reflective pedagogical engagement; conversely, they may be more willing to respond to research-supported pedagogies of the sort shared in this volume and elsewhere (e.g., Vee et al., 2023). These examples also intersect with competing values of individualism versus collectivism: many academics operate as independent contractors, focused on their areas of expertise, whereas departments or institutions must work collectively and proactively to respond to generative AI. Faculty also bring values from their family, cultures, faiths, and communities; to help faculty name such values, I often share James Clear's (n.d.) list of core values and encourage them to identify one or two that they hold dear.

Because of these many values, it behooves CCL professionals to begin conversations about generative AI with reflections on values, so that they may be made more explicit and therefore open to discussion. After all, people rarely change their minds by being told their ideas—and those ideas' underlying values—are wrong. Instead, we need to open relational spaces where, even amid disagreement, we can understand and speak to one another's perspectives. The ethical principle at work here is one of negotiation, rather than imposition: if, as CCL professionals, we want to manage conceptual, pedagogical, curricular, and policy change regarding generative AI, then we need to engage others in principled dialogue by ensuring their values have a seat at the table.

Center Intellectual Commitments

In addition to core values, faculty members and administrators bring intellectual commitments to pedagogical and curricular conversations. The threshold concepts theory has taught us that faculty think and work with intellectual frameworks that have become naturalized (Adler-Kassner & Wardle, 2015; Adler-Kassner & Wardle, 2019; Meyer & Land, 2005). CCL professionals can engage faculty in intellectually rich conversations about these literacy technologies by considering them through the lens of their disciplinary concepts. One way I have done so is to select data from a published article in a given discipline and invite faculty to compare the published analysis with a ChatGPT-generated analysis. I ask faculty to identify the conceptual and discursive differences between human- and AI-generated writing within their disciplinary territory. I also explain that a similar activity could help them teach their students disciplinary knowledge, including writing, in a low-stakes way, without overhauling a course completely to address generative AI. Such techniques acknowledge faculty expertise and create space for a critically pragmatic approach to the technology.

While this principle certainly intersects with Tarabochia's (2017) principle of negotiating expertise, it also prompts CCL professionals to recognize that faculty can draw on critical theory, problem-solving, the scientific method, or most other intellectual frameworks to build productive responses to generative AI in classrooms and curricula. Ethically speaking, it empowers faculty to make decisions about generative AI using their own ways of thinking and doing.

Recognize Different Levels of Comfort

Our responses to generative AI are affective as much as they are intellectual and values-driven. When facilitating conversations, we may face audiences who are alternately panicked, excited, or a combination of both. Transparency about our own feelings can create a sense of solidarity and promote engagement at the same time. For example, when Packback, an educational technology company, announced the release of the Writing Lab, which they described as an AI writing tutor, I immediately feared for the future of our writing center. However, in conversations with my team and with the University Writing Committee, we acknowledged the ongoing benefits of human tutors, including an empathetic touch, real readership, and rich contextual awareness, all of which are difficult, if not impossible, for generative AI to mimic. Those discussions provided a sense of solidarity and helped us refine how we talk about writing center work. In other cases, play may be an optimal approach because it can give faculty and other stakeholders permission to learn about the technology without necessarily endorsing its widespread use, thus diffusing fear.

Whereas intellectual labor is part and parcel of academia, and values also figure in our work, emotions are too often ignored in academic spaces. By recognizing them, we can round out a relational ethic toward generative AI.

Conclusion

In his contribution to a special section of *Composition Studies* on generative AI, Johnson (2023) urged the field to remember what we already know about teaching writing with and through technologies: "[W]hile this iteration of AI technology is new and needs to be addressed on its own terms," he wrote, "our general approach to AI and writing should follow core tenets set out and cited in decades of scholarship and pedagogy" in the field (p. 169).

For instance, literacy technologies are not neutral tools for reading and composing. Rather, they influence our rhetorical, epistemological, and ideological choices (e.g., Baron, 2009; Johnson, 2023; Jones & Hirsu, 2019; New London Group, 1996; Sheridan et al., 2012). To take one example, the introduction of the pencil with eraser enabled revision to play a stronger role in writing processes, and for that reason "was initially greeted with suspicion … because critics charged that erasers would adversely affect the quality of writing" (Baron, 2009, p. 43). Today, revision is part and parcel of writing pedagogy, regularly viewed as essential to quality writing.

Similar changes are underway with generative AI. When leading campus conversations about this technology, I have tried to remain mindful of decades of WAC scholarship that recommends ethical means of engaging with faculty when seeking pedagogical and curricular change. I have had to be aware of my own instincts to assert my disciplinary perspectives on generative AI unthinkingly, lest I colonize the disciplines with my ways of knowing and teaching (Farris, 1992). When faculty express opinions that I find short-sighted or dismissive of students, I have tried to practice deep listening so I can better understand their underlying motivations (Mullin, 2008), and then respond. Through these reflective practices, I have also sought to empower faculty to consider for themselves what it means to teach writing in the disciplines (Flash, 2016; Flash, 2021; Glotfelter et al. 2020; Wardle, 2019). And I have found them to be "practices" in a deep sense: I have to attend to them mindfully, habitually, and recognize both when I succeed and when I fail to act on the theoretical and ethical commitments they represent.

After all, these ideas have served us through many literacy crises, from the beginning of the WAC movement through an earlier generation of technological changes (e.g., new media, web 2.0, social media) that produced similar panics (see, e.g., Trimbur, 2015). Still, to echo Johnson (2023), I have also seen that this latest crisis deserves to be addressed not only through the strategies that have long served CCL professionals but also in its own right, given the range of responses faculty hold and the depth of the challenge generative AI poses for higher education. It touches on so many aspects of our being, not just as writers and communicators, but as thinkers and teachers, as embodied people living in the world. By adding concerted attention to values, intellectual commitments, and affect to our pedagogical ethics, we can respond humanely and ethically to this emerging technology.

Notes

1 Tarabochia (2017) uses *cross-curricular literacy* (CCL) as a blanket term for literacy-focused programs and projects that do not reside within, or work in the confines of, a singular departmental structure. Principally, CCL includes WAC and its many permutations (writing in the disciplines, communication across the curriculum, writing enriched curriculum) and writing centers. It may also include community literacy, communication across the curriculum, and even quantitative literacy programs.
2 Change in faculty perspectives can be difficult to identify because such changes may happen tacitly or over long periods of time (see Walvoord et al., 1997), although reflective narratives may provide one means of gauging shifts in conceptions of writing pedagogy (Basgier & Simpson, 2019, 2020). Still, multi-part professional development experiences centered on discipline-specific concepts have been shown to contribute to changes in writing pedagogy (Glotfelter et al., 2020).
3 This activity was suggested by my colleague Luca Guazzotto, Professor of Physics at Auburn University.

References

Adler-Kassner, L., & Wardle, E. (Eds.). (2019). *(Re)Considering what we know: Learning thresholds in writing, composition, rhetoric, and literacy.* Utah State UP.

Adler-Kassner, Linda, & Wardle, Elizabeth. (2015). *Naming what we know: Threshold concepts of writing studies.* Utah State UP.

Anderson, P., Anson, C. M., Gonyea, R. M., & Paine, C. (2016). How to create high-impact writing assignments that enhance learning and development and reinvigorate WAC/WID programs: What almost 72,000 undergraduates taught us. *Across the Disciplines, 13*(4), 1–18. https://doi.org/10.37514/ATD-J.2016.13.4.13

Baron, D. (2009). *A better pencil: Readers, writers, and the digital revolution.* Oxford University Press.

Basgier, C. (2023). Continuing writing across the curriculum programs amid the contraction of higher education: Vision, mission, and strategy. In R. McCabe & J. Juszkiewicz (Eds.), *Composition and Rhetoric in Contentious Times* (pp. 69–89). Utah State UP.

Basgier, C., & Simpson, A. (2019). Trouble and transformation in higher education: Identifying threshold concepts through faculty narratives about teaching writing. *Studies in Higher Education, 45*(9), 1906–1918.

Basgier, C., & Simpson, A. (2020). Reflecting on the past, reconstructing the future: Faculty member's threshold concepts for teaching writing in the disciplines. *Across the Disciplines, 17*(1/2), 6–25. https://doi.org/10.37514/ATD-J.2020.17.1-2.02

Clear, James. (n.d.). Core values list. *James Clear.* Retrieved October 26, 2023, from https://jamesclear.com/core-values

Farris, C. (1992). Giving religion, taking gold: Disciplinary cultures and the claims of writing across the curriculum. In J. Berlin & M. Vivion (Eds.), *Cultural studies in the English classroom* (pp. 112–122). Boynton/Cook.

Flash, P. (2016). From apprised to revised: Faculty in the disciplines change what they never knew they knew. In K. B. Yancey (Ed.), *A rhetoric of reflection* (pp. 227–249). Utah State UP.

Flash, P. (2021). Writing-enriched curriculum: A model for making and sustaining change. In C. M. Anson & P. Flash (Eds.), *Writing-enriched curricula: Models of faculty-driven and departmental transformation* (pp. 17–44). The WAC Clearinghouse; University Press of Colorado. https://doi.org/10.37514/PER-B.2021.1299.2.01

Glotfelter, A., Updike, A., & Wardle, E. (2020). Something invisible… Has been made visible for me: An expertise-based WAC seminar model grounded in theory and (cross) disciplinary dialogue. In L. E. Bartlett, S. L. Tarabochia, A. R. Olinger, M. J. Marshall (Eds.), *Diverse approaches to teaching, learning, and writing across the curriculum: IWAC at 25* (pp. 167–192). The WAC Clearinghouse and University Press of Colorado.

Johnson, G. P. (2023). Don't act like you forgot: Approaching another literacy "crisis" by (re)considering what we know about teaching writing with and through technologies. *Composition Studies, 51*(1), 169–175.

Jones, J., & Hirsu, L. (2019). *Rhetorical machines: Writing, code, and computational ethics.* University of Alabama Press.

Maimon, E. P. (2006). It takes a campus to teach a writer: WAC and the reform of undergraduate education. In S. H. McLeod & M. Soven (Eds.), *Composing a community: A history of writing across the curriculum* (pp. 16–31). Parlor Press.

Marche, S. (2022, December 6). The college essay is dead. *The Atlantic.* https://www.theatlantic.com/technology/archive/2022/12/chatgpt-ai-writing-college-student-essays/672371/

Marshall, D. T., & Naff, D. B. (2024). The ethics of using artificial intelligence in qualitative research. *Journal of Empirical Research on Human Research Ethics, 19*(3), 92–102. https://doi.org/10.1177/15562646241262659

Meyer, J. H. F., & Land, R. (2005). Threshold concepts and troublesome knowledge (2): Epistemological considerations and a conceptual framework for teaching and learning. *Higher Education, 49*(3), 373–388.

Mullin, J. A. (2008). Interdisciplinary work as professional development: Changing the culture of teaching. *Pedagogy: Critical Approaches to Teaching Literature, Language, Composition, and Culture, 8*(3), 495–508.

New London Group. (1996). A pedagogy of multiliteracies: Designing social futures. *Harvard Educational Review, 66*(1), 60–92.

Palmquist, M., Childers, P., Maimon, E. P., Mullin, J. A., Rice, R., Russell, A., & Russell, D. R. (2020). Fifty years of WAC: Where have we been? Where are we going? *Across the Disciplines, 17*(3/4), 5–45. https://doi.org/10.37514/ATD-J.2020.17.3.01

Sheridan, D. M., Ridolfo, J., & Michel, A. J. (2012). *The available means of persuasion: Mapping a theory and pedagogy of multimodal public rhetoric.* Parlor Press.

Statement of WAC Principles and Practices. (2014). Retrieved from https://wac.colostate.edu/principles

Tarabochia, S. L. (2017). *Reframing the relational: A pedagogical ethic for cross-curricular literacy work.* CCCC/NCTE.

Trimbur, J. (1989). Consensus and difference in collaborative learning. *College English, 51*(6), 602–616.

Trimbur, J. (1991). Literacy and the discourse of crisis. In R. H. Bullock & J. Trimbur (Eds.), *The politics of writing instruction: Postsecondary* (pp. 277–296). Boynton/Cook.

Trimbur, J. (2015). Revisiting "literacy and the discourse of crisis" in the era of neoliberalism. In L. C. Lewis (Ed.), *Strategic discourse: The politics of (new) literacy crises.* Computers and Composition Digital Press/Utah State University Press. Retrieved April 10, 2024, from https://ccdigitalpress.org/book/strategic/afterword.html

Vee, A., Laquintano, T., & Schnitzler, C. (Eds.). (2023). *TextGenEd: Teaching with text generation technologies.* The WAC Clearinghouse. https://doi.org/10.37514/TWR-J.2023.1.1.02

Vieira, K., Heap, L., Descourtis, S., Isaac, J., Senanayake, S., Swift, B., Castillo, C., Kim, A. M., Krzus-Shaw, K., Black, M., Oladipo, O., Yang, X., Ratanapraphart, P., Tiwari, N. M., Velarde, L., & West, G. B. (2019). Literacy is a sociohistoric phenomenon with the potential to liberate and oppress. In L. Adler-Kassner & E. Wardle (Eds.), *(Re)considering what we know: Learning thresholds in writing, composition, rhetoric, and literacy* (pp. 36–55). Utah State UP.

Walvoord, B. E., Hunt, L. L., Dowling, Jr., H. F., & McMahon, J. D. (1997). *In the long run: A study of faculty in three writing-across-the-curriculum programs.* NCTE.

Wardle, E. (2019). Using a threshold concepts framework to facilitate an expertise-based WAC model for faculty development. In L. Adler-Kassner & E. Wardle (Eds.), *(Re)considering what we know: Learning thresholds in writing, composition, rhetoric, and literacy* (pp. 295–312). Utah State UP.

Winkelmes, M. A. (2013). Transparency in teaching: Faculty share data and improve students' learning. *Liberal Education, 99*(2)., 48–55.

Wood, D. A., Achhpilia, M. P., Adams, M. T., et al. (2023). The ChatGPT artificial intelligence chatbot: How well does it answer accounting assessment questions? *Issues in Accounting Education,* 1–28. https://doi.org/10.2308/ISSUES-2023-013

7

GENERATIVE AI AND THE WRITING CENTER

A New Era of Peer-Tutor Professionalization*

Ghada Gherwash and Joshua M. Paiz

Introduction

OpenAI's ChatGPT has undeniably triggered a paradigm shift in the way humans engage with technology in educational settings. One significant consequence of this technological advancement is the transformation it has brought to how Writing Program Administrators (WPAs) and Writing Center Administrators (WCAs) engage in discussions about the writing process with colleagues, students, and writing center tutors. This transformation is most evident within the core of the writing center practice, where traditional pedagogical practices must be reevaluated to align with our new technological landscape. We see that the confluence of human expertise and machine learning provides a fertile ground for WPAs to explore the intriguing interplay between generative AI and WCAs to rethink and redefine the terrain of writing support. The premise of this chapter is not driven by concern that our tutors' roles will become obsolete. We firmly believe that "[w]hat students do when working collaboratively on their writing is not write or edit, or least of all, proof. What they do is converse...[T]hey converse about and as a part of writing" (Bruffee, 1984, p. 645). Our motivation for this premise stems from our sincere curiosity about what an AI-informed tutor training program might look like. An obvious step toward that goal is through peer-tutor professionalization. Our inquiry here goes beyond the mere examination of technology. Instead, we encourage readers to think pragmatically about the future of writing tutor professionalization in the age of AI. We envision the creation of a liminal tutor training space where generative AI and human expertise collaborate to shape a new narrative of student learning and agency.

With that in mind, this chapter will explore how WCAs could ethically incorporate generative AI tools in their practice both to design tutor professional development opportunities and to raise awareness about critical AI literacy among the tutoring staff. Following Long and Magerko's (2020) definition of AI literacy "as a set of competencies that enables individuals to critically evaluate AI technologies; communicate and collaborate effectively with AI; and use AI as a tool online, at home, and in the workplace" (p. 598), this could

---

* OpenAI was used to generate parts of this manuscript.

DOI: 10.4324/9781003426936-10

potentially alleviate training design and delivery stress that are well documented among WCAs in the literature (e.g., Jackson et al., 2016). We will begin by providing a brief history of the emergence of generative AI tools. We will subsequently explore how AI compels us to reevaluate the traditional writing center practice, especially concerning the fundamental skills required for effective tutoring. We conclude by providing top-down, hands-on, dialogic training scenarios WCAs could use to familiarize tutors with generative AI tools to foster their continuous professional growth. We believe that we can enhance student writers' understanding of these tools by preparing tutors to guide discussions about AI and how it can be critically and responsibly deployed in the composition process. Through the process of preparing tutors to guide these discussions, the writing center can influence broader conversations around AI, potentially driving instructional design decisions to prepare students for critically AI-integrated professional spaces. The rhetorical situation has evolved, and writing centers must adapt.

Exigence: The Seemingly Staggering Advent of Generative AI

Undoubtedly, the arrival of OpenAI's ChatGPT as an easily accessible and initially free model caught many of us in higher education by surprise. One need only look at the vociferous, at times reactionary, response across traditional and social media for proof of this (c.f., Caplan, 2023; Grobe, 2023; McMurtri, 2022). Indeed, this collection is part of that reaction, and we, the chapter's authors, are voices in that chorus. We would be remiss if we did not acknowledge the, at times, emotionally charged reality that we inhabit—replete as it is with stories of professorial over-reaction (Verma, 2023), concerns over learning loss (Office of Educational Technology, 2023), dread over professional replacement (Farnell, 2023), and ruminations on ethics and user privacy (Acquisit et al., 2022). Admittedly, these concerns are legitimate ones, even if we may feel that the positive or negative reaction has been rather outsized, and they are not without historical precedent. Very similar reactions emerged in the early days of computers in the classroom (c.f., Cuban, 1993; Dreyfus & Dreyfus, 1984). Nevertheless, we begin from a simple premise: generative AI is undoubtedly revolutionary, but therein lies the crux. The field of computer science has been building toward generative AI for some time, with incremental developments going all the way back to the 1960s—tracing its lineage back to the Restricted Boltzmann Machine, a form of artificial neural network for unsupervised machine learning (Hinton & Sejnowski, 1986) and ELIZA, the original chatbot that many thought came close to passing the Turing Test because human users had issue telling they were talking to a machine in early turns of the conversation(Weizenbaum, 1966). While generative AI is certainly a seismic shift, its emergence has been clearly presaged in the field of computer sciences and computational linguistics for quite some time.

AI: The Case of Yet Another Alphabet Soup

It is in recognition of this need to "catch up" that we approach the current section. Before addressing the question, "how can I ethically leverage AI for better writing center practice?" we believe it is helpful to first explore what AI is and how it operates. Our goal is to provide you with a basic understanding (compared to that of AI designers, computer engineers, and data scientists) so that you can (a) speak confidently about AI and (b) participate in discussions—verbal or written—as a critically engaged member. In other words, engaging with AI agents and having critical dialogue about them may soon become a new baseline social literacy necessary for participating in broader disciplinary and national discourses (see Alexander, 2008; Gee, 2015).

Artificial intelligence can best be understood as the capacity for a machine or computer program to learn from experience, adapt to new inputs, and create novel outputs to accomplish tasks traditionally associated with human intelligence (though this distinction is debated [see de Waal, 2016]). For instance, determining if a text is positive or negative in emotional content was once seen as uniquely human, until the development of sentiment analysis allowed machines to do this. This technology, when paired with others like collaborative and content filtering, supports recommender systems used by Amazon and Netflix (Liu, 2020). Emulating human cognition has long been a goal in computer science. Early visionaries like Charles Babbage and Ada Lovelace, 18th-century mathematicians, laid the foundation for machines capable of symbolic manipulations similar to how humans use language for complex tasks (Vardi, 2016)—even if AI as we understand it now is a more modern development.

Addressing the question, "How does AI work?" is complex and varies depending on the type of AI system. However, modern AI generally relies on key technologies: machine learning, which involves automatic learning from experience; neural networks, which mimic the human brain to process information; and natural language processing, allowing AI to understand and generate human language (Crawford, 2022; Mitchell, 2020). These components form the backbone of most AI systems today.

AI agents like ChatGPT and Google Gemini represent a new evolution of AI, using Large Language Models (LLMs) trained on vast amounts of text data—much of it from public sources but also from specialty documents (Zhao et al., 2023). These models use context to enhance their understanding of text, generating outputs that align more frequently with Gricean Maxims. What makes models like ChatGPT revolutionary is their use of Generative Pre-trained Transformers (GPTs), a specialized type of neural network designed to understand word relationships across sentences and generate novel outputs. These models, trained on hundreds of billions of tokens, are known as generative AI or genAI and may also produce voice, music, and images (Ghahramani, 2023; Zhao et al., 2023). With this understanding, we turn our attention to the writing center and AI's potential role in writing.

AI Tools and the Writing Process

In the late 20th century, writing center research underwent a significant transformation known as the social turn (Geller et al., 2007; McComiskey, 2000). This shift aligns with broader developments in writing studies and represents a departure from the traditional cognitive approach to text production, which portrays the writer as "isolated from the social world," a "solitary author [who] works alone within the confines of his [sic] own mind" (Cooper, 1986, p. 356). Instead, there has been a growing emphasis on socio-ecological approaches that focus on the writer as an active participant in various communities of practice, each characterized by its own unique context and dynamics (Wenger, 1998; Geller et al., 2007). This shift challenges the notion of the writer as a solitary figure working in isolation and instead highlights the collaborative and dialogic nature of the writing process. Scholars such as Bruffee (1987) and Elbow (1973) have emphasized the importance of dialogic and interaction in writing. According to the socio-ecological model, writing is not solely the product of individual effort but rather emerges from ongoing engagement with social systems and relationships (Cooper, 1986, p. 367). This perspective underscores the interconnectedness between writers, their peers, other stakeholders, and the context where writing takes place, emphasizing the role of social dynamics in shaping the writing process.

The turn to this collaborative, process-based aspect of writing has demanded a shift in writing center practice from their initial function as "labs," which were extensions for writing classes, to independent centers (Bouquet, 1999). This separation of the writing lab from the classroom, which previously shaped the educational goals of lab writing sessions, required that autonomous writing centers establish their independent pedagogical strategies, philosophies, and tutoring staff. One of the early proponents of developing tutor training programs for writing center staff was Bruffee (1980), who notes that "peer tutors tend to enhance the quality of the service as an alternative to classroom learning" (p. 77). Bruffee advocates for staffing writing centers with graduate and professional tutors, as well as undergraduate peer tutors. According to Bruffee, the latter group is "more likely to be perceived as 'something else'—not teachers exactly, but helpers, friends, at best intellectual companions' (p. 77). Tutoring staff must receive appropriate training to provide feedback, with the primary objective of this training being to increase tutors' respect for other students' minds, and to increase their ability to work collaboratively" (Bruffee, 1980, p. 78; see also Gillespie & Lerner, 2003).

As we delve into the importance of tutor training and its role in enhancing the quality of writing center support, it is crucial to recognize the evolving landscape of education and technology. While we recognize the importance of traditional tutor training programs where tutors are trained to work collaboratively with student writers and to respect their intellect, it is important for us to think about the role generative AI tools might play in the drafting process. This raises the question: If we have embraced the writing-as-a-process model for decades now, why can't we accept AI tools as yet another affordance in the writer's socio-ecological environment? It is important to emphasize here that our intention is not to promote unguided student use of AI, nor is it to suggest that AI output should be used uncritically or in place of student-generated writing and cognition. Instead, we aim to draw attention to the undeniable prevalence of an array of technological tools and that students already actively employ them to varying degrees in their writing and compositional processes (e.g., Sheridan & Inman, 2010). For us, we see AI as one more technological tool, albeit one novel and untested. Thus, our task is to confront a pertinent issue: whether we are comfortable with it or not, students are already seeking assistance from AI tools (see Terry, 2023; McVay, 2022). So how can we initiate constructive discussion about responsible use with writing center tutors? Before we return to this question and present potential solutions, we will first present what researchers had already been forecasting about the potential impact of generative AI tools on writing instruction.

AI Tools and Writing Studies

Prior to the launch of OpenAI's ChatGPT in November 2022, writing scholars have predicted what writing instructors and WPAs are wrestling with today: the impact of AI tools on writing instruction. Porter (2018), for example, foresaw that "very soon our students will have bots available to 'assist' their academic writing—and that will become a perfectly reasonable thing for them to be doing, not unlike their current use of spelling and grammar checkers" (Para. 3). Hart-Davidson (2018) suggests a future where initial drafts, except for artistic texts, are rarely manually composed. Instead, writers could rely on writing software to start drafts, potentially restricting it to the author's vocabulary or incorporating external texts, with writers retaining control over the revision process (p. 252). Regardless of our willingness to adopt AI tools, these predictions have become a plausible reality. Therefore, as writing instructors and WCAs, our foremost concern should revolve around the question: how can we provide our students with the necessary skills to utilize AI tools with expertise? Or as Porter (2018) puts it: "we and our professional writing students need to know how to teach bots to write, because it is bots who are increasingly handling basic writing/communication tasks such as customer service, technical documentation, and news and report writing" (Para. 2).

When examining the interplay between human and machine-generated writing, Porter (2002) emphasizes the importance of adopting Katherine Hayles' (1999, p. 3) perspective on technology from an ethical standpoint. This perspective, he asserts, draws from Donna Haraway's (1991) concept of the cyborg, which challenges the traditional human-machine dichotomy and reconsiders conventional notions of bodily boundaries and the identity of the writer as solely human. By embracing a posthuman approach, one delves into the hybrid nature of cyborgs and the interconnectedness between humans and machines (Porter, 2002, p. 387). According to Hayles (1999), "there are no essential differences or absolute demarcations between bodily existence and computer simulation, cybernetic mechanism and biological organism, robot teleology and human goals" (p. 3; as cited in Porter, 2002, p. 387). This post-humanist perspective on AI-generated text highlights a pertinent ethical concern regarding the blurred lines of authorship within texts produced collaboratively by humans and machines. McKee and Porter (2020) articulates the critical modern concern of human-machine interaction by stating that "the ethics of human-machine writing requires of both humans and machines a deeper understanding of context and commitment to being a good human, a good machine, and a good human-machine speaking together" (p. 111). Although we, as writing instructors and WCAs, lack the ability to instill ethics in machine training directly, we believe that we are ethically obliged to initiate open and transparent dialogue with tutors as part of tutor professionalization, which by extension will enable tutors to have these conversations with student writers. These conversations will enable us to understand the extent to which AI is involved in our students' writing processes. Unless we actively encourage such discussions, students may remain hesitant to disclose their use of AI tools. And, given the already fraught nature of the writing classroom and conversations about academic integrity and plagiarism, this becomes an even more salient need in light of colleges' and universities' disparate responses to the advent of generative AI. Therefore, it becomes important to not only equip students with an understanding of the tools available but also to teach the ethical use of said tools and their potential rhetorical impacts.

To offer a metaphorical example, we would encourage you to think back to the turn of the 20th century and the emergence of the Industrial Revolution. This was another moment of radical automation of previously inherently human creative/generative labor. Throughout much of human history, pre-Industrial revolution, the textile industry represented highly skilled labor, with particularly skilled sewists being able to demand a high premium for their art. However, the emergence of automation during the Industrial Revolution led to a deskilling of the labor needed for basic clothes construction, giving rise to the problematic industry of fast fashion that we see today. It should be noted that this hasn't led to the deletion of sewing as a skill, but instead to a seismic shift in how the textiles industry operates and in our, the consumer's, relationship to it. Now, fast fashion is crafted in highly automated environments by low-skill labor in exploitative conditions, and you, the consumer, imbue little value on its outputs. To be honest, when was the last time you wept at the destruction of your Old Navy or Zara sweater in the wash? However, in this new environment, the home sewist, who can leverage skill (human labor and expertise) with automation (computerized sewing and pattern-cutting machines), represents a new class of semi-skilled labor that can produce custom pieces that carry more inherent social and personal value. And, the skilled sewist or tailor, now taking on a role akin to a textile artist can not only eschew automation altogether, if they wish, they have hard-won disciplinary expertise that allows them to create highly custom pieces that have the highest personal and social value for the consumer.

It is, with relatively little imagination, that we can apply this example to one possible future of writing. Yes, automation, in the form of generative AI, can produce massive amounts of novel, yet-to-exist, text. However, we would argue this text will be imbued with little social, commercial, or personal value. However, by teaching students critical AI literacy and how to incorporate this new socio-ecological tool into their workflows, we equip them to become like the home sewist in the earlier example. They are able to deploy their journeyman expertise and automation to produce novel text that meets an immediate and personal rhetorical need in a way that facilitates connection communication and carries greater value than mere AI-produced text. And, it will be the skilled writer, with rich life experiences, hard-won disciplinary expertise, and written communicative ability that will emerge as the textual artisan of the future. Indeed, even tech companies see this value, as AI training companies are beginning to hire writers, poets, and rhetors to help train future generative AI models and to stave off model collapse (see Malleck, 2023). This shows that the ability to engage in the act of writing sans automated assistance will become highly valued, but in different ways and for different purposes.

Transitioning now to the discussion of AI-focused training for writing center tutors on generative AI tools, we delve into how peer tutors, knowledgeable in guiding conversation with students and faculty, can extend their expertise to include discussions on AI in writing. Additionally, we will explore how WCAs can leverage AI tools to provide professional development opportunities for tutors. This proactive approach positions writing centers to influence faculty discussions, leading to better instructional designs for students in AI-influenced professional realms post-graduation. The rhetorical landscape has evolved, and writing centers must adapt. Central to this is the belief that humans remain essential, with AI serving to enhance our cognitive and creative capacities.

On Stage: AI and the Writing Center Administrator

We don't believe that it would be a radical statement to say that the role of the WCA is one that could be described as either having to wear, and balance multiple hats (optimistically), or one so multivariate that the risk of burnout is ever-present as the WCA is pulled in scores of different directions each time they set foot in the office or open their email. This raises a legitimate question: how can we create space for the human expertise of the WCA and their ability to create meaningful connections between human agents and disciplinary expertise to facilitate tutor training and student success while still acknowledging the time-poor nature of

WCA labor (i.e., never enough hours in the day)? We believe that AI represents a tool to help address this time-poor state and to help encourage greater work-life balance for the WCA, which will ultimately allow them to function more effectively. And, understand, we are not arguing that AI should replace the WCA. Rather, the WCA can use AI in ways that ethically and meaningfully support their professional efforts. In doing so, the WCA can model the use of AI tools for their tutors who can then consider how to discuss AI use with their tutees. To highlight this, we will describe a short vignette, connecting it to our socio-ecological framework.

At a small writing center at a liberal arts college in the Midwest, a WCA needs to prepare for a tutor training session on AI, a session that their staff has been calling for since the beginning of the term. The WCA, while curious about AI, is not a computer scientist, nor are they a digital humanities specialist. So, somewhere between teaching their course load, which is three courses this semester because of budget cuts at the college; managing the day-to-day operations of the center; and representing the center in various meetings across campus, the WCA must plan an effective training session to help prepare tutors for an AI-rich world. With the writing-to-learn framework in mind, the WCA decides that instead of pre-planning every element of the workshop, they would instead model the use of AI tools and critically explore them with their tutors. So, to prepare, knowing that the day-of outputs will be different, the WCA decides to explore AI tools and how they might be presented to the tutors.

Hence, considering the AI tool as an eco-social affordance, a digital, robotic partner of sorts, the WCA opts to begin by leaning into the conversational style encouraged by the chatbot style UI of many modern generative AI, such as ChatGPT, Google Gemini, and Anthropic Claude2. The WCA poses a simple question to the AI:

> I'm a writing center administrator and need to prepare my tutors to have conversations with students about using AI as part of the writing process. I'm a bit ambivalent about the whole thing myself. So, I'd like you to act as my tech-savvy colleague, as another writing center specialist with a most optimistic, yet critical view of AI, to help me think through this training session.

While using a tool like ChatGPT (GPT-4), the system decides to be overly helpful and produces an outline of a potential workshop instead of merely acknowledging the role that we have created for it—acting a step ahead of what we were expecting/needing from just this prompt. The WCA, while not having asked for a workshop outline, does find it to be a useful starting point (see Figure 7.1, below).

Now, while our imaginary WCA remains somewhat ambivalent about AI, it has provided some useful food for thought, so the WCA decides to dig deeper through follow-up prompting, this time asking:

> So, this idea of using AI to help brainstorm and organize thoughts is rather interesting. What would be an effective way of introducing this skill to tutors? What is some advice that I can give them to help them learn, practice, and master this skill?

Here, the AI response is less helpful, or at least not aligned with what the WCA was hoping for. The AI has produced another list of general ideas, and not specific recommendations.

It's great that you're looking to prepare your tutors for this emerging topic. AI can indeed be a double-edged sword in the educational arena, particularly in writing centers. Here's how you might approach the training session, focusing on the optimistic yet critical perspective on AI.

1. Introduction to AI:

- **Definition and Overview:** Briefly introduce Artificial Intelligence, its capabilities, and its applications in writing and education.
- **Recent Advancements:** Talk about the advancements in AI technology such as GPT-3 or GPT-4, and how they are being used in writing aids like Grammarly, or even as virtual tutors.

2. Benefits of AI in the Writing Process:

- **Assistance and Efficiency:** Emphasize how AI can help in brainstorming, organizing thoughts, checking grammar and style, thus making the writing process smoother and more efficient.

- **Accessibility:** Explain how AI can provide immediate feedback, making tutoring resources more accessible.

3. Critical Engagement with AI:

- **Dependency:** Discuss the risk of over-reliance on AI, which may hinder the development of critical thinking and writing skills.

- **Authenticity and Originality:** Engage with the concern that AI might encourage plagiarism or diminish the originality and personal touch in writing.

FIGURE 7.1   Sample GPT-4 output in response to prompt.

The WCA revises their prompting, just as they would if talking with a colleague who misunderstood the intent behind their original question (Figure 7.2).

> Ok, but if I wanted to show them how to do this through guided practice, how could I do this? Can you help me develop an action plan for how to model using AI to come up with ideas for writing in a way that helps tutors learn how to do it by watching it being done?

Now, the AI has produced a more useful outline that the WCA can actually implement during the upcoming training session, and more importantly, they now have an example of working with AI that they can share and discuss with their tutors as they consider the rhetorical and discoursal skills necessary to engage in effective AI use. It is not so detailed that anyone could just read from the outline to deliver the session; it still requires considerable experience and expertise in the fields of writing center administration and rhetoric and composition, but it's a good start. At this point, the WCA has only been talking with the AI for about 10 minutes. To have reached this point on their own may have taken a few hours. They now have more time to dedicate to preparing for the training session, or other professional demands—or to

---

(§) **ChatGPT**

Certainly! To effectively model the use of AI for brainstorming and organizing ideas in writing, you can develop a structured action plan that involves demonstration, participation, and reflection. Here's a step-by-step guide to help you:

Action Plan for Modeling AI Use in Brainstorming

Step 1: Pre-Session Preparation
- **Select a Tool:** Choose an AI writing tool that is accessible and offers features like brainstorming assistance, Idea generation, and outline creation.
- **Prepare Topics:** Select a range of topics or use past assignments for demonstration. These topics should vary in complexity and subject matter to show the tool's versatility.

Step 2: Live Demonstration
- **Introduction:** Start by introducing the selected AI tool, discussing its features, capabilities, and limitations.
- **Live Demo:** Conduct a live demonstration where you input a topic into the AI tool and show how It generates ideas, key points, or an outline. Explain each step:
- **Input Process:** Show how to input prompts effectively.
- **Interpretation:** Demonstrate how to interpret the AI's output.
- **Selection and Modification:** Show how to select useful ideas and modify others to fit the writing goals.

Step 3: Guided Practice
- **Hands-on Practice:** Allow tutors to use the AI tool themselves. Give them a topic and guide them through the process of generating ideas using the tool.
- **Group Activity:** Break the tutors into small groups and assign each group a different topic. Have them use the AI to generate a structured outline.
- **Discussion:** After the activity, discuss what ideas the AI generated, which were useful, and how they could be integrated into a writing piece.

Step 4: Role-Playing Exercises
- **Scenario-Based Role Play:** Create scenarios where tutors play the role of both the student and the tutor. The 'student' uses the AI tool to generate ideas while the 'tutor' guides and provides feedback.
- **Swap Roles:** Allow roles to swap to give each tuttor the prespective of using the tool and teaching how to use it.

FIGURE 7.2 Action plan for modeling AI use in brainstorming.

actually take a needed break to avoid burnout. More importantly, they have realized something important about AI and writing—AI is most effective when prompted properly. This means providing plenty of contexts and approaching the tool not as an answer engine (like a Google search), but like a live conversation. Richer output is arrived at through careful conversation—through follow-up questions, additional context, and redirection where needed. And, herein the WCA has arrived at a key insight to share with their tutors when it comes to helping them reflect on AI's potential role in the writing process and how they discuss this tool with the students who visit the writing center.

Behind the Scenes: AI and the Writing Center Administrator

To build on the example in the previous section, the WCA can effectively utilize AI generative tools to preplan targeted and efficient tutor training materials. Here, we present two additional scenarios through which WCA can employ AI technologies for designing professional development content for tutors and tutors-in-training:

1 **Content Generation**: AI tools can be leveraged to generate written materials tailored to the specific objectives of a training session. For example, during a tutor norming session centered on Standardized Academic English, the WCA can supplement a student's draft with an AI-generated draft on the same topic. The WCA should not disclose to the tutors the involvement of AI in text generation at this stage of the training. Instead, tutors can be encouraged to compare the two drafts, focusing primarily on the texts' stylistic features such as voice, flow, and diction. After facilitating a guided discussion, the WCA can then reveal the authors of each draft. Subsequently, the discussion can shift toward how tutors should interact with AI-generated texts, especially when a student writer discloses their use of such tools during a tutoring session.

   Another application of text generation involves using AI to create a text with specific weaknesses aligned with the training's focus. These weaknesses might include the overuse of the passive voice, run-on sentences, inadequate transitions, or any other writing issue pertinent to the training. Tutors then can collaborate, using these AI-generated drafts to brainstorm effective feedback strategies for assisting students who may seek help with similar writing challenges. It is important to emphasize that the WCA should leverage its expertise to review and refine the AI-generated text to ensure it fulfills its intended purpose effectively.

2 **Content Adaptation**: The WCA can also use AI-driven applications like Twee to formulate discussion prompts based on YouTube videos. For example, the WCA might use John Baugh's TEDx presentation on linguistic profiling to raise tutors' awareness about issues related to linguistic diversity. Additionally, the WCA can employ Twee to create a transcript of the talk, offering an alternative or supplementary resource for tutors who prefer reading over or alongside listening to the presentation.

By integrating AI-generated content in these ways, WCAs can enhance the quality of their tutor training materials while also encouraging thoughtful discussions about the role of AI in the writing center and how tutors can best assist students who integrate AI tools into their writing processes.

Closing Remarks

The advent of generative AI marked a significant juncture in the academic sphere. What some perceived as an unexpected emergence not only brought innovative functionalities but also sparked various responses across higher education (e.g., Anson, 2022). The accessibility and capabilities of such AI tools were met with varying degrees of reception, from enthusiastic adoption to critical scrutiny. It is within this juxtaposition of surprise and varied sentiment that we hope we were able to illustrate some modest measures WCAs can employ to raise writing center tutors' awareness about the transformative potential of generative AI and its implications for contemporary writing center practices.

The integration of artificial intelligence, particularly the advancements brought about by generative models, has the potential to profoundly reshape the operational socio-ecological environment of writing center practice. These changes encompass various dimensions of writing center administration and pedagogy. From an administrative perspective, the incorporation of AI could facilitate a more streamlined approach to WCA labor. One of the greatest advantages lies within the domain of professional development. With the assistance of AI-driven analytics and automated modules, administrators can now devise targeted training programs, ensuring that tutors and staff are equipped with the most up-to-date critical AI literacy tools. This not only simplifies the often complex and time-consuming process of curriculum design but also ensures that training materials are consistently aligned with the evolving demands of the academic environment. This efficiency has freed up valuable resources, allowing writing centers to invest in other critical areas of growth and development. Furthermore, the introduction of AI into writing centers enhances their role as hubs for continuous learning and adaptation within writing center cultures. In this new paradigm, learning is not viewed as a one-time event but as an ongoing journey. Tutors and staff can be encouraged to engage with AI tools regularly, benefiting from real-time feedback and adaptive learning pathways. This ensures that they remain at the forefront of educational innovation, ready to meet the diverse and evolving needs of students.

Integrating AI into tutor training and professionalization ushers a new set of considerations and imperatives. Historically, the core competencies of effective tutoring were largely rooted in interpersonal skills, content knowledge, and collaborative pedagogical strategies. However, with the growing conversations around the use of AI in educational settings, there is an emerging need to reassess and expand this skill set. The presence of AI, therefore, demands a recalibration of what constitutes essential skills for modern tutors. It's no longer sufficient to solely rely on traditional tutoring techniques; tutors must now also possess a foundational understanding of AI-driven tools and their potential applications in the educational context. This includes not only the technical aspects of operating such tools but also an appreciation of their underlying algorithms and decision-making processes.

It is in this new reality that we delineated a hands-on, dialogic training approach that becomes crucial in this context. Dialogic training emphasizes active engagement and open dialogue between WCAs and tutors, ensuring a deeper and more nuanced understanding of the subject matter. Through such interactive sessions, tutors can gain firsthand experience with AI tools, exploring their functionalities, strengths, and limitations. This experiential learning approach ensures that tutors are not merely passive recipients of knowledge but active participants in their own professional development journeys. Moreover, familiarity with AI's capabilities is just the starting point. Tutors must be trained to adeptly integrate these tools into their existing tutoring methodologies. This involves understanding when to rely on AI for assistance, how to interpret AI-generated feedback, and how to seamlessly blend traditional and AI-enhanced techniques to create a holistic tutoring experience that caters to the diverse needs of students. In essence, the evolution of AI in educational settings doesn't just add another tool to a tutor's toolkit; it reshapes the very fabric of tutoring pedagogy, prompting a shift toward a more integrated, adaptive, and technologically informed approach.

In light of the new AI-rich world, it is crucial to re-theorize writing center practices. We suggest adopting a socio-ecological lens to understand AI's role in writing. This perspective views writing as a dynamic mix of social and ecological elements, not just a static product. Historically, writing centers focused on the individual writer's skills and voice. But with advanced AI tools, there's a paradigm shift. Writing isn't just about individual thought—it's an evolving process influenced by AI. These tools not only aid in mechanics but also shape a writer's choices and content, reflecting the socio-ecological perspective. AI's influence on writing practices manifests in several ways. For instance, AI-driven tools offer real-time feedback, predictive text suggestions, and advanced grammar checks, all of which subtly guide and shape the writing process. These tools not only aid in the mechanical aspects of writing but also influence the writer's choices, style, and even content direction. This dynamic interaction between the writer and AI tools exemplifies the socio-ecological perspective, highlighting the interconnectedness of individual agency and external ecological factors. Furthermore, this evolving landscape underscores the need for a more holistic approach to understanding writing. It's not just about the writer or the written text but about the entire ecosystem that influences the act of writing. From the algorithms that suggest the next word to the databases that provide research material, AI is intricately woven into the modern writing process. In essence, the socio-ecological lens illuminates the complexities of the contemporary writing landscape. It challenges us to move beyond traditional dichotomies and embrace a more integrated view, recognizing writing as a continually evolving process shaped by both human agency and technological advancements like AI.

The integration of AI into writing centers signifies a notable shift in educational methodologies. As technological advancements continue to shape various sectors, education—specifically writing practices—are not exempt from this influence. The evidence suggests that AI-driven tools offer tangible benefits in terms of administrative efficiency and enhanced learning experiences (Fatima et al., 2024; Fillippi et al., 2023; Felten et al., 2019; Diamandis, 2023; Zarifhonarvar, 2023). However, the full implications of these tools, both positive and potential challenges, require careful consideration. It's essential for educators and administrators to approach the integration of AI with a balanced perspective, prioritizing empirical evidence and best practices. While the potential of AI to augment writing centers is evident, it's equally crucial to ensure that such integrations align with educational goals and values. As the landscape of writing practices evolves, a proactive approach to understanding and adapting to these technological shifts is advisable. Such an approach will likely ensure that writing centers remain effective and relevant in an increasingly digital academic environment.

References

Acquisit, A., Brandimarte, L., & Hancock, J. (2022). How privacy's past may shape its future. *Science*, *375*(6578), 270–272. https://doi.org/10.1126/science/abj0826

Alexander, J. (2008). *Literacy, sexuality, pedagogy: Theory and practice for composition studies*. Provo, US: Utah State University Press.

Anson, C. (2022). AI-based text generation and the social construction of "fraudulent authorship": A revisitation. *Composition Studies, 50*(1), 37–46

Bouquet, E. (1999). "Our little secret": A History of writing centers, pre- to post-open admission. *College composition and Communication, 50*(3), 463–482.

Bruffee, K. (1980). Two related issues in peer tutoring: Program structure and tutor training. *College Composition and Communication, 31*(1), 76–80.

Bruffee, K. (1984). Collaborative learning and the "conversation of mankind". *College English, 43*(7), 635–652.

Bruffee, K. A. (1987). The art of collaborative learning: Making the most of knowledgeable peers. *Change: The Magazine of Higher Learning, 19*(2), 42–47

Caplan, N. (2023, April 30). Why I'm not excited by (or even using) generative AI. *Nigel Caplan*. Retrieved from: https://nigelcaplan.com/2023/04/30/why-im-not-excited-by-or-even-using-generative-ai/

Cooper, M. (1986). The ecology of writing. *College English*, 48(4), 364–375.

Crawford, K. (2022). *Atlas of AI: Power, politics, and the planetary costs of artificial intelligence*. New Haven, US: Yale University Press.

Cuban, L. (1993). Computers meet classroom: Classroom wins. *Teachers College Record*, 95(2), 185–210.

de Waal, F. (2016). *Are we smart enough to know how smart animals are?*. New York, US: Norton.

Diamandis, P. (2023). Embracing the future-don't fear it! Retrieved from: https://www.diamandis.com/blog/embrace-the-future-summit-2023

Elbow, P. (1973). *Writing without teachers*. New York, NY: Oxford University Press.

Farnell, A. (2023, January 19). AI will replace academics unless our teaching challenges students again. *Times Higher Education*. Retrieved from: https://www.timeshighereducation.com/opinion/ai-will-replace-academics-unless-our-teaching-challenges-students-again

Fatima, H., Jan, S. M. H. A., Khan, A. K., Javed, S., & Rashid, M. (2024). Effect of artificial intelligence on the human workforce. *International Journal of Contemporary Issues in Social Sciences*, 3(1), 1197–1203.

Felten, E. W., Raj, M., & Seamans, R. (2019). The occupational impact of artificial intelligence: Labor, skills, and polarization. *NYU Stern School of Business*.

Filippi, E., Banno, M., & Trento, S. (2023). Automation technologies and their impact on employment: A review, synthesis and future research agenda. *Technological Forecasting and Social Change*, 191, 122448.

Gee, J. P. (2015). *Social linguistics and literacies: Ideology in discourses* (5th ed.). New York, US: Routledge.

Geller, A., Eodice, M. Condo, F., Carroll Boquet, E. (2007). *Everyday writing center*. US: Utah State University Press.

Ghahramani, Z. (2023, May 10). Introducing PaLM2. *The Keyword*. https://blog.google/technology/ai/google-palm-2-ai-large-language-model/

Gillespie, P., & Lerner, N. (2003). *The Allyn & Bacon guide to peer tutoring* (2nd ed.). Longman.

Grobe, C. (2023, January 18). Why I'm not scared of ChatGPT: The limits of technology are where real writing begins. *The Chronicle of Higher Education*. Retrieved from: https://www.chronicle.com/article/why-im-not-scared-of-chatgpt

Hart-Davidson, W. (2018). Writing with robots and other curiosities of the age of machine rhetorics. In *The Routledge handbook of digital writing and rhetoric* (pp. 248–255). New York: Routledge.

Hinton, G. E., & Sejnowski, T. J. (1986). Learning and relearning in Boltzmann machines. In D. E. Rumelhart, J. L. McClelland, and the PDP Research Group (Eds.), *Parallel distributed processing: Explorations in the microstructure of cognition*, vol. 1 (pp. 282–317). Cambridge, US: MIT Press.

Jackson, R., Grutsch-McKinney, J., & Casewell, N. (Summer 2016). Writing center administration and/as emotional labor. *Composition Forum*. Retrieved from: https://www.compositionforum.com/issue/34/writing-center.php

Liu, B. (2020). *Sentiment analysis: Mining opinions, sentiments, and emotions* (2nd ed.). Cambridge, UK: Cambridge University Press.

Long, D. & Magerko, B. (2020, April). What is AI literacy? Competencies and design considerations. In *Proceedings of the 2020 CHI conference on human factors in computing systems* (pp. 1–16).

Malleck, J. (2023, September 26). AI companies are hiring creative writers and here's what they're looking for. *Quartz*. https://qz.com/ai-companies-hiring-creative-writers-1850873456

McComiskey, B. (2000). *Teaching composition as a social process* (1st ed.). Utah State University Press. https://doi.org/10.2307/j.ctt46nx11

McKee, H., & Porter, J. E. (2020, February 7–8). Ethics for AI writing: The importance of rhetorical context. In *Proceedings of 2020 AAAI/ACM conference on AI, ethics, and society (AIES'20)*. New York. Retrieved from: https://doi.org/10.1145/3375627.3375811

McMurtri, B. (2022, December 13). AI and the future of undergraduate writing: Teaching experts are concerned, but not for the reasons you think. *The Chronicle of Higher Education*. Retrieved from: https://www.chronicle.com/article/ai-and-the-future-of-undergraduate-writing

McVay, C. (2022, December 5). Artificial intelligence is changing writing at the university, let's embrace it. *Boston University Today*. https://www.bu.edu/articles/2022/pov-artificial-intelligence-is-changing-writing-at-universities/

Mitchell, M. (2020). *Artificial intelligence: A guide for thinking humans.* New York, US: Pelican.

Office of Educational Technology. (2023). *Artificial intelligence and the future of teaching and learning: Insights and recommendations* [government report]. Retrieved from: https://www2.ed.gov/documents/ai-report/ai-report.pdf

Porter, J. (2002). Why technology matters to writing: A cyberwriter's tale. *Computers and Composition, 20.* 375–394.

Porter, J. E. (2018, April 25). The impact of AI on writing and writing instruction. *Digital Rhetoric Collaborative.* https://www.digitalrhetoriccollaborative.org/2018/04/25/ai-on-writing/

Sheridan, D. M., & Inman, J. A. (Eds.). (2010). *Multiliteracy centers: Writing center work, new media, and multimodal rhetoric.* Hampton Press

Terry, O. K. (2023, May 12). I'm a student: You have no idea how much we're using ChatGPT. *The Chronicle of Higher Education.* https://www.chronicle.com/article/im-a-student-you-have-no-idea-how-much-were-using-chatgpt

Vardi, M. Y. (2016). The moral imperative of artificial intelligence. *Communications of the ACM, 59*(5), 5. https://doi.org/10.1145/2903530

Verma, P. (2023, May 18). A professor accused his entire class of using ChatGPT, putting diplomas in jeopardy. *The Washington Post.* Retrieved from: https://www.washingtonpost.com/technology/2023/05/18/texas-professor-threatened-fail-class-chatgpt-cheating/

Weizenbaum, J. (1966). ELIZA—A computer program for the study of natural language communication between man (sic) and machine. *Communications of the ACM, 9*(1), 36–45. https://doi.org/10.1145/365153.365168

Wenger, E. (1998). *Communities of practice: Learning, meaning, and identity.* Cambridge, U.K.; New York, N.Y.: Cambridge University Press.

Zarifhonarvar, A. (2023). Economics of ChatGPT: A labor market view on the occupational impact of artificial intelligence. *Journal of Electronic Business & Digital Economics, 3*(2), 100–116. https://doi.org/10.1108/JEBDE-10-2023-0021

Zhao, W., et al. (2023). A survey of large language models. *arXiv preprint. 2303.18223.*

8

AI-POWERED READING ASSISTANTS

A Tool for Equity in First-Year Writing

Marc Watkins

The exponential growth of generative artificial intelligence is transforming education. With the advent of large language models like GPT-3, new opportunities have emerged to support students' reading comprehension and engagement. Yet with these opportunities come critical challenges. How can educators thoughtfully integrate AI reading assistants while safeguarding close reading skills and artistic intent? This article explores a pilot study conducted with first-year college students using AI-powered apps to scaffold a complex reading assignment. The small sample size of three first-year writing courses class and reliance on self-reported student reflections represent key limitations. As such, findings should be considered preliminary impressions rather than conclusive outcomes. Further research across diverse educational contexts with larger samples will be essential to fully understand the promise and perils of this emerging application. Educators should work with developers to promote mindful innovation that harnesses AI's potential to make education more equitable and accessible without diminishing the development of essential literacies.

The widespread release of OpenAI's Generative Pretrained Transformer through a chatbot interface the public has come to know as ChatGPT created an existential crisis in education about machines generating text. So much focus was placed on ChatGPT's capabilities to mimic human writing, that many came to see the tool as synonymous with the underlying technology of generative AI. This is unfortunate because ChatGPT is but one interface of the technology and much of the critical discourse fails to focus on the lack of affordances offered by the chatbot interface. In reality, thousands of developers have now used OpenAI's API to develop their applications that enable AI-powered writing, research, feedback, and reading assistants. Many of these developers used customized interfaces to support human interaction, augmenting an existing skill instead of offloading it through an increasingly automated process.

How AI-Assisted Reading Tools Can Be Used to Promote Equity

AI reading assistants have remarkable potential to expand accessibility for students with disabilities in K-12 and higher education. Many of the tools use underlying language models to help users explore texts with features like text-to-speech, summarization, and vocabulary

DOI: 10.4324/9781003426936-11

simplification. Using such features can make dense, specialized texts more manageable for diverse learners. For example, OpenAI's Whisper model offers text-to-speech, allowing students with visual impairments or processing disorders to listen to the content read aloud, focusing on comprehension rather than decoding. Summarization condenses key ideas into more understandable overviews depending on the user's reading level, potentially assisting students with attention deficit disorder, executive functioning challenges, or learning disabilities in grasping the main concepts of challenging texts. Likewise, vocabulary simplification rephrases difficult terminology that students may be unfamiliar with due to knowledge gaps and varying degrees of preparedness. Because AI reading assistants transform textual material into multiple formats while reducing barriers to understanding, they may create more entry points into learning content. This flexibility shows promise for enabling students with disabilities to participate more fully in academic reading (Rajagopal et al., 2023).

For English language learners and multilingual students, AI reading assistants that offer multiple languages provide invaluable aid in comprehending complex academic texts. By generating summaries, defining vocabulary, and clarifying concepts in students' native languages, AI tools may remove language barriers to deciphering readings outside of a user's main language. Because academic prose is often discipline-specific, even esoteric and erudite, translating key passages on demand could make the content more accessible. Students can also toggle back and forth between languages in certain interfaces, using their stronger native language skills to clarify concepts in their developing second language. This promotes deeper engagement with course materials by allowing multilingual students to code-switch. Given the predominance of English-only curricula in the United States, AI reading assistants that facilitate comprehension in diverse languages have exciting potential to serve traditionally underrepresented bilingual and multilingual students.

AI reading assistants can provide vital scaffolds for students who lack the skills or background knowledge to fully grasp college-level readings independently. Many first-generation, low-income, or minority students arrive underprepared for the advanced literacy demands of higher education. This is especially true in junior and community colleges, where completion to degree rates remain below 30% nationally (Schneider & Yin, 2012). Many students may lack strategies for tackling difficult texts or be unfamiliar with academic vocabulary and conventions. Adult learners who are reentering college may also struggle with balancing the time needed to harness the close reading skills necessary for their courses. Generative AI-powered reading assistants may help bridge these gaps by actively clarifying concepts, genres, and terminology—all on demand. The interactive features let students target the sections of reading that they struggle with most. This personalized support promotes comprehension and may help close skill gaps for students who need it most. Unlike remedial courses that can stigmatize students, AI reading assistants are discrete tools that subtly provide built-in scaffolds for students who need to develop college readiness. Their potential to unobtrusively level the playing field makes them a promising innovation.

Affordable AI reading assistants have the potential to help learners overcome cost barriers that prevent some students from accessing academic support services. Private tutoring, learning specialists, writing centers, and disability services often involve fees that many low-income students cannot afford. However, free reading assistant apps like Explainpaper, SciSpace, and Microsoft's Immersive Reader may democratize access to the innovative features noted above. While not nearly as robust as one-on-one human services, their availability helps offset socioeconomic inequities that exclude students without financial means from support. By automating some reading support, AI assistants may reduce teacher work-loads so instructors can focus on providing individualized attention to students who need it most. Teachers often struggle to accommodate diverse learners within large classes and providing structured interventions and timely support is often not possible in these instances. AI reading assistants may alleviate some burdens by offering personalized clarification tailored to students' needs. Teachers can then dedicate their expertise to in-depth instruction and conferencing with students who need more individualized support. Implementing AI reading assistants strategically as part of a comprehensive support system can help institutions better identify and assist students who require such human intervention (Cummings et al., 2024).

The goal should be to use technology to complement human services and strengthen the teacher-student relationship, as AI-powered tools will likely never match a caring teacher but can aid in freeing up their availability. Thoughtfully implemented AI reading assistants promote self-directed learning, learner autonomy, and metacognition. Students take ownership of their reading process by selectively using interactive features only when they feel the need for clarification. This fosters metacognitive awareness and strategy development as students determine how to best leverage the technology for themselves. Teachers can structure activities where students reflect on and track their usage. Unlike passive forms of reading assistance, interactive AI tools empower diverse learners to become active participants in scaffolding challenges. By facilitating comprehension and reducing barriers, they place agency in the students' hands. AI reading assistants shift away from a remedial paradigm to one of independent self-improvement if students are guided to value their emerging skills over convenience.

Computer-Assisted Reading

Computer-assisted reading and writing have a long history, with early examples being successfully piloted in many forms for decades. Notable pilots include Carnegie Mellon University's Literacy Innovation that Speech Technology ENables and more recently the personalized reading offered by Dreambox (Mostow et al., 2013). Such systems focused on helping young students develop basic literacy and fluency skills; however, fewer studies explored computer-assisted reading to offer adult learners support in higher education. Before OpenAI deployed GPT-3's API in 2021 and 2022, the most widespread use of an automated system designed to support students' reading occurred in Georgia's K-12 schools with the introduction of the avatar Amira in 800 public schools, with promising results in increasing students' literacy and fluency scores (Mader, 2021). Many different systems used older forms of machine learning and natural language processing techniques to provide readers with some type of automated support (Lenhard et al., 2011; Heilman et al., 2010), but none engaged large language models. Since previous systems did not rely on transformer-based architecture and were limited in terms of scope and personalization of content, often being piloted in closed systems, using generative AI as a reading assistant with adult learners is likely a newer use case (Chace, 2020).

Large language models offer new opportunities for computer-assisted reading at scale unrealized by earlier systems. Some of the early research into GPT-3 suggests that the model is capable of producing high-quality and situation-specific reading summaries for grade-school learners, structured interventions, automated feedback, and support for language learning (Srinivasan, 2022; Risher, 2023; Cavalcanti et al., 2021; Gayed et al., 2022; Vee, 2023) beyond basic literacy instruction. Indeed, the public can now interact with generative AI at scale using a variety of apps, allowing developers to experiment with more and more use cases. Some of the most recent research has shown the promise of LLMs to aid assessment through reading passage generation, suggesting malleable and adaptive usage of the tool in an educational context (Bezirhan & Von Davier, 2023).

Finding the Tools

At the time of my pilot, very little research had been done on using large language models to support users outside of writing assistants. One of the few articles I found that served as a lodestar was "Beyond Text Generation: Supporting Writers with Continuous Automatic Text Summaries" (Dang et al., 2022). The authors developed an interactive text editor powered by generative AI that provided users with continuous text summaries to support a writer as they wrote and a reader as they read the work. The findings of their study found that automatically generated summaries helped facilitate reflection and provide a reader with a clearer understanding of the text. More pointedly, the study called for more developers to reconsider interfaces for generative AI beyond simple text generation.

In August of 2022, I began to work with the developers of an AI-powered tool called Fermat. Fermat used GPT-3 to power actions on a spatial canvas, allowing users to interact with AI generation alongside their writing. The user interface was thoughtfully designed as an evolution of Apple's now-defunct Hypercard. I developed a scaffolded brainstorming activity as a framework to design an assignment for my first-year students to explore counterarguments; unfortunately, many students found the interface to be a radical departure from the linear interfaces they were accustomed to (Watkins, 2023). However, one of the chief developers at Fermat, Max Drake, began to design and implement new features within Fermat's spatial canvas that followed many of the design principles Dang and his research team had identified as supporting writing and readers with automated feedback. Drake created an Implicit Reaction tool that used generative AI to produce tailored summaries of a user's writing. One of the key features of the tool was an automatic counterargument or opposing opinion box that generated live counterarguments during the writing process (Drake, 2023). Ultimately, Fermat's spatial canvas and reactive writing tools proved too exotic for students to use effectively during the fall pilot, but the design and experimentation were vital in understanding how interfaces using generative AI could support users by providing summaries for them to read.

By October of 2022 two grad students had come to a similar conclusion with a project called Explainpaper. The app was built by Aman Jha and Jade Asmus and launched for under $400. Both developers were students pursuing their graduate degrees in computer science and were frustrated and overwhelmed by the amount of material they had to read each week and the generally inaccessible jargon-laden prose of the writing within the articles. Instead of building an app that generated text, they decided to build one that could call upon generative AI to synthesize complex readings and create approachable and concise summaries based on a user's reading level. Unlike the prototype built by Dang and his team, a user in Explainpaper could use the technology to help them explore a word, phrase, paragraph, or even entire pages of text using their natural language. What's more, the generative summaries could themselves be queried for further insights into a selected reading.

Less than a month later, the developers of Explainpaper had a competition. A new app called SciSpace built by Saikiran Chandha took the concept and use case pioneered by Jha and Asmus and integrated it directly into a database of open-access scholarly articles. What's more, SciSpace's tool was multilingual, and a user only needed to toggle to the language of their choice and query the language model about a particular article.

I contacted both developers to test each app and provided them feedback that they often attempted to implement in a few hours. As a teacher of writing without a technical background in computer science, it was humbling to see tools develop before my eyes with such profound implications. The launch of ChatGPT caused many to question what it meant to write, now, two small apps were taking shape that were causing me to question what it meant to read.

Fostering Inclusion through Universal Design for Learning

One of the troubling areas with generative AI tools is their public release under the auspices of experimentation. For the developers to know how the public will use the tools, they argue that they must first test them as widely as possible. This ethos is troubling for inclusion and Universal Design for Learning (UDL). An experimental tool may not be designed with affordances to help those with differential learning needs. Basic tools many have come to rely on to assist them with technology, such as immersive readers, are often incompatible with many of these tools. Furthermore, one does not need to spend long with a chatbot interface, like ChatGPT, to realize that many students find the very nature of repetitive prompting to be cognitively overloading in learning environments. Amelia Wattenberger (2023) critiques this lack of affordances in chatbot design, arguing that "users can learn over time what prompts work well and which don't, but the burden to learn what works still lies with every single user. When it could instead be baked into the interface." As such, this presents numerous barriers for generative AI tools to be adopted in education.

However, tools like ExplainPaper and SciSpace align well with UDL guidelines by promoting flexibility and accessibility through their interactive features. Students can actively control how information is presented to them by customizing text simplification and clarification to match their proficiency level. This adheres to UDL principles such as providing options for perception, action, expression, engagement, and comprehension (UDL, 2018). The personalized scaffolding creates multiple entry points into the reading by reducing barriers, focusing engagement, and minimizing distraction. This provides more equitable access to learning materials. Additionally, the reading assistants allow instructors to implement UDL strategies such as providing alternatives for language and symbols. By facilitating learner autonomy while providing tailored support, AI tools may enable more universally designed, student-centered reading experiences. Their capacity to make the text more accessible and manageable demonstrates their value in promoting equity through UDL implementation.

Establishing a Tentative Approach: Scaffolding Skills through Gradual Release Modeling

To leverage AI-enabled tools effectively with students, I worked alongside Dr. Stephen Monroe and Dr. Robert Cummings at the University of Mississippi to establish a framework for faculty to define and evaluate different technologies that used generative AI and tie those tools to existing student learning outcomes. We then asked students to explore and reflect on how that tool impacted their learning. The define, evaluation, exploration, reflection approach, which we refer to as the DEER praxis, allowed us to establish working guidelines for a variety of AI assistance (Cummings et al., 2024). Initially, using the DEER praxis for a writing assignment provides students with a heavier scaffolding to clarify unfamiliar concepts and complex vocabulary in structured assignments, like the one outlined below. Over time, as students gained familiarity with the tools and use cases, I gradually shifted responsibility to my student learners to practice close reading strategies with AI assistance as they deemed necessary for their individualized learning needs. This developmental approach provided equity of access to students who needed more initial support and guidance versus students who might otherwise feel too constrained with such an ongoing approach.

The overall DEER praxis borrows concepts from constructivist learning approaches, by allowing students to learn through doing and exploring concepts at their own pace and style, creating a learner-centered environment that is highly adaptive to individual learning needs (Jonassen & Rohrer-Murphy, 1999). Constructivist approaches encourage active learning and exploration, qualities that can be enhanced through AI reading tools, which provide personalized, adaptive learning experiences. This can foster deeper engagement and understanding in students (Grubaugh et al., 2023). While I wholeheartedly support this approach, it is not without the potential perils of students becoming over-reliant on technology and potentially leading to deskilling close reading skills.

In anticipation of some students becoming too reliant on adopting AI reading assistants, I explicitly advised them to use the AI tools only when encountering pain points in comprehending the text, not as a shortcut to avoid close reading. I attempted to monitor usage through close check-ins with students and intervened if students seemed overly reliant on the technology. We held several in-class discussions and I met privately with students in conferences, where I asked them about their overall experience using AI assistants, including the AI reading assistants. However, these conversations and open-ended reflective assignments merely elicited perceived experiences from students rather than measurable assessment data. While this provided subjective insights about learner reactions, incorporating surveys, interviews, and usage analytics are valuable tools in objectively confirming many of these self-reported student observations.

For this pilot, I selected an existing reading assignment in my Hybrid Writing 102 course that students often struggled with as one of three required sources for their synthesis essay assignment. A synthesis essay within a first-year writing course calls upon a writer to synthesize three different texts into a coherent essay. The assignment occurs in scaffolded stages, starting with close reading and discussion of artifacts, a written brainstorming activity, several written synthesis exercises, a rough draft, and a final draft, followed by a reflection on what the writing process taught the student. For the purpose of this pilot, students were allowed and encouraged to use the AI reading assistant on one of the three required artifacts they were to use as sources for their synthesis essay.

For many years, I have assigned my students Neal Postman's "Judgment of Thamus" in my pop culture-themed course as an introduction to how new technologies alter our existing habits. Since we were talking broadly about how generative AI was impacting our culture in the wake of ChatGPT's launch, assigning students a reading about technological change made for a good fit. The problem I'd previously encountered with assigning this reading is that it is quite old, being published in the early 1990s, and it uses the Greek myth from Plato's *Phaedrus* about King Thamus. Most students were not enthused nor partially engaged because of these factors. In past semesters, some students misidentified Thamus as Thanos from the Marvel films.

I developed the following assignment for my students to use paired with the reading. Students had previously been introduced to several types of AI-powered text generation and used several in brainstorming assignments, so they were familiar with what AI could do in terms of generating text but had no idea about how it could be used to support reading.

AI Reading Assistant Assignment

Explainpaper works by uploading a PDF and using the power of AI to scan it and a conversational interface that allows you to explore the text, ask questions about difficult terms within the paper, or if you run across a concept or theme in one section and would like to know how it relates to the overall paper.

- Sign up for a free account using your go.olemiss.edu credentials, then download the paper (must be a PDF). Once you've downloaded a PDF, you then need to upload it to Explainpaper and follow the instructions.

Directions

Neil Postman's "The Judgement of Thamus" can be challenging to read. It has terms used within the essay that are unfamiliar and concepts that might be equally challenging to explore. This exercise invites you to download the essay, then create a free account with Explainpaper, an AI reading assistant, and use the app to help you explore the essay. Engage AI assistance as needed once you hit a pain point in your reading process. Once you have used the app to help you read the essay, respond to some of the reflection questions below.

Reflection Questions

- How did the AI app Explainpaper enhance my understanding of the difficult PDF I was reading?
- What were some of the key features of the AI app that made it easy for me to read and comprehend the PDF?
- Did the AI app provide additional resources or contextual information that helped me better understand the content of the PDF?
- Did the AI app help me to focus and stay engaged with the challenging content of the PDF? Why or why not?
- Did using an AI app like Explainpaper change the way I typically approach reading difficult material?
- What was my overall experience using an AI app like Explainpaper, and how would I rate its effectiveness?
- Did the AI app help me retain more information from the PDF than I typically would have?
- Do you see yourself using an AI app like Explainpaper in your future reading activities?
- Did the AI app like Explainpaper help to reduce the stress and anxiety associated with reading difficult material? Why or why not?
- Would you recommend an AI app like Explainpaper to others who struggle with reading and understanding complex PDFs?

Student Impressions: Simplifying Complex Text

The AI reading tools helped simplify dense, complex texts into more comprehensible language tailored to each student's personal reading level. As one student reflected, "All I had to do was highlight the text I wanted, and it reworded it to be more comprehensive." The AI rephrased confusing vocabulary and passages in "layman's terms," as noted by another student. This clarified concepts that would normally "go over my head," according to another student's response. The interactive highlighting also lets students focus on understanding challenging sections, with one sharing that "it was challenging to focus on the task without being able to markup text." While the AI tools filled this need by simplifying complex sections, they did not reduce the scope or meaning of the assigned reading. More students came to class prepared to talk about the reading and the core concepts within the essay than in previous semesters. I'm not certain if this shift was due to the AI reading assistants, or the students being excited about using a new technique to augment their reading for the first time. During class discussion, students said they used the feature sporadically and as needed in their reading exploration, simplifying phrases or even entire paragraphs when they felt it benefited them the most.

One area that impressed me was the language model's ability to change the wording, tone, and even style of certain sentences to meet the learning needs of the students and still capture the essence and meaning behind that sentence. An important note is that no students reported hallucinations or fabricated responses from the AI in their reflections; however, that does not mean it did not happen. I was not able to manually review each student's interaction with the AI reading assistance and instead told them to tread cautiously, reviewing outputs carefully for accuracy and not be swept up in the speed of a generated response. Such reminders are necessary for any user to develop adequate AI literacy.

Improving Focus and Engagement

The reading tools likewise appeared to have helped improve student focus and engagement with the assignment. One student explained the AI "helped me stay focused because I was finally able to use something that could translate text into something that I could understand." This positive response was shared by several other students; many of whom complained about being assigned material in other classes that used language in ways they were unfamiliar with and caused them to disengage. Another shared that the reading assistant enabled them to comprehend the text enough to "pre-plan my own ideas," enhancing engagement. The same student added, "readings like this one can be hard to follow, especially with multi-page counts and it is entirely beneficial to be able to go back and recall what stuck out during your initial read." The interactive features found within ExplainPaper and SciSpace required highlighting text, which also promoted active reading, rather than passive skimming. Students repeatedly referenced how much easier it was for them to stay on track and not lose focus during the course of the reading.

At least one student self-identified as suffering from a disability in their reflection, saying,

I have always struggled with reading comprehension because of my learning disabilities so using an app that analyzes a paper is very helpful for me. The process of shortening down a reading into an understandable paragraph definitely helped me understand the main claims of each section of the reading. I think that this is extremely helpful because when I read, I tend to lose focus which causes me to completely zone out for most of the reading. A shorter, clearly explained paragraph is much easier to focus on and understand than a long, wordy essay or article.

While only one student response indicated the support they received from AI was helpful to them because of an existing disability, I believe including the response in full is an important touchstone that captures the promise these tools have to offer.

Another potential benefit to using AI reading assistants is that they discreetly offer the potential to reduce negative stereotypes and stigmas that some students face when seeking help (Wolfner et al., 2023). Students with disabilities, multilingual learners, low-income populations, and minorities often feel self-conscious about accessing accommodations and services for fear of being perceived as less capable. AI reading assistants allow students to address challenges privately without disclosing disability status or other factors. Ideally, classroom culture may one day normalize AI support as a component of AI literacy, so all students utilize technology to enhance learning without judgment. Although best implemented alongside inclusive messaging, AI tools alone cannot transform mindsets. With care not to overstate capabilities, they may subtly help convey reading difficulties as navigable challenges rather than fixed deficits, benefiting vulnerable student groups.

Reducing Anxiety and Stress

As an educator, I often forget how much anxiety a student feels when being assigned a reading. There's not only the time involved, but also the complex planning of scheduling for that time, finding a quiet and comfortable space that isn't noisy or distracting, and then the cognitive process of taking physical and mental notes from the text itself. Multiple students reported feeling less anxious and stressed when using the AI reading assistants. A student confessed, "When I first looked at the reading we were supposed to read, I thought to myself, 'omg, this is going to take me so long. What am I even reading?' Using the AI reduced my stress and anxiety because I was finally able to use something that could translate text into something that I could understand." One student gave the reading assistant a "10/10" rating, explaining it helped them "get past this barrier in my learning" and "this helps relieve the stress that comes with reading a complex document because typically for me to really understand a reading, I have to read over every section many times before even knowing what it says." Another found it made the essay "much easier and enjoyable to read," easing their normal reading anxiety. A third student reflected that "using AI reduced the amount of stress I had about being able to deeply comprehend the article." The reading assistants allowed students more flexibility in how they read the material, and this likely helped give them more agency and control over how they read and, remarkably, how the writing on that reading was structured and worded.

Retaining More Information and Saving Time

Students consistently reported that the AI tools enabled them to retain more information from the readings. One explained it "100% helped me retain more information than I usually would" by simplifying the text and highlighting the main ideas. Another shared that "I was able to retain much greater amounts of information" compared to just reading the full text. By making complex readings more understandable, students could better comprehend and recall the core concepts. Providing each user a structured summary of key concepts helped students explore complex terms and subjects; however, I did not quiz the students about the content of the essay, only asked them to discuss and reflect on it in class, so it is possible that students felt like they retained more information than they did.

The AI tools helped some students streamline the reading process. As one reflection noted, "These apps helped because they summarized it to where I did not feel like I was reading for so long. It helped me get a quicker understanding of what I was reading." Rather than painstakingly rereading dense sections, the AI summaries enabled students to understand the core ideas more efficiently. This saved time compared to repeated close rereadings. The interactive features also enabled students to target the most confusing sections, rather than wasting time on clearer passages. One fear I had during the initial planning stage of the pilot was students offloading too much of their close reading skills to the AI reading assistant. While that did not appear to happen in this case, I foresee several critical challenges that I explore in-depth in the critical discussion sections.

From my perspective, students appeared more engaged in discussion than in previous semesters when I assigned this reading. They responded to their peers with quotes from the text and the AI-generated summaries. I also observed one student in class who may have not completed the reading attempting to use the AI reading assistant to catch up and not fall further behind while the class was having a discussion. While certainly not unusual, it was fascinating watching the students try to use the AI assistant in class to try and engage with the conversation, even though they were not prepared.

Since the spring pilot concluded, both tools have continued to develop and enhance their existing features with new ones. ExplainPaper is now beta testing a method where users can self-select their reading level for tailored feedback. Likewise, SciSpace has also expanded the multilingual offerings of their tool, going from a few languages during the spring to supporting well over two dozen languages now. These further refinements allow users to customize their reading experience in ways only envisioned in science fiction. Generative AI used in customized applications to support reading may well be the closest we've come to a technology that engages universal communication for text.

Other applications with similar features are now being deployed and scaled through established tech companies. Microsoft is currently piloting Reading Coach and Reading Progress as paired tools to help K-12 students achieve reading success at their grade level. Both tools use generative AI and other machine learning features to support students at their unique reading level in an experience often mimicking the personalized support reading intervention specialists provide to students. Used in this manner, generative AI may be a powerful tool to improve equity throughout the global south (Gates, 2023).

Critical Discussion

While this study suggests positive outcomes, integrating AI reading assistants risks detrimental overuse within and beyond the classroom. Students may become over-reliant on simplification and summarization, losing incentives to develop close reading skills essential for academic success. It is also possible that the quality of comprehension is reduced when relying solely on condensed summaries rather than wrestling with texts firsthand. I am unsure how primary analysis will be fair unless it is conducted in class. While my scaffolded approach attempted to promote balance, students exposed to apps through social media without thoughtful guidance may prioritize expediency over sustained engagement. There are no easy safeguards against students utilizing shortcuts that deskill them. Beyond comprehension, extensive processing of language is critical for growth in vocabulary, writing style, and analytical thinking for maturing readers and writers. If students predominantly consume AI summaries in place of full texts, the associated cognitive benefits may decline sharply. While AI assistants have the potential as reading aids, widespread adoption without careful integration could undermine the very literacies meant to be supported (Adisa et al., 2024).

More research is needed to prevent unintended consequences in the classroom, but it is unclear if any intervention or strategy will be impactful in curbing students' engagement with generative AI technologies on their own. Warning students not to overuse the AI reading feature is likely not enough of a barrier against potential deskilling; specific scaffolds are needed to foster metacognitive awareness and ethical usage. This may involve direct modeling, monitoring comprehension with and without AI support, and emphasizing reflection activities that are siloed from computer-assisted technology, such as reading and writing by hand in class for five or ten minutes.

Close Reading Needs to Be Protected

A major threat posed by AI reading assistant is that it potentially offloads the close reading skills educators try to teach students. Just as many feared ChatGPT would lead to a loss of writing skills, so too will many fear a similar loss of close reading skills with AI reading assistance. Many students do not view completing assigned readings as anything more than a transactional task, one they are required to complete in a course and their degree paths. Having a technology that can easily summarize material into compressible and concise summaries is a massive temptation to save time, but also a threat to the valuable skills and learning that come from close reading. My earlier anecdote of seeing a student in class using the tool to try to catch up echoes this fear; students who are unprepared and have not completed the work will simply turn to AI assistance to catch up and not fall behind.

One technique I employed with my students to discourage this was to encourage them to only engage AI assistance in their coursework when they reached a pain point within their reading assignment that would have otherwise caused them to disengage from the text or skip over the passage. Doing so emphasized that AI reading assistance is a tool to augment and enhance the student's reading experience, not offload it entirely. I have no means to gauge if such messaging is effective for students, but I imagine individual conferencing with students will remain an important pedagogical tool in helping guide students to the ethical and pragmatic use of generative AI tools in education.

Copyright and Artistic Intent

Another area to be thoughtful about is teaching students AI literacy about their use of generative AI tools so they understand that they may not have the right to scan anyone else's words in systems notorious for scraping billions of words without consent. Such conversations are necessary and deserve more time and space than what any individual educator can offer in a single course and must be part of a compressive approach at all institutions of higher education. I do not foresee many students adopting AI literacy about copyright or fair use on their own.

As a published writer of fiction and creative nonfiction, this pilot has caused me to pause and reflect on what my own feelings would be if someone uploaded one of my published works to an AI-powered reading app. I do not believe that I would be concerned if a non-native speaker or someone suffering from a disability used such a feature, but what if it was just a reader using it to generate summaries of my work? I, like all other writers, took care in crafting those words, thinking about style, tone, audience, and dozens of other things. Now a machine can scan and synthesize my words and the audience gets to choose the language and the reading level. What will this do to nuance and meaning? After all, writers are not simply content producers. Higher education should explore creating guidelines for humanities to carefully integrate generative AI tools to see if they can maintain artistic integrity by ensuring summarization does not override nuance and authorial style.

Stephen King's recent piece in the *Atlantic* "My Books Were Used to Train AI" describes AI's threat to artists in simple terms: "These programmers can dump thousands of books into state-of-the-art digital blenders. Including, it seems, mine. The real question is whether you get a sum that's greater than the parts when you pour back out." (S. King, 2023). The fundamental question we must ask when using these tools to augment our existing skills, such as reading, is what is gained and what is lost. AI-powered reading apps may indeed be transformative and help improve equity, but that transformative power may come at a profound cost to our ability to read closely and render the artistic intent of an author to simple information. King further reflects

> Would I forbid the teaching (if that is the word) of my stories to computers? Not even if I could. I might as well be King Canute, forbidding the tide to come in. Or a Luddite trying to stop industrial progress by hammering a steam loom to pieces.

We cannot stop progress, nor can we inhibit a technology or tool's influence. The most we can do is help shape our student's use of it by helping them to see the pragmatic and ethical implications, shaping their understanding of what it means to be AI literate.

Conclusion

While AI reading assistants hold profound promise to increase accessibility, streamline comprehension, and enhance focus for diverse learners, integration requires caution. Educators in the humanities have a daunting task before them, navigating the tension between generative AI's potential to help or hard students. We must take care to develop students' AI and close reading literacies in tandem, fostering agency and metacognition. Consulting with disability professionals and copyright experts can inform ethical implementation and should be considered before adopting any new tool. Despite valid concerns, the thoughtful use of these technologies may provide more students the support needed to deeply engage with academic content. By personalizing the reading experience and reducing barriers, AI tools can help make education more inclusive. Yet skillful integration is key to realizing these benefits, guiding students to read both with machines and on their own critical terms. Only by embracing emerging technologies' potential thoughtfully and progressively can we ensure education elevates the many, not just the few.

Author Note

Some portions from this pilot about AI reading assistants were accepted for publication in *Teaching and Generative AI: Pedagogical Possibilities and Productive Tensions*, for a short 2000-word reflective article "Automated Aide or Offloading Close Reading: Student Perspectives on AI Reading Assistants."

IRB "AI and the Student Writing Process" (Protocol #23x-068) has been determined as Exempt under 45 CFR 46.101(b)(#1).

The MLA/CCCC AI Taskforce also requested that I include the reading assistant assignment in a forthcoming digital resource under a Creative Commons license, with a short 250-word reflection framing the assignment. https://exploringaipedagogy.hcommons.org/2023/11/27/reading-assistants-explainpaper-and-scispace/#comments

References

Adisa, K., Byrd, A., Flores, L., Green, D., Hassel, H., Johnson, S. Z., Kirschenbaum, M., Lockett, A., Mathews Losh, E., & Mills, A. (2024). Initial guidance for evaluating the use of AI in scholarship and creativity – MLA-CCCC joint task force on writing and AI. *Initial guidance for evaluating the use of AI in scholarship and creativity.* https://aiandwriting.hcommons.org/2024/01/28/initial-guidance-for-evaluating-the-use-of-ai-in-scholarship-and-creativity/

Bezirhan, U., & Von Davier, M. (2023). Automated reading passage generation with OpenAI's large language model. *Computers & Education: Artificial Intelligence, 5,* 100161. https://doi.org/10.1016/j.caeai.2023.100161

Cavalcanti, A. P., Barbosa, A., Carvalho, R., Freitas, F., Tsai, Y., Gašević, D., & Mello, R. F. (2021). Automatic feedback in online learning environments: A systematic literature review. *Computers & Education: Artificial Intelligence, 2,* 100027. https://doi.org/10.1016/j.caeai.2021.100027

Chace, C. (2020, October 29). *The impact of artificial intelligence on education.* Forbes. https://www.forbes.com/sites/calumchace/2020/10/29/the-impact-of-artificial-intelligence-on-education/?sh=68906fe750df

Cummings, R., Monroe, S., & Watkins, M. (2024). Generative AI in first-year writing: An early analysis of affordances, limitations, and a framework for the future. *Computers and Composition.* https://doi.org/10.1016/j.compcom.2024.102827

Dang, H., Benharrak, K., Lehmann, F., & Buschek, D. (2022). Beyond Text Generation: Supporting Writers with Continuous Automatic Text Summaries. *UIST '22: Proceedings of the 35th annual ACM symposium on user interface software and technology.* https://doi.org/10.1145/3526113.3545672

Drake, M. (2023). Spatial canvases and large language models. *Fermat Research.* https://research.fermat.app/spatial-canvases-and-large-language-models

Gates, B. (2023, April 19). *A fireside chat on education, technology, and almost everything in between.* gatesnotes.com. https://www.gatesnotes.com/ASU-and-GSV?WT.mc_id=20230419100000_ASU-GSV-2023_BG-EM_&WT.tsrc=BGEM

Gayed, J. M., Carlon, M. K. J., Oriola, A. M., & Cross, J. S. (2022). *Exploring an AI-based writing Assistant's impact on English language learners. Computers & Education: Artificial Intelligence, 3,* 100055. https://doi.org/10.1016/j.caeai.2022.100055

Grubaugh, S., Levitt, G., & Deever, D. (2023). Harnessing AI to power constructivist learning: An evolution in educational methodologies. *EIKI Journal of Effective Teaching Methods.* https://doi.org/10.59652/jetm.v1i3.43

Heilman, M., Collins-Thompson, K., Callan, J., Eskénazi, M., Juffs, A., & Wilson, L. (2010). Personalization of reading passages improves vocabulary acquisition. *Artificial Intelligence in Education, 20*(1), 73–98. https://doi.org/10.3233/jai-2010-0003

Jonassen, D., & Rohrer-Murphy, L. (1999). Activity theory as a framework for designing constructivist learning environments. *Educational Technology Research and Development, 47,* 61–79. https://doi.org/10.1007/BF02299477

King, S. (2023, September 1). Stephen King: My books were used to train AI. *The Atlantic.* https://www.theatlantic.com/books/archive/2023/08/stephen-king-books-ai-writing/675088/

Lenhard, W., Baier, H., Endlich, D., Schneider, W., & Hoffmann, J. (2011). Rethinking strategy instruction: Direct reading strategy instruction versus computer-based guided practice. *Journal of Research in Reading*, 36(2), 223–240. https://doi.org/10.1111/j.1467-9817.2011.01505.x

Mader, J., (2021, September 8). Can an AI tutor teach your child to read? *The Hechinger Report.* https://hechingerreport.org/can-an-ai-tutor-teach-your-child-to-read/

Mostow, J., Nelson-Taylor, J., & Beck, J. E. (2013). Computer-guided oral reading versus independent practice: Comparison of sustained silent reading to an automated reading tutor that listens. *Journal of Educational Computing Research*, 49(2), 249–276. https://eric.ed.gov/?id=EJ1076364

Rajagopal, A., Nirmala, V., Jebadurai, I., Vedamanickam, A., & Kumar, P. (2023). Design of Generative Multimodal AI Agents to Enable Persons with Learning Disability. *Companion publication of the 25th international conference on multimodal interaction.* https://doi.org/10.1145/3610661.3617514

Risher, D. (2023, April 11). Artificial intelligence could make a difference for young readers around the world–or make literacy even less equitable. *Fortune.* https://fortune.com/2023/04/11/artificial-intelligence-young-readers-world-literacy-equitable-tech-ai-education-david-risher/

Schneider, M., & Yin, L. (2012). *Completion matters: The high cost of low community college graduation rates.* Education outlook. No. 2. American Enterprise Institute for Public Policy Research.

Srinivasan, V. (2022). AI & learning: A preferred future. *Computers & Education: Artificial Intelligence*, 3, 100062. https://doi.org/10.1016/j.caeai.2022.100062

The UDL Guidelines. (2018). https://udlguidelines.cast.org/

Vee, A. (2023). Large language models write answers. *Composition Studies.* https://compositionstudiesjournal.files.wordpress.com/2023/06/vee.pdf

Watkins, M. (2023) AI in first year writing courses. *TextGenEd*. The WAC Clearinghouse. https://wac.colostate.edu/repository/collections/textgened/ethical-considerations/ai-in-first-year-writing-courses/

Wattenberger, A. (2023). Why chatbots are not the future of interfaces. https://wattenberger.com/thoughts/boo-chatbots

Wolfner, C., Ott, C., Upshaw, K., Stowe, A., Schwiebert, L. M., & Lanzi, R. G. (2023). Coping strategies and help-seeking behaviors of college students and postdoctoral fellows with disabilities or pre-existing conditions during COVID-19. *Disabilities*, 3(1), 62–86. https://doi.org/10.3390/disabilities3010006

9

GENERATIVE ARTIFICIAL INTELLIGENCE IN WRITING

ChatGPT and Critical Questioning for Multilingual Learners

Allessandra Elisabeth dos Santos, Paulo Boa Sorte, and Luciana C. de Oliveira

Introduction

Among the numerous social practices embedded in our daily routine, writing serves as a technology that enables us to actively engage in ongoing discussions and disseminate knowledge across a wide array of communities (Bazerman, 2016). When it comes to writing as a social practice, it is not simply a matter of completing sentences, summarizing, and translating texts. The challenge is: Who will pose issues that really matter to humanity? After asking questions and seeking answers, students would be better able to develop collaboration, creativity, and critical thinking. The pedagogical approaches toward the teaching of writing within academic and research domains significantly support the cultivation of critical inquiry among learners. Writing is not merely a tool for communication but also a means to engage in higher-order thinking, argumentation, and the dissemination of knowledge.

Technology has always played a significant role in addressing the challenges associated with the instruction and practice of writing. Acknowledging the presence of Generative Artificial Intelligence (GenAI) and other technological tools in education is essential since schools are impacted by changes in society. The various forms of using GenAI nowadays are both a pathway toward simplification and time efficiency in completing human tasks, whether they are professional or personal, and they also reveal the social intricacies in diverse contexts. As content-generating platforms and applications within GenAI become more accessible to the public, the demand for text-generating assistants is becoming a noticeable trend in the field of education (Boa Sorte et al., 2021; dos Santos et al., 2023a, 2023b). A vivid recent representative example is ChatGPT, which is causing controversial reactions worldwide in educational systems as well as in other instances of our society. Taking this into consideration, this chapter shares pedagogical approaches to incorporating ChatGPT into the teaching of writing in order to raise awareness of how to critically ask questions. In this praxis piece, we address writing focusing on critical thinking development and share a plan for an academic writing course in which ChatGPT is integrated in the writing of review articles within a multilingual learner's dominant higher education institution.

DOI: 10.4324/9781003426936-12

We continue this chapter by contextualizing ChatGPT, the most well-known large language model in the current GenAI setting, an AI-text generator whose writing may be confused with human texts.

Generative Artificial Intelligence: Situating ChatGPT

Historically, researchers have tried to guide our understanding of AI by defining AI into four categories: systems that think like humans, systems that act like humans, systems that think rationally, and systems that act rationally (Russell & Norvig, 2021). Even though AI cannot yet be compared to human reasoning, as we explore the latest potential of GenAI technologies, it is clear that the advancements are indisputable.

The multifaceted uses of GenAI depict the pursuit of simplifying and optimizing time for the completion of human tasks, whether professional or personal. On the other hand, they expose the ethical, privacy, and employment challenges inherent in various societal contexts. As GenAI-based platforms and applications become increasingly accessible, there is an evident shift toward seeking text-generating assistants in the educational domain, which is the case of ChatGPT. GenAI is centered on the creation of systems proficient in generating new content, encompassing domains such as texts, images, videos, and musical compositions. Within the educational sector, this technology can be leveraged to craft individualized and adaptive educational resources. For instance, a GenAI system could design a series of exercises and activities tailored to a student's writing needs, based on their performance history, or even develop pedagogical simulators and games (dos Santos et al., 2023b).

It is clear that GenAI, specifically ChatGPT, presents capabilities to produce what has been identified as new content. However, its limitations are clearly described by the company that developed it (OpenAI, 2022): ChatGPT generates human-like texts, but some of these answers are incorrect and lack factual information; the model tends to repeat phrases and vocabulary constantly; when a user creates an ambiguous prompt, the model does not ask for clarification, and automatically responds acting as if the user's intention is guessed clearly; the model does not refuse inappropriate requests, but might respond to harmful instructions and express biased behavior; the chatbot often acts inconsistently during a human-machine interaction generating completely opposite responses even if a prompt is slightly rephrased.

Among the current versions, there are ChatGPT (GPT-4o and GPT-3.5 models) and ChatGPT Plus (GPT-4o and GPT-4 models), which primarily differ in terms of access and service levels. ChatGPT is a free-of-cost model, offering the core functionality of generating fast human-like text that easily impresses and deceives us. ChatGPT Plus is a subscription-based model that provides additional benefits, including priority access to the model during peak times, faster response speeds, and early access to new features and improvements: DALLE-3 AI image generator and some capabilities such as image recognition and voice processing (OpenAI, 2023a).

As seen previously, a prompt is an essential aspect of this interaction with ChatGPT, and defining it is necessary to make the most of its capabilities. Writing prompts describe a statement or a question with the purpose of inspiring the writer to initiate a text. In the context of ChatGPT or other large language models, a prompt can be defined as information provided to the model, also called input text, used to generate the output or response desired.

Writing for Critical Questioning: ChatGPT and Special Considerations

Given that there are different conceptions of language, the attitude toward writing will change the approach to the teaching of writing. Therefore, in this section, we address writing as a social practice bearing in mind the need to focus on critical thinking development in all formal educational levels. Our discussion concentrates on writing in higher education directing the preparation of individuals to navigate and contribute to the scholarly discourses prevalent within their respective fields. This approach is fostered by posing meaningful questions that initiate a meaning-making process aiming to achieve social goals.

The act of writing is easily associated with a combination of words, sentences, and phrases whose focus is primarily on grammar and lexical structures. This view is supported by those who understand language in a more abstract way, considering the teaching of language as neutral and objective by presenting information as it is described in grammar books and dictionaries. Another conception of language is language as a means of communication. Based on this perspective, every text written will be understood by all readers similarly. Therefore, the teaching of language highlights the importance of identifying what messages an author seeks to convey. This viewpoint emphasizes the development of critical reflection and the ability to recognize the author's intentions and potential manipulation in texts. The third and last conception of language we intend to mention does not take for granted the fact that every reader manages comprehension differently. The origins of meanings we create from texts (verbal, non-verbal, verb-visual) represent the various ways we engage with reading and explain why we read in different ways influenced by each reader's socio-historical and cultural contexts (de Souza, 2018).

Writing as a social practice involves much more than sentence and word-level work, that is, putting words and sentences together to form a whole. Writing must be connected with social purpose, audiences, and meaning-making. The work on multiliteracies is especially relevant in this conception of writing as a social practice developed by the New London Group (Cazden et al., 1996). As a result of its visionary, paradigm-shifting, and innovative approach, this pedagogy acknowledges the changing environment of communication and literacy in the digital age, offering a comprehensive perspective on education that goes beyond what is called traditional literacy, i.e., having a primary focus on reading and writing. It advocates for fostering multiliteracies to prepare students for the complex demands of contemporary society. Communication in this era is multifaceted, encompassing not just written language but also symbolic representation, auditory components, and visual elements. A more expansive concept of literacy is important to understand the cultural and social contexts in which communication occurs. Interpretation of texts and the meaning-making processes are deeply influenced by the cultural and social factors surrounding them. In this regard, this pedagogy encourages students to actively participate in today's culture and emphasizes the importance of incorporating various forms of literacy into the curriculum (Cazden et al., 1996; Cope & Kalantzis, 2000; Kalantzis et al., 2020). Continuous teacher development is a critical component, aiming to cultivate flexible learning abilities in students and prepare them for the ever-changing digital landscape.

The pedagogy of multiliteracies is based on a Freirian perspective (Freire, 1985) delving into the principles of critical pedagogy. Centering on the concept of liberatory education, questioning is a potent instrument for both empowerment and transformation by challenging the traditional notion of education as a unidirectional process in which knowledge is merely imparted to students passively (Freire & Faundez, 1992). Freire supports a dynamic and interactive educational experience that cultivates critical thinking, promotes inquiry, and stimulates active engagement. In this environment, teachers and students engage in meaningful conversations to collectively explore and question the world. This may be done, for instance, by challenging the unfair systems and inequalities in society; taking the lead in making positive changes in their own lives and communities, and seeing education as the way to achieve freedom for both individuals and groups.

The concept of the banking system of education (Freire, 1970) represents what is known as a traditional approach to teaching, where teachers deposit knowledge into students' minds as if they were uninvolved recipients, thinking of them as empty containers. In this system, students are required to remember and repeat facts without thinking deeply or actively taking part in the learning process. Freire criticizes this method as dehumanizing and oppressive, emphasizing the need for a more student-centered and participatory educational model that fosters critical thinking, dialogue, and empowerment. He advocates for a pedagogy that values the student's experience, encourages questioning, and promotes the development of critical consciousness, ultimately leading to social transformation and liberation.

One of the examples of how the US Departments of Education may not have engaged their policies around practices of critical pedagogy was featured in the news in January 2023. The New York City Department of Education implemented a ban on the use of ChatGPT within its schools' devices and networks due to concerns of potential academic dishonesty and a perceived lack of support for critical thinking skills (Rosenblatt, 2023). While opinions among experts varied regarding the educational impact of these chatbots, with some proposing their integration into the curriculum rather than a complete ban, it took four months before the ban was lifted.

For the purpose of exploring the resources that GenAI, such as ChatGPT, provides in the classroom, it is crucial to consider what we call a task assigned by the Freirian approach to education: Without reevaluating our practices, we may be destined to continually prohibit and fight against the introduction of new resources into classrooms, whether through student initiatives or government technology funding initiatives.

ChatGPT: Applications and Limitations for Academic Writing

ChatGPT serves multiple functions, primarily focusing on interactive conversational responses to our questions. In this interaction, it generates coherent and cohesive texts with answers spanning multiple areas of knowledge. It assists in problem-solving, creates scripts, articles, essays, and stories, edits, revises, translates texts, and provides definitions of terms and concepts.

In spite of ChatGPT limitless potential, the responses or information generated by the system are not always accurate, correct, or based on real facts. This phenomenon, known in the field of AI as "hallucination," occurs when the language model produces results that are untrue or entirely fabricated. Such hallucinations happen when the model is exposed to incorrect, biased, or ambiguous data during training. Hence, as ChatGPT does not disclose the sources of the information it generates, it is essential to verify its reliability outside the platform.

Once again, the need for multiliteracy practices in education is discussed. Even if we ask ChatGPT to generate initial ideas for writing a paragraph, for example, the chatbot cannot observe the real world and, therefore, is not able to generate new knowledge or critical thinking based on observation. We are talking about codes generated by algorithms taken from existing databases. This means that in the context of scientific research in higher education, which continually demands new discoveries, ChatGPT may not be as effective. As a GenAI tool, ChatGPT can help with writer's block and provide ideas for paragraph construction, but it does not generate research questions stemming from real-world observations and analysis. From this perspective, formulating pertinent questions requires specialized knowledge and human understanding in each field of expertise.

To claim, in the past, that education and knowledge are about answers and not questions, Freire (1970) anticipated the role that ChatGPT would assume today, highlighting the importance of promoting an education that values the practice of questioning pedagogy. One must know how to inquire, even when using GenAI. It is no wonder that after ChatGPT's release, advertisements for prompt engineering courses attracted attention on social media. However, despite involving the careful formulation of prompts to influence the model in producing desired outputs, prompt engineering still does not assist us in the task of questioning based on observation.

Thus, as we navigate the evolving landscape of GenAI, such as ChatGPT, and its applications to generate written texts, we are reminded of the foundational elements of academic writing. Academic writing encompasses the concept of authorship and, being influenced by post-structuralist principles needs to consider the concept of ethical appropriation, which goes beyond being merely a law-guided process (Boa Sorte et al., 2021). Ethical appropriation involves the concern to recognize that every act of creation has its roots in a specific context, is interconnected with other productions, and acknowledges the references used. With the emergence of contemporary technologies, it is critical to dedicate spaces for discussions on digital texts and practices in the field of education (Burwell, 2013). Furthermore, a reflection on the convergent relationship between digital and non-digital texts is necessary, as ChatGPT does not serve for plagiarism detection. For instance, if you input a text of your own authorship into the platform and ask who wrote it, the language model will likely say that it wrote it itself.

Addressing this aspect involves recognizing the active participation of the author in the intellectual creation process, requiring a stance rather than adopting a supposed neutrality. Authorship is linked to defining the writer's identity in the production as well as the concern for presenting original work free from plagiarism-related issues (dos Santos et al., 2023a, 2023b).

Even before the advent of ChatGPT, various methods of promoting academic writing were under debate. These approaches included establishing support groups that offered activities such as peer review, constructive feedback, and formal and informal mentorship, in addition to providing emotional support. These activities serve as supplements to conventional guidance, aiming to enhance the development of authorship by researchers.

Integrating ChatGPT into Critical Writing

In this section, we aim to share an academic writing course plan whose focus is on preparing multilingual learners (MLs) in higher education to write a review article. The course was designed taking into consideration cognitive as well as emotional challenges of developing academic writing texts (Casanave, 2019; Russell-Pinson & Harris, 2019). Also, we cannot deny the language barriers encountered, not only by MLs but also by English language native speakers due to the fact that academic language is different from everyday language (Schleppegrell, 2004). Academic language is much more than vocabulary and includes broader language aspects, grammatical, and linguistic components (de Oliveira, 2023). Our objective is to develop an academic course in which ChatGPT is incorporated into writing as a scaffolding strategy.

Course Design with ChatGPT

In this subsection, we detail our approach to designing an academic writing course using ChatGPT as a central pedagogical tool. The context involves a professor from the Department of Teaching and Learning at a North American university and a group of 20 students enrolled in the course. Among these students are MLs from Asian, European, and Latin American countries. The objective of the course is to enable students to effectively use ChatGPT to organize their thoughts, refine arguments, and ensure clarity and coherence to write review articles. This course lasts 30 hours and is divided into 10 days. In order to experience planning and writing with ChatGPT, we decided to plan each module of the course with the assistance of ChatGPT (GPT-4 model).

To start interacting with any AI-text generator, a user needs to create a prompt. A prompt is a sentence or set of sentences provided by the user, serving as a command for the GenAI platform to generate a response. As we know, this kind of large language model does not understand what we are saying. The "magic" happens as a consequence of patterns and associations the model learned during its training or through examples of human interactions. In fact, when ChatGPT generates text, it calculates the probability of a word appearing next in a sequence of text (OpenAI, 2023b).

Overall, although there is no limited number of prompts we can use, the first prompt represents a key planning stage for users of large language models. The crafting of a prompt depends on the nature of the task, and it implies the selection of central and basic aspects so that the language model can process the user's request. Effective prompt engineering requires an understanding of the intended audience, purpose, and social context in educational and communicative practices. Connecting Freire's pedagogical strategies with the concept of multiliteracies (Cazden et al., 1996) in the age of GenAI provides a comprehensive framework for education that prepares students not just to navigate but also to critically assess and shape the evolving digital communication and information landscape.

To make the most of ChatGPT's generative capabilities, we created a descriptive prompt (see Figure 9.1) that depicts a suggestion for this academic writing program. Besides requesting this large language model to generate contents, objectives, and lesson plans, we supplied the AI-text generator with some background information aiming to obtain a more suitable curriculum and course design.

GPT-4

 You

I am a professor in a Department of Teaching and Learning in a North American university. I teach an undergraduate course on writing to a group of 20 students. Among the 20 students, there are multilingual learners from Asian, European, and Latin American countries. I am preparing an academic writing project in which my students are supposed to write and submit a scientific paper to a journal. For most learners, this will be their first time submitting a manuscript to a scientific journal and it is acknowledged how important publishing is in the academic scenario. My View on writing is connected to a critical perspective. It is writing for questioning aspects in our society from a critical standpoint so writing is taught to these multilingual learners as a social practice. Since I am aware not only of the cognitive but also the emotional challenges of writing. I see scaffolding strategies as essential to my planning of this course. Also, we cannot deny the presence of language barriers, not thinking only about the multilingual learners but having in mind that academic language is different from everyday language, my objective is to develop this course integrating ChatGPT as a scaffolding strategy. This is a 30-hour course, so create a 10-day course, including contents, objectives and lesson plans.

FIGURE 9.1   First prompt: initial user-ChatGPT interaction.

Although we agree that the previous prompt (see Figure 9.1) offers detailed context, we decided to interrupt the generation of content to create a supplementary prompt, informing that the content of the course needed to concentrate on review articles. This decision was made to provide essential clarification that had been omitted in the initial prompt, ensuring the generated course content aligned with the specific focus. Additionally, since ChatGPT retains a memory of the user-ChatGPT interaction, there was no need to reintroduce the same detailed context, as the system could recall the information already provided. Consequently, we maintained the interaction with straightforward language, given that the chatbot's conversational capabilities eliminate the need for restarting a new user-ChatGPT conversation. The second, augmenting prompt instructed to "Create another course bearing in mind that the articles will be review articles" generated these components (see Figure 9.2): a course title, an overview paragraph, the structure of ten modules/days, and a concluding note with final considerations.

Analyzing Day 1 (see Figure 9.2), what the chatbot generates as a lesson plan cannot be described as one, after all it only frames three vague steps and a homework assignment at the end. Even though ChatGPT generated suitable contents and appropriate objectives, the lesson plans did not include all the necessary information, and most importantly, the guidance to use scaffolding strategies was absent.

Upon further analysis of the remaining nine modules, we concluded that some decision-making was necessary regarding the course framework to better align with our course objective: to enable students to effectively use ChatGPT to organize their thoughts, refine arguments, and ensure clarity and coherence to write review articles. Therefore, we decided to continue interacting with the model to gather more detailed ideas for planning that would offer clearer guidance for students. Specifically, we chose to develop the lesson plan for Day 6, *Drafting the Introduction and Objectives*, using the following prompt: "Create a detailed

"Scaffolding Scientific Writing for Multilingual Learners: A 10-Day Course with ChatGPT"

Overview:
This course aims to equip multilingual learners with the tools and strategies necessary to write and submit a scientific paper to a journal. Emphasis is on understanding academic writing as a social practice that critiques and questions societal aspects, integrating both cognitive and emotional support.

Day 1: Introduction to Academic Writing

Objective: Understand the nature and purpose of academic writing, especially from a critical perspective.

Contents
1. What is academic writing?
2. The importance of publishing in academia.
3. Writing as a social practice.
4. The crucel perspective in academic writing.

Lesson Plan:

1. Introduction to the course and its objectives.
2. Discussion: Differences between everyday language and academic language.
3. Group activity: Critiquing a sample paper.
4. Homework: Read an assigned scientific paper.

FIGURE 9.2   ChatGPT output: creating an academic writing course.

lesson of Day 6. Focus on the step-by-step of how ChatGPT can be used." Both the third prompt and its output can be seen in Figure 9.3.

When analyzing the output (see Figure 9.3), we observed that although the algorithm had miscalculated the three-hour period for a module, suggesting a plan for 140 minutes instead of the intended 180 minutes (3 hours), it generated a more complete and structured lesson plan that outlines objectives and meaningful tasks to assist users in achieving their goals. We decided to start planning the course with the ideas generated for Day 6 because this plan better suits our course objective and framework. Day 6 was also chosen to exemplify the pedagogical applications of ChatGPT in teaching how to write a review article in the next subsection.

Incorporating ChatGPT into the planning of this academic writing course has raised our awareness about the importance of not only designing prompts carefully but also crafting a well-structured initial prompt. Based on our experience with prompt engineering in the context of planning this course, we identified three essential elements to consider when crafting an effective prompt. These elements are presented in our Prompt Creation Reference Chart (see Figure 9.4). We developed this chart based on these insights.

Accordingly, by following the Prompt Creation Reference Chart (see Figure 9.4), we recommend structuring an initial prompt considering (1) some background information about

Create a detailed lesson plan for day 6. Focus on the step by step of how ChatGPT can be used.

ChatGPT

Lesson Plan: Day 6 - "Drafting the Introduction and Objectives"

Objective: Students will be able to articulate the purpose and importance of their review article through a well-crafted introduction and clear objectives.

Warm-up (15 minutes)
- Begin with a brief discussion about the importance of first impressions.
  Share excerpts from renowned review articles and discuss what makes the introduction compelling.

Crafting an Impactful Introduction (30 minutes)
- Lecture (10 minutes):
  - Importance of setting the context.
  - Strategies to grab the reader's attention.
  - Providing an overview of what will be covered in the review.
- Activity: Initial Drafting (20 minutes)
  - Students start drafting their introductions.
  - While drafting, students are Arcouraged to use ChatGPT to:
    - Ask questions or clarify doubts.
    - Seek examples or guidance on phrasing
    - Review their drafted sentences for clarity or coherence.

Defining Clear Objectives (30 minutes)
- Lecture (10 minutes):
  - The importance of having clear objectives.
  - Differentiating between broad aims and specific objectives.
- Activity: Objective Setting (20 minutes):
  - Students draft 2-3 objectives for their review article.
  - During this process, students use ChatGPT to:
    - Refine and rephrase objectives for clarity.
    - Ensure their objectives align with the scope of their review.
    - Check if the objectives are neither too broad nor too narrow.

Incorporating ChatGPT Feedback (30 minutes)
- Activity: ChatGPT Review Session (20 minutes):
  - Students copy their drafted introduction and objectives into ChatGPT.
  - They ask ChatGPT for feedback, improvements, and suggestions.
  - Students make real-time revisions based on the feedback.
- Group Discussion (10 minutes):
  - A few volunteers share the feedback they received from ChatGPT.
  - The class discusses common challenges and beneficial suggestions.

FIGURE 9.3 Planning an academic writing course in collaboration with ChatGPT.

Peer Feedback (20 minutes)
    Pair & Share (10 minutes):
        • Students pair up and share their introductions and objectives.
        • They provide each other with feedback, keeping in mind what they learned and the feedback from ChatGPT.

    Whole Group Reflection (10 minutes):
        • Discussion on the feedback process.
        • Students reflect on the changes they plan to make based on peer suggestions and ChatGPT feedback.

Wrap-up and Homework Assignment (15 minutes)
    Recap the importance of a compelling introduction and clear objectives.
    For homework, students will:

        • Finalize their introductions and objectives based on feedback.
        • Prepare a first draft of their first thematic section.
        • Use ChatGPT as needed for refining language, coerence, and clarity.

Note: Throughout the lesson, the instructor should emphasize the importance of using ChatGPT as a tool for refining their writing and seeking clarity. The objective is to make students comfortable with leveraging technology for academic writing support.

FIGURE 9.3   (Continued)

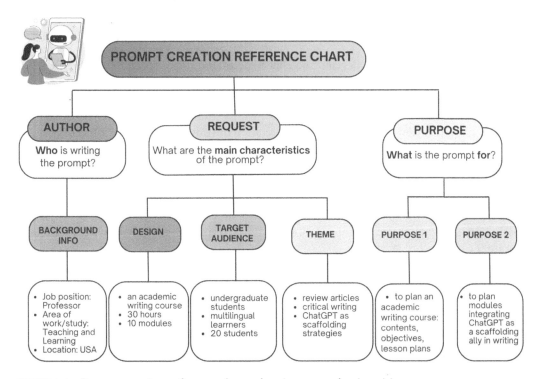

FIGURE 9.4   Prompt creation reference chart: planning an academic writing course.

the user, the prompt's *author*, (2) the main characteristics of the *request*, which in the context of this study involve design, target audience, and theme, (3) and the *purpose* which replies the question "what is this prompt for?" Our experience designing this course, with ChatGPT as a scaffolding tool for refining ideas and making decisions, has better equipped us to guide our students in the art of crafting prompts.

We continued planning the course by using prompts tailored to the remaining modules. These subsequent prompts were crafted to focus on key aspects of the academic writing course, such as teaching specific elements of review articles. To maintain consistency and ensure a focused output, we utilized the prompt: "Create a detailed lesson of Day __. Focus on the step-by-step process of how ChatGPT can be used." By specifying each day and leveraging ChatGPT's memory capabilities, we were able to streamline the process and produce detailed, structured lesson plans that aligned with the course objectives. This method allowed us to refine and develop the course progressively, with each subsequent prompt addressing distinct elements necessary for writing review articles, thereby ensuring a coherent course structure.

Teaching Review Article with ChatGPT

Throughout the course, we encourage students to use ChatGPT aiming to diminish stress and anxiety possibly caused by a high level of expectation and perfection commonly present during the writing stages of academic texts (Casanave, 2019). We intend to explore additional benefits of this integration, specifically within one of the modules. Given its relevance, the plan is to model the "thinking aloud" process during the human-AI interactions whenever possible or required. This integration is promoted by posing significant inquiries, which lead to a meaning-making process used to achieve social goals (Cazden et al., 1996; Cope & Kalantzis, 2000; Freire, 1985).

To exemplify, we chose to develop the Day 6 module in this subsection (see Figure 9.5). Day 6 focuses on drafting the introduction of a review article. The contents addressed are the purpose and importance of a review, crafting an impactful introduction, and clearly defining objectives. This module has a seminar format in which students will be able to articulate the purpose of their review article through a well-crafted introduction and clear objectives.

The seminar is divided into five moments (see Figure 9.5) beginning with activating prior knowledge regarding review articles they have as mentor texts. Students briefly discuss their first impressions in groups, identifying topic sentences and commenting on their role and relevance in the text. Then comes the first student-ChatGPT interaction: still in their groups. Either using ChatGPT Plus (GPT-4o or GPT-4) or ChatGPT free version (GPT-4o or GPT-3.5), students create prompts following the Prompt Creation Reference Chart (see Figure 9.6).

The information given (see Figure 9.6) about each essential element—*author*, *request*, and *purpose*—helps structure the prompt. To better visualize the three key elements of a prompt (see Figure 9.7), we employed distinct shades of the color gray. The excerpts highlighted in light gray refer to background information about the *author*. The excerpts highlighted in medium gray detail the main characteristics of the *request*. Based on our experience, some of these characteristics can be altered depending on the specific context. Finally, the sentences highlighted in dark gray present the *purposes*. It is important to note that the number of purposes may vary depending on the context.

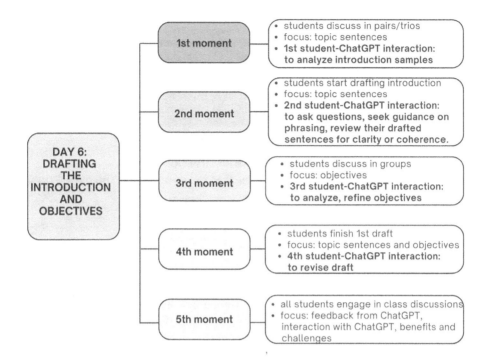

FIGURE 9.5 Day 6: drafting the introduction and objectives.

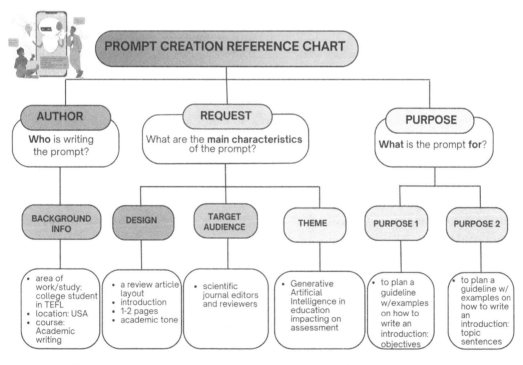

FIGURE 9.6 Prompt creation reference chart: review article introduction.

Prompt —

I am a **college student** in **the USA, minoring in Teaching English as a Foreign Language**. I am enrolled in an **Academic Writing course** and have been assigned to **draft the introduction of a review article**, aiming for a length of **1 to 2 pages**. This introduction is part of a larger review article that will be submitted to a scientific journal for **editorial and peer review**. The choice of an **academic tone** is crucial to align with the expectations. My chosen theme is **Generative Artificial Intelligence in Education, focusing on its impact on assessment**. Generate a guideline on how to write compelling topic sentences for the introduction of a review article, including one or to mentor texts as references for these topic sentences.
(ChatGPT 4, April 23, 2024)

AUTHOR (WHO): BACKGROUND INFORMATION

REQUEST (MAIN CHARACTERISTCS): DESIGN – TARGET AUDIENCE – THEME

PURPOSE (WHAT FOR): PURPOSE 1 + PURPOSE 2...

FIGURE 9.7 Visualizing the prompt: 1st student-ChatGPT interaction.

During the crafting of the prompt and the analysis of its output, we recommend engaging in "thinking aloud" and encouraging active interaction between students and teachers, as well as human-AI interactions while discussing the output. These practices naturally develop creativity and critical thinking through collaboration and the questioning of ideas (Freire, 1985). The output (see Figure 9.8) generated from this prompt provides students with additional examples of introductory sections, allowing them to analyze and organize key elements of an effective introduction. This step represents the first scaffolding strategy, preparing students for the subsequent phase of drafting their own introductions.

Before trying to write their introduction individually, students start to draft the topic sentence by interacting with their groups. While drafting, students are encouraged to use ChatGPT to ask questions or clarify doubts, seek examples or guidance on phrasing, and review their drafted sentences for clarity or coherence. This teaching strategy encourages active participation in debates, where the main focus is on posing relevant questions and pursuing significant responses to cultivate critical thinking abilities in both students and teachers.

In the third section of this module, we draw students' attention to another essential element of an introduction for any research: the objectives of a study. Defining clear objectives requires reflection on the selection of the verbs that will connect future readers to read the review article. Understanding the importance of having clear objectives and differentiating between general and specific objectives are crucial to the writing of an introduction. During this process, students use ChatGPT to (1) refine and rephrase objectives for clarity, (2) ensure their objectives align with the scope of their review, (3) and check if the objectives are neither too broad nor too narrow.

The fourth stage is when the groups finish working on their first draft. This phase consists of editing, paraphrasing, and discussing language choices. Students are supposed to revise their pieces and seek feedback. Here the feedback is enhanced when students copy their drafted introduction and objectives into ChatGPT creating prompts that request improvements and suggestions. Students make real-time revisions based on the feedback and discussions in groups.

In the final moment of this module, the group discusses common challenges and beneficial suggestions. Students are paired up with students from other groups in order to share their

ChatGPT

To create compelling topic sentences for the introduction of a review article on Generative Artificial Intelligence (AI) in Education with a focus on its impact on assessment, consider these steps:

1. **Contextualize the Topic**: Begin with a broad context to set the stage for your theme. You might mention trends, broader impacts, or key definitions.
   - *Example*: "In recent years, the rise of generative artificial intelligence has significantly influenced educational practices, reshaping how educators assess student learning outcomes."
2. **Introduce the Specific Focus**: Narrow the context to the particular angle of your review article.
   - *Example*: "Among the various applications of AI in education, its impact on assessment has sparked considerable debate, raising questions about fairness, reliability, and ethical considerations."
3. **Identify the Gap or Problem**: Highlight why this review is essential. This can involve pointing out existing challenges or limitations in current research or practice.
   - *Example*: "Despite its growing adoption, the use of AI in educational assessment lacks comprehensive analysis, with many educators uncertain about its long-term implications for learning quality and academic integrity."
4. **State the Aim or Thesis**: Conclude the introduction by indicating what your review article aims to accomplish.
   - *Example*: *This review aims to explore the various ways generative AI impacts educational assessment, examining both the potential benefits and the risks it poses to traditional assessment methods."

FIGURE 9.8   ChatGPT output: 1st student-ChatGPT interaction (OpenAI, 2023c).

introductions and objectives, and most importantly, keeping in mind what they learned and the feedback from ChatGPT.

Upon reflecting on the use of the *Prompt Creation Reference Chart*, we realized that while most of the elements—*author*, *purpose*, design and theme—in the *request* remained consistent, the element of the target audience could vary depending on the user's specific context. In our discussions, we found that substituting "target audience" with "journal criteria or requirements" was more beneficial, particularly when guiding students in the context of writing review articles. This adjustment allowed the prompts to be more tailored to the context, thus yielding more focused and relevant outputs.

During the reflection process, students analyzed how these variations impacted their interaction with ChatGPT, which provided more consistent and practical guidance. This reflective practice not only reinforced their understanding of prompt creation but also allowed them to adapt their approach based on the specific needs of their writing tasks. A final whole group discussion ends this module with a reflection on the changes they plan to make based on peer suggestions and ChatGPT feedback.

Our chapter explores effective strategies for integrating this GenAI technology into both writing instruction and course design. By leveraging ChatGPT for tasks such as outlining, editing, and paraphrasing, we enhance the scaffolding support available to students throughout the writing. Furthermore, ChatGPT proves invaluable in aiding educators and instructional designers in developing curricula and creating mentor texts that familiarize MLs with specific genre expectations. Therefore, we advocate for the adoption of GenAI technologies in both the planning and execution phases of educational settings.

Conclusion

Our experiences integrating ChatGPT into writing instruction reveal that ethically employing GenAI tools for planning, editing, or revising texts, or for overcoming challenges like writer's block, significantly enhances collaboration and creativity. This pedagogical approach promotes active engagement in discussions, where asking pertinent questions and seeking meaningful answers serve as the primary means of developing critical thinking skills among students and educators.

There are various challenges to acknowledge GenAI technologies in educational settings and then integrate them as teaching and learning resources. The possibilities of achieving this integration adequately for educational-specific purposes are influenced by our knowledge of these tools and our conception of language. Also, it is essential to understand that academic language poses challenges for both MLs and English language native speakers. Furthermore, familiarizing teachers and students with the strengths as well as the ethical implications of these large language models is crucial for learning how to converse with these chatbots and ultimately be capable of creating prompts that serve as scaffolding for writing.

This book chapter shares pedagogical approaches to incorporating ChatGPT into the teaching of writing in order to raise awareness of how to critically ask questions. We develop an academic course in which ChatGPT is incorporated into writing as a scaffolding strategy. Therefore, we adopt this GenAI technology as a pedagogical resource in essential planning stages as well as performing phases. For this, we need to devote time to the planning and writing of prompts considering aspects such as (1) the prompt's author: background information, (2) the main characteristics of the request: design, target audience, and theme, (3) and the purpose of the prompt: what the prompt is for, what the user wants to achieve. These are the three essential elements that form the Prompt Creation Reference Chart, our principle to promote the crafting of well-structured and effective initial prompts.

Recognizing the need for scaffolding strategies while performing writing, we show MLs how to use ChatGPT in order to lower the cognitive and emotional challenges we all face. Through the seminars, we model the thinking aloud of the human-AI interaction by reviewing the essential elements of a prompt as described in the Prompt Creation Reference Chart. We activate prior knowledge about review articles, the focus of this course. We encourage learners to work collaboratively and along with the chatbot to draft prompts for elaborating topic sentences. This scaffolding strategy increases confidence to develop their individual writing piece at a later stage. During the drafting phases, ChatGPT serves as a scaffolding element to ask questions or clarify doubts, seek examples or guidance on phrasing, and review sentences for clarity or coherence. In the third stage, we incorporate ChatGPT so that students can refine the writing of their review article objectives. After the groups conclude the first draft of the review article's introductory section, it is time to revise. Editing, paraphrasing, and making new language choices are strategies scaffolded by more interaction with ChatGPT. The final stages consist of learners creating prompts to help them make real-time revisions based on the AI feedback about their texts and, especially, on the critical analysis of this feedback by the group discussions.

We understand the relevance of creating a prompt that is detailed enough to initiate a human-AI interaction and generate a reasonable response. However, in most cases, this initial prompt will either have to be rewritten or completed to be able to generate a more effective and contextualized output. This is why we recommend the adoption of the Prompt Creation Reference Chart providing guidelines to facilitate this first interaction. It is crucial to bear in mind that making the most of what AI-text generators can perform requires deep, analytical, and critical thinking from humans in order to complete the final required task.

Incorporating ChatGPT to provide scaffolding in writing helps reduce the language barriers that often block writers from expressing what they truly wish to convey. The inclusion of GenAI in educational practices bridges gaps in writing development and fosters collaboration, creativity, and critical thinking among MLs. Therefore, it ultimately prepares them to navigate and contribute meaningfully in an increasingly interconnected AI-driven world.

References

Bazerman, C. (2016). What do sociocultural studies of writing tell us about learning to write? In C. A. MacArthur, S. Graham, J. Fitzgerald (Eds.), *Handbook of writing research* (pp. 17–31). The Guilford Press.

Boa Sorte, P., de Freitas Farias, M. A., dos Santos, A. E. do Carmo Andrade Santos, J., & dos Santos Rodrigues Dias, J. S. (2021). Artificial intelligence in academic writing: What is in store with the GPT-3 algorithm? *Revista EntreLinguas, 7,* 1–22. https://doi.org/10.29051/el.v7i00.15352

Burwell, C. (2013). The pedagogical potential of video remix: Critical conversations about culture, creativity and copyright. *Journal of Adolescent & Adult Literacy, 57*(3), 205–213.

Casanave, C. P. (2019). Performing expertise in doctoral dissertations: Thoughts on a fundamental dilemma facing doctoral students and their supervisors. *Journal of Second Language Writing, 43,* 57–62.

Cazden, C., Cope, B., Fairclough, N., Gee, J., Cook, J. (1996). A pedagogy of multiliteracies: Design social futures. *Harvard Educational Review, 66*(1), 60–93. https://doi-org.proxy.library.vcu.edu/10.17763/haer.66.1.17370n67v22j160u

Cope, B., & Kalantzis, M. (2000). *Multiliteracies: Literacy learning and the design of social futures.* Routledge.

de Oliveira, L. C. (2023). *Supporting multilingual learners' academic language development: A language-based approach to content instruction.* Routledge.

de Souza, M. A. A. (2018). Formação de professores de inglês: Buscando caminhos para uma educação linguística crítica [English teacher training: Seeking paths for a critical linguistic education]. In R. R. Pessoa,V. P. V. Silvestre, & W. M. Mór (Eds.). *Perspectivas críticas de educação linguística no Brasil: Trajetórias e práticas de professoras/es universitárias/os de inglês [Critical perspectives on linguistic education in Brazil]* (pp 163–186). Pá de Palavra.

dos Santos, A. E., Olesova, L., Vicentini, C., & de Oliveira, L. C. (2023a). ChatGPT in ELT: Writing affordances and activities. *TESOL Connections.* May 2023. http://newsmanager.commpartners.com/tesolc/issues/2023-05-01/2.html

dos Santos, A. E., Silva, L. G. V., & de Siqueira, N. R. (2023b). ChatGPT e Implicações na Educação: o cenário da escrita acadêmica. [ChatGPT and implications in education: The context of academic writing]. In C. Porto, A. Chagas, & K. E. Oliveira (Eds.). *Educiber: Educação e divulgação científica em plataformas digitais [Education and scientific dissemination on digital platforms].* (pp. 204–222). Edunit. https://editoratiradentes.com.br/wp-content/uploads/2023/08/Educiber-5-Final.pdf

Freire, P. (1970). *Pedagogia do oprimido. [Pedagogy of the oppressed].* Paz e Terra.

Freire, P. (1985). *Educação como prática da liberdade. [Education as the practice of freedom].* Paz e Terra.

Freire, P., & Faundez, A. (1992). *Por uma pedagogia da pergunta. [Toward a pedagogy of the question].* Paz e Terra.

Kalantzis, M., Cope, B., & Pinheiro, P. (2020). *Letramentos. [Literacies].* Editora da Unicamp.

OpenAI. (2022). *Introducing ChatGPT.* Retrieved October 25, 2023, from: https://openai.com/blog/chatgpt

OpenAI. (2023a). *ChatGPT can now see, hear, and speak.* Retrieved September 28, 2023, from: https://openai.com/blog/chatgpt-can-now-see-hear-and-speak

OpenAI. (2023b). *GPT-4.* Retrieved October 13, 2023, from: https://openai.com/research/gpt-4

OpenAI. (2023c). *ChatGPT (GPT-4 model, Sep 25 version)* [Large language model]. Retrieved October 10, 2023, from: https://chat.openai.com/chat

Rosenblatt, K. (2023, January 5). ChatGPT banned from New York City public schools' devices and networks. *NBC News.* https://www.nbcnews.com/tech/tech-news/new-york-city-public-schools-ban-chatgpt-devices-networks-rcna64446

Russell, S. J., & Norvig, P. (2021). *Artificial intelligence: A modern approach.* Prentice Hall.

Russell-Pinson, L., & Harris, M. L. (2019). Anguish and anxiety, stress and strain: Attending to writers' stress in the dissertation process. *Journal of Second Language Writing, 43*(1), 63–71. https://www-sciencedirect-com.proxy.library.vcu.edu/science/article/pii/S1060374317302977

Schleppegrell, M. J. (2004). *The language of schooling: A functional linguistics perspective.* Erlbaum.

AFTERWORD I

Second Language Writing in an AI and Multilingual World

Robert Godwin-Jones

Writing in all genres and in all languages is undergoing a significant transformation through the arrival of generative AI. AI systems like ChatGPT are able to generate texts that appear in their coherence, fluidity, and grammatical accuracy to have been created by competent human writers. That development has occurred in parallel with a growing recognition of the reality of multilingualism today across the globe, along with the realization in SLA (second language acquisition) theory that individual plurilingualism needs to be integrated into instruction (Byrnes, 2020). Both developments have been underway for some time. AI-powered writing assistance has been enabled through advances in machine learning, resulting in digital writing tools able to provide auto-completion and real-time spelling, grammar, and style suggestions and corrections (Godwin-Jones, 2022). Now AI systems can generate output on virtually any given subject in multiple languages and at any given length and proficiency level, while also enabling L2 (second language) learners to check the accuracy and stylistics of their own writing. At the same time, in applied linguistics there has been a growing recognition that monolingualism is the exception rather than the rule in human society (Ortega, 2017) and that we need to recognize in SLA the plurilingual nature of language learning (and of most individuals' real lives). That has led to the practice of pedagogical translanguaging (Wei, 2018) in which a learner's first language is not banned from instruction but rather is used as a mediating and scaffolding tool (Cenoz & Gorter, 2017). Translanguaging and generative AI have enabled and invited – although in quite different ways – new and alternative writing practices. These changes are explored from various perspectives in this volume, with the authors offering both theoretical explorations and practical pedagogical suggestions.

Writing educators have reacted to these developments in a variety of ways. As has been the case with the arrival of machine translation, simply banning the use of AI is not feasible and at any rate would not help prepare students for a work world in which AI features prominently, especially in any profession involving writing. Instead, instructors should rethink goals and assignments related to L2 writing. An initial step is the recognition of how learners are likely to use AI. While teachers may anticipate that students will simply copy and paste AI-generated output to turn in as their own work, evidence from studies demonstrates a different pattern of use. As in studies of the student use of machine translation (Hellmich & Vinall,

DOI: 10.4324/9781003426936-13

2023), studies of AI have shown more selective and sophisticated uses, which often involve learners querying for specific words or phrases, as well as editing substantially AI-generated text to fit their own voice and style (Jacob et al., 2023). Writers will tend to go back and forth among different writing tools, content sources, and their own drafts (Vogel et al., 2018). That process, in its complexity and distributed agency, points to how the concepts of authorship, authenticity, and creativity need to be re-thought in the age of AI (O'Gieblyn, 2021). In that process, the West may broaden its scope of authorship by considering perspectives from China (Pennycook, 1996) and the global South (McKinley, 2022) that have long had different concepts of imitation, the use of model texts, and the importance of tying academic writing to long-standing cultural traditions and values (Canagarajah, 2021).

The availability of AI to assist writers in the mechanics of writing has consequences for both assessment and the kinds of writing tasks to assign. As discussed in this volume, the focus should no longer be on surface-level features (grammar, spelling) or on other aspects of form and structure for which AI can provide assistance (genre markers and conventions, for example). In an age of machine translation and proficient AI text generation, linguistic/grammatical accuracy "can no longer be viewed as a synonym of learning and excellence" (Klekovkina & Denié-Higney, 2022, p. 107). Assignments should target opportunities for personal engagement (autobiographical incidents, family connections) and human creativity (unconventional storylines, breaking genre conventions; see Kalan, 2022). It may be premature to proclaim the death of the conventional five-paragraph essay, particularly not until standardized testing and university entry procedures are changed to reflect the new AI reality. But it is time to expand beyond the essay (Vicentini et al., 2022). As emphasized in this volume, it behooves educators – in assigning and assessing tasks – to highlight writing's essential socio-ecological character, as well as the variety of forms/genres it can take. That translates into placing emphasis on the recipients of the written texts, looking at purpose, strategy, and audience. AI is proficient in genre signaling, generating texts that simulate genre conventions and associated rhetorical moves, but its lack of audience awareness leads to output that is bland, generic, and socially inauthentic (Omizo & Hart-Davidson, 2024). In addition to having students generate a variety of genres (and expand characteristics beyond their traditional confines), assignments might also involve writing to engage in real-world activities, such as participation in online communities (Reddit, fanfiction sites, social media) in which writers consider language register and site-specific cultures-of-use (Thorne & Reinhardt, 2008). That kind of engagement can provide feedback on writing as well as an apprenticeship into real-world authorship. In that way, students can see that writing is not just an academic exercise but also an essential life skill. Engagement with others on an affinity site or social media has the added benefit of alerting students to real-world issues and social concerns (Ortega, 2017).

In instructional settings, it will be important to provide students opportunities to reflect on their experiences with AI, through group discussions and writing journals (Tarabochia, 2017). An important theme in that reflective process will likely be the role that AI can play in various kinds of writing and as used in different stages of text development (idea generation, drafting, editing). In addition, students should discuss editing choices related to AI, for example, why they accepted or rejected the provided output. In that way, students gain better insights into both the benefits and limitations of AI. That is an important step on the way to developing critical AI literacy (Darvin, 2023). That kind of critical consciousness will also involve gaining an appreciation of how AI has developed its language abilities and what that means for its effectiveness in particular domains (Godwin-Jones, 2024). Humans develop language in social settings, first in the family, then expanding to school, friends, and later social and work worlds. In the process we are socialized into using all of our semiotic resources (verbal languages, nonverbal behaviors, paralanguage) to communicate meaning, negotiating common ground with our interlocutors through the theory of mind, i.e., reading cues and clues of the other's emotional state and way of thinking. Large language models in AI systems have not had the advantage of sensorimotor experiences or the dynamic give and take of human conversations (Kosinski, 2023). Through its training data, AI systems do have sufficient information on forms and formulas to use in interactions with humans (i.e., pragmalinguistic information, such as how to frame requests). However, as studies have shown, they lack the ability to use language to mediate and negotiate meaning in nuanced social and cultural contexts (Chen et al., 2024). That deficiency (along with AI's Western-oriented and Anglocentric training) limits AI's abilities as a reliable and authentic written or spoken conversation partner for L2 learners, especially for low-resource languages (Godwin-Jones, 2025).

Given the artificiality of AI output, the development of interactional, pragmatic, and strategic competencies in an L2 is best developed in authentic and meaningful human-to-human communication, rather than in chats with synthetic interlocuters. There are rich opportunities for that experience in online environments, particularly by participating in virtual exchange (O'Dowd, 2021). Online exchanges can also provide an experience not likely to be found in the classroom, namely of language use that is frequently multilingual (Oliver & Nguyen, 2017). That has been shown to be the case for *Facebook* (Lee, 2016), as well as for other social media (Barrot, 2022). Integrating plurilingualism into the classroom through pedagogical translanguaging can have a variety of benefits for learners. Those include building self-confidence through validation of the learners' everyday language practices, as well as the opportunity to mix languages playfully (Belz, 2002). By accepting learners' plurilingual communicative abilities, they no longer are viewed as deficient L2 users, but as emergent multilingual writers and "skilled communicators" (Cenoz & Gorter, 2017, p. 75). Studies have shown that translanguaging can benefit both content learning and language skills (Byrnes, 2020). It may be easier for learners to engage in plurilingualism online than in the classroom, where the dominance of the Communication Method has discouraged the use of the L1 (Cook, 2001). Engaging in code-switching and in language play/humor are not areas in which AI has much to contribute (Li et al., 2023). Plurilingual practices are highly individualized, dependent on contextual factors such as social relationships/hierarchy, communication medium/device, and emotional/psychological state (Kramsch, 1998). That kind of complexity in shaping and understanding human discourse is well beyond the current abilities of AI.

Future developments in AI will likely lead to improved performance in a number of areas. Multimedia input and output will likely enhance AI's ability to understand human nonverbal communication patterns (Xu et al., 2023). That may result in a better AI capacity to infer meanings and to respond more appropriately in pragmatic contexts. It is likely as well that AI systems will offer greater personalization than is currently available, building a user profile that includes information about individual interests/hobbies and language abilities. That will also mean that we see generative AI functioning more as an enhanced voice assistant or personal agent, interacting intimately with the user, as well as serving as a buffer and interface with third-party tools and services. A more complete profile of a user will enable AI systems to provide more appropriate and contextual assistance with writing and other activities.

That will further complicate questions of authorship and authenticity, as AI becomes a real collaborator with human authors (Godwin-Jones, 2024). That will make the development of critical AI literacy all the more vital in instructional settings.

References

Barrot, J. S. (2022). Social media as a language learning environment: A systematic review of the literature (2008–2019). *Computer Assisted Language Learning, 35*(9), 2534–2562. https://doi.org/10.1080/09588221.2021.1883673

Belz, J. A. (2002). Second language play as a representation of the multicompetent self in foreign language study. *Journal of Language, Identity, and Education, 1*(1), 13–39. https://doi.org/10.1207/s15327701jlie0101_3

Byrnes, H. (2020). Navigating pedagogical translanguaging: Commentary on the special issue. *System, 92*, 1–12. https://doi.org/10.1016/j.system.2020.102278

Canagarajah, S. (2021). Rethinking mobility and language: From the Global South. *The Modern Language Journal, 105*(2), 570–582. https://doi.org/10.1111/modl.12726

Cenoz, J., & Gorter, D. (2017). Minority languages and sustainable translanguaging: Threat or opportunity? *Journal of Multilingual and Multicultural Development, 38*, 901–912. https://doi.org/10.1080/01434632.2017.1284855

Chen, X., Li, J., & Ye, Y. (2024). A feasibility study for the application of AI-generated conversations in pragmatic analysis. *Journal of Pragmatics, 223*, 14–30. https://doi.org/10.2139/ssrn.4545327

Cook, V. (2001). Using the first language in the classroom. *Canadian Modern Language Review, 57*, 402–423. https://doi.org/10.3138/cmlr.57.3.402

Darvin, R. (2023). Moving across a genre continuum: Pedagogical strategies for integrating online genres in the language classroom. *English for Specific Purposes, 70*, 101–115. https://doi.org/10.1016/j.esp.2022.11.004

Godwin-Jones, R. (2022). Partnering with AI: Intelligent writing assistance and instructed language learning. *Language Learning & Technology, 26*(2), 5–24. https://doi.org/10125/73474

Godwin-Jones, R. (2024). Distributed agency in language learning and teaching through generative AI. *Language Learning & Technology, 28*(2), 5–31. https://doi.org/10125/73570

Godwin-Jones, R. (2025). Technology integration for less commonly taught languages: AI and pedagogical translanguaging. *Language Learning & Technology, 29*(1), 11–34. https://hdl.handle.net/10125/73609

Hellmich, E. A., & Vinall, K. (2023). Student use and instructor beliefs: Machine translation in language education. *Language Learning & Technology, 27*(1), 1–27. https://hdl.handle.net/10125/73525

Jacob, S., Tate, T., & Warschauer, M. (2023). Emergent AI-assisted discourse: Case study of a second language writer authoring with ChatGPT. arXiv. https://doi.org/10.48550/arXiv.2310.10903

Kalan, A. (2022). Negotiating writing identities across languages: Translanguaging as enrichment of semiotic trajectories. *TESL Canada Journal, 38*(2), 63–87. https://doi.org/10.18806/tesl.v38i2.1357

Klekovkina, V., & Denié-Higney, L. (2022). Machine translation: Friend or foe in the language classroom?. *L2 Journal, 14*(1), 105–135. https://doi.org/10.5070/l214151723

Kosinski, M. (2023). Theory of mind might have spontaneously emerged in large language models. arXiv. https://arxiv.org/abs/2302.02083

Kramsch, C. (1998). *Language and culture.* Oxford University Press.

Li, B., Bonk, C. J., & Kou, X. (2023). Exploring the multilingual applications of ChatGPT: Uncovering language learning affordances in YouTuber videos. *International Journal of Computer-Assisted Language Learning and Teaching (IJCALLT), 13*(1), 1–22. https://doi.org/10.4018/ijcallt.326135

McKinley, J. (2022). An argument for globalized L2 writing methodological innovation. *Journal of Second Language Writing, 58*, 100945. https://doi.org/10.1016/j.jslw.2022.100945

O'Dowd, R. (2021). Virtual exchange: Moving forward into the next decade. *Computer Assisted Language Learning, 34*(3), 209–224. https://doi.org/10.1080/09588221.2021.1902201

O'Gieblyn, M. (2021). *God, human, animal, machine: Technology, metaphor, and the search for meaning.* Doubleday.

Oliver, R., & Nguyen, B. (2017). Translanguaging on Facebook: Exploring Australian aboriginal multilingual competence in technology-enhanced environments and its pedagogical implications. *Canadian Modern Language Review, 73*(4), 463–487. https://doi.org/10.3138/cmlr.3890

Omizo, R., & Hart-Davidson, B. (2024). Is genre enough? A theory of genre signaling as generative AI rhetoric. *Rhetoric Society Quarterly, 54*(3), 272–285. https://doi.org/10.1080/02773945.2024.2343615

Ortega, L. (2017). New CALL-SLA research interfaces for the 21st century: Towards equitable multilingualism. *CALICO Journal, 34*(3), 283–316. https://doi.org/10.1558/cj.33855

Pennycook, A. (1996). Borrowing others' words: Text, ownership, memory, and plagiarism. *TESOL Quarterly, 30*(2), 201–230. https://doi.org/10.2307/3588141

Tarabochia, S. L. (2017). *Reframing the relational: A pedagogical ethic for cross-curricular literacy work.* CCCC/NCTE. https://publicationsncte.org/content/books/9780814100653

Thorne, S. L., & Reinhardt, J. (2008). "Bridging activities," new media literacies, and advanced foreign language proficiency. *CALICO Journal, 25*(3), 558–572. https://www.jstor.org/stable/calicojournal.25.3.558

Vicentini, C., de Oliveira, L. C., & Gui, J. (2022). Integrating technology into genre-based writing instruction for multilingual learners. *GATESOL Journal, 32*(2), 27–42. https://doi.org/10.52242/gatesol.167

Vogel, S., Ascenzi-Moreno, L., & García, O. (2018). An expanded view of translanguaging: Leveraging the dynamic interactions between a young multilingual writer and machine translation software. In J. Choi, S. Ollerhead (Eds.), *Plurilingualism in teaching and learning* (pp. 89–106). Routledge. https://doi.org/10.4324/9781315392462-6

Wei, L. (2018). Translanguaging as a practical theory of language. *Applied Linguistics, 39*(1), 9–30. https://doi.org/10.1093/applin/amx039

Xu, Q., Peng, Y., Wu, M., Xiao, F., Chodorow, M., & Li, P. (2023). Does conceptual representation require embodiment? Insights from large language models. arXiv. https://arxiv.org/abs/2305.19103

AFTERWORD II

Reflecting on the Role of AI in the Evolution of Writing Support Tools

Curtis J. Bonk

In my youth, personal computers did not exist, and I had to write my thoughts out by hand or use a typewriter. Unfortunately, I had extremely poor handwriting that even I had trouble interpreting, and I received my only C+ in high school in typing; my lowest grade. As a result, none of my teachers pegged me as a writer. This perception continued to limit me in my later work settings, as bad handwriting was often equated with incoherent writing. What was clear to me was that many people of influence thought that I could not write.

What they did not perceive was that writing was in my veins. I was always a writer. In fact, I would be trained to be an accountant and later become a CPA. Little did I realize that ancient Sumerian accountants were thought to be the first writers as they recorded accounting transactions more than 5,000 years ago. With an accounting degree, I received four full years of training in organized writing.

Unfortunately, I was a total wipeout in my first job as an accountant at Vrakas, Blum and Company in Waukesha, Wisconsin in the early 1980s, as my supervisors thought that I could not write. Nevertheless, I did learn some important lessons. Among them, I noticed that there were people employed at the firm who interestingly were titled "Word Processors." Such a person, and we had two of them, would type up our auditing and tax reports and other documents, as needed, into a machine using a software application. At the time, the popular applications for word processing were WordPerfect and WordStar, and by 1983, Microsoft Word was invented. What is striking, in retrospect, was that we had designated positions for these "word processors" and they were assigned premium office space near the tax accountants, auditors, supervisors, and company partners. Despite their secretarial pay, they had status; everything seemed to flow through them.

A few years later, after a brief stint at a company that designed and fabricated the densest printed circuit boards in the world, I would find myself in graduate school at the University of Wisconsin in Madison studying educational psychology and educational technology. It was the mid to late 1980s and I was soon using these early word processing tools myself; in particular, WordPerfect. At the time, writing across the curriculum was a hot topic. Also prominent was the process model of writing by Linda Flower and Richard (Dick) Hayes (1981). Writing was becoming promoted as a tool for supporting and elevating one's thinking, which was

DOI: 10.4324/9781003426936-14

increasingly obvious as one made revisions in WordPerfect; especially, if one tracked or high-lighted changes. With such technology, I no longer needed to rely on a typewriter and cor-rection tape. More importantly, I no longer worried about my sloppy handwriting (other than being able to decipher the points on my notecards or handwritten annotations and insertions on the research papers that I studiously read and accumulated).

At that time, writing was starting to be augmented by various technology tools in addition to word processors. An article in 1981 in the *Journal of Educational Technology Systems*, "On the road to computer assisted composition," by Earl Woodruff, Carl Bereiter, and Marlene Scardamalia from the University of Toronto (Woodruff et al., 1981) discussed how computer prompts might help an individual reflect on one's writing plans and approaches at a higher, more metacognitive, level (Bonk & Reynolds, 1992). Technology tools for creating outlines and concept maps of one's paper were posited to help writers to better organize, structure, and visualize one's thoughts when writing (Scardamalia & Bereiter, 1982) and help with reprocessing (Bonk, Reynolds, & Medury, 1996) and revisioning one's writing (Scardamalia, & Bereiter, 1986). Technology tools might prompt the writer at random moments or require self-prompting since the tools embedded in the writing systems were not that intelligent. AI in education was only speculative at that point.

In Israel, Gavriel Salomon (1988) focused on developing computer-based reading and writing tools that could reduce working memory constraints of the learner by functioning as a type of collaborative partner when one was reading or writing. Such goals could be accom-plished by explicitly displaying complex cognitive operations inherent in the reading or writ-ing process. When I wrote to Salomon at the time, he informed me that his "Writing Partner" tool was built on a low budget and was basically held together with band-aids. What he did with his limited funding was create computerized prompts that could be invoked during the writing process to facilitate metacognitive awareness of diverse writing strategies.

Salomon claimed that computer prompting programs acted as intellectual partners that could pose questions within writers' zones of proximal development. In Salomon's studies, prompts or procedural facilitators acted as temporary supports for student thoughts, thereby encouraging the internalization of these strategies; a rationale essentially drawn from neo-Vygotskian theories of learning and development (Vygotsky, 1978, 1986). In updating Vygotsky's ideas from the 1920s and 1930s for the digital age, Salomon argued that interac-tions with a supportive partner could include computer prompts and other instructional scaf-folds that could enhance the interpersonal processing of the learner. The intelligence was embedded and displayed in the computer prompts for learners to use and hopefully internal-ize. Again, at that time, there was no AI in the available educational tools or platforms to help, though many educators expressed interest in what AI might eventually provide for the learners.

As many millions of personal computers arrived on the scene during the 1980s and 1990s, the technologies for writing support began to arrive in a trickle that soon exploded into a flood. One of my professors at UW-Madison, Richard Lehrer, was using an early text-to-speech software package to research the impact of hearing one's writing spoken auditorily on early elementary student revisionary processes and writing strategies (Lehrer, Levin, DeHart, & Comeaux, 1987; Lehrer, & Randle, 1987). That got me intrigued into exploring not just writing as a tool for thinking but also tools for writing that might inspire critical and creative thinking long before the present age of pervasive AI in education.

Soon my colleague, Tom Reynolds, and I were experimenting with ways to embed critical and creative thinking prompts into WordPerfect 4.2 (released in 1986) and later WordPerfect

5.1 (released in 1989) through a set of keyboard macro commands. We were looking to foster generative thinking (i.e., fluency, flexibility, originality, and elaboration) as well as evaluative thinking (i.e., logical flow and cohesion, relevancy, assumptions and bias, and conclusions) (Reynolds & Bonk 1996a, 1996b). We also designed a second macro application to record all student keystrokes as a means to better understand student writing development and revisionary practices. With the emergence of such tools, there were myriad experimentations with technology-enhanced pedagogical strategies for teaching writing.

As Tom Reynolds and I conducted our research using WordPerfect, we discovered many other software tools that could benefit writers and facilitate the writing process. In less than a few years, Planet Earth was awash with a multitude of writing tools for brainstorming, knowledge representation and concept mapping, collaborative document creation and editing (also known as groupware), synchronous conferencing (Bonk, 2020), commenting on and annotating documents, hyperlinking documents, knowledge construction, idea outlining, and grammar and spell checking (Bonk, Medury, & Reynolds, 1994); as David Wiley and I retrospectively wrote a few years ago, educational technology tools and resources were coming in endless waves (Bonk & Wiley, 2020). One might argue that it was the golden age of technology-assisted and enhanced writing. It was as if, if you dreamed of it or thought about it long enough, the writing tool or aid you wanted would eventually appear. These now feel like enchanted times akin to the magical moments we are now witnessing in the early stages of generative AI in education.

The goal of the computer prompting and keyboard mapping system that Tom Reynolds and I developed was to utilize technology to support and hopefully elevate one's thinking processes. We were using technology to not only augment the writing process and amplify human intelligence but to see thoughts evolve over time. These were human thoughts, not ones generated with an AI engine. At the time, technology tools were not taking over writing one's papers and then creating summaries of them or questions about them. Perhaps, as a result, there was no one calling into question the authorship of documents that were written with the support of word processing software and thought visualization technology. Prompts intended to foster critical or creative thinking, like those we designed for WordPerfect, were accepted as useful innovations and often celebrated. If lingering thoughts existed in the writer's mind, it was important to find ways to get them out; in effect, computer prompts were deemed valued writing support mechanisms.

Such prompts and other aids were support tools to improve human writing and were hopefully internalized to make users better writers, thinkers, and learners for the years to come and were not tools to deskill us or take over total writing responsibilities. However, with the advent of generative AI, as discussed in this wonderful book by Tian and Wang and countless educational journal articles, magazines, and technical reports on generative AI, the embracement of technology-enhanced writing and thinking has caused some to pause and ask about the purpose of generative AI support and who benefits from it. It is like we have come back to the basic questions the Founding Fathers of Artificial Intelligence, John McCarthy, Marvin Minsky, Allen Newell, and Alan Turing, must have been asking back in the 1950s (Markoff, 2015). Is AI in education going to be a tool to replace human beings (i.e., the instructor) in their job roles and responsibilities, or will it supplement and support the user (i.e., the learner)?

Alternatively, AI might become integrated into society and individual tasks as an augmentative device to enable us to more effectively and productively accomplish different tasks as Douglas Engelbart (Engelbart, 1962) envisioned long ago. Will it augment human intelligence and competencies to enable us to solve extremely complex problems, comprehend difficult texts, synthesize a range of facts and data, compare and contrast what previously seemed like highly disparate information sources, and so on? For the purposes of this book, "Rethinking Language Education in the Age of Generative AI" edited by Zhongfeng Tian and Chaoran Wang, we must ask, will AI tools and resources serve as augmentative devices for more effective writing? At the time of this writing, the jury is still out and likely will be out for decades to come.

According to my friend Ray Schroeder (2023) at the University of Illinois Springfield, faculty members are not immune from these changes; generative AI tools and platforms can now "conduct research, write reports, create curricula and courses, teach and tutor students, and provide detailed reports on student progress with active, adaptive paths to ensure all students meet essential outcomes." Not only can AI do many common faculty tasks, but the jobs that faculty might be applying for are increasingly requiring that they have sufficient AI literacy and competencies (Swaak, 2024).

Without a doubt, knowledge of AI will provide new opportunities and perhaps even a sense of job security, however brief. As Phil Hill stated in Inside Higher Education, "It's a gold rush…But it's a gold rush where you don't know where the gold mine is or how to get the gold" (D'Agostino, 2023). Hill's AI gold rush is now in full display, and countless institutions and organizations are rushing to find the best AI talent in the land. Given the history of writing tools described above, many of the resources of this gold rush are likely to be allocated to hiring those who can help design innovative generative AI tools and features for writing and language learning.

Unfortunately, the seemingly rapid emergence of generative AI tools has at least momentarily blinded many people from the quest to create, find, and experiment with technology tools for intelligence enhancement, augmentation, and amplification to a more cautionary stance and see generative AI as something to definitely be wary and suspicious of. We likely all have heard a colleague or acquaintance implying that there are cheaters, tricksters, and scammers out there who will happily let AI pull the majority of the weight for an educational task and then turn in unethically produced work as if they had done it themselves. Instead of embracing the possibilities, such naysayers find AI cheaters under every manuscript submitted, student email received, and class project deposited. It is akin to a five-alarm fire drill repeated daily at every institution of higher learning (Huang, 2023; Terry, 2023) and K-12 school (Cutler, 2023). The frustration among some instructors is so high that they now ask if ChatGPT is simply a plagiarism machine (Keegin, 2023) and whether professors are simply grading robots (McMurtrie, 2024).

Student plagiarism and cheating issues are not new. Advice, strategies, and guidelines related to plagiarism and cheating have existed for decades and were in place well before the pocket calculators of the 1970s (Whitfield, 2014). There are dozens of strategies to attempt to prevent it or at least reduce it (e.g., plagiarism detection tools, setting clear guidelines and policies, requiring drafts of work, looking for patterns in the writing, etc.) (Cotton, Cotton, & Shipway, 2023). These guidelines and examples might find renewed use in this AI in education age and help temper concerns about generative AI to a low enough level that one can begin to focus on when and where generative AI makes a difference in the writing process and in the development of a student as an effective writer.

Recently, one of my research teams found the opposite of all the ethical concerns; students seemed cautious and hesitant to utilize generative AI like ChatGPT even when instructors encouraged them to do so (Li, Wang, & Bonk, 2025). While the ethical concerns were varied in that study, students were candid about their concerns and fears related to the ethical use of AI for learning. Many expressed concerns about fairness and equal access to learning or had concerns about the misuse of generative AI tools like ChatGPT for plagiarism.

In another study that this research team conducted at about the same time with 384 post-secondary writers, we found that over 90 percent of them were positive about the impact of ChatGPT on their writing (Wang, Li, & Bonk, 2024). In particular, they appreciated the specific nature and immediacy of the feedback generative AI offered, as well as the ability to stimulate ideas in one's head when suffering from writer's block and helping them outline their thoughts once their ideas started flowing. Overall, Wang et al. (2024) found ChatGPT to be a helpful tool for their writing development. Not too surprisingly, it was useful both for higher-order thinking activities like brainstorming and seeking inspiration for ideas as well as lower-level tasks such as grammar checking, improving sentence structure, and refining one's wording. These tools helped these learners focus and spend more time writing and revising that writing. On average, they relied on generative AI on a weekly or monthly basis for their writing episodes, not daily. In addition, due to the fact that a non-human entity was perceived to be less stressful to them and resulting in lower social pressure and anxiety, ChatGPT allowed them to be more self-directed in their writing pursuits.

Much more research is needed. As Beth McMurtrie (2023) points out, there is much conversation, concern, and experimentation related to generative AI writing tools and resources. Let's have those conversations. Let's share our concerns. Let's continue to experiment and hopefully discover generative AI writing aids that can effectively augment the writing process for young as well as more experienced learners. Instead of concerns about "writing plagiarizers," it is time to create effective "writing partners" that Salomon and many other scholars were attempting to build with paperclips and band-aids three to four decades ago. May such AI-based writing tools enable each of us to dream up and compose novel thoughts and ideas that are our own and then utilize still other technology tools to globally share those thoughts and effectively integrate them with the work of others.

References

Bonk, C. J. (2020). Pandemic ponderings, 30 years to today: Synchronous signals, saviors, or survivors? *Distance Education, 41*(4), 589–599. https://doi.org/10.1080/01587919.2020.1821610

Bonk, C. J., Medury, P. V., & Reynolds, T. H. (1994). Cooperative hypermedia: The marriage of collaborative writing and mediated environments. *Computers in the Schools, 10*(1/2), 79–124.

Bonk, C. J., & Reynolds, T. H. (1992). Early adolescent composing within a generative-evaluative computerized prompting framework. *Computers in Human Behavior, 8*(1), 39–62.

Bonk, C. J., Reynolds, T. H., & Medury, P. V. (1996). Technology enhanced workplace writing: A social and cognitive transformation. In A. H. Duin & C. J. Hansen (Eds.), *Nonacademic writing: Social theory and technology* (pp. 281–303). Erlbaum.

Bonk, C. J., & Wiley, D. (2020). Preface: Reflections on the waves of emerging learning technology. *Educational Technology Research and Development* (ETR&D), *68*(4), 1595–1612. https://doi.org/10.1007/s11423-020-09809-x

Cotton, D. R., Cotton, P. A., & Shipway, J. R. (2023). Chatting and cheating: Ensuring academic integrity in the era of ChatGPT. *Innovations in Education and Teaching International*, 1–12.

Cutler, D. (2023, January 26). Grappling with AI writing technologies in the classroom. *Edutopia*. https://www.edutopia.org/article/chatgpt-ai-writing-platforms-classroom

D'Agonstino, S. (2023, May 19). Colleges race to hire and build amid AI 'Gold Rush'. *Inside Higher Ed*. https://www.insidehighered.com/news/tech-innovation/artificial-intelligence/2023/05/19/colleges-race-hire-and-build-amid-ai-gold

Englebart, D. (1962). *Augmenting human intellect: A conceptual framework.* Stanford Research Institute. https://www.dougengelbart.org/pubs/augment-3906.html

Flower, L., & Hayes, J. R. (1981). A cognitive process theory of writing. *College Composition and Communication, 32,* 365–387.

Huang, K. (2023, January 16). Alarmed by A.I. chatbots, universities start revamping how they teach. *The New York Times.* https://www.nytimes.com/2023/01/16/technology/chatgpt-artificial-intelligence-universities.html

Keegin, J. M. (2023, May 23). ChatGPT is a plagiarism machine. *The Chronicle of Higher Education.* https://www.chronicle.com/article/chatgpt-is-a-plagiarism-machine

Lehrer, R., Levin, B. B., DeHart, P., & Comeaux, M. (1987). Voice-feedback as a scaffold for writing: A comparative study. *Journal of Educational Computing Research, 3,* 335–353.

Lehrer, R., & Randle, L. (1987). Problem solving, metacognition and composition: The effects of interactive software for first-grade children. *Journal of Educational Computing Research, 3,* 401–425.

Li, Z., Wang, C., & Bonk, C. J. (2025). *Learners' perspectives on the ethical use of AI in learning: A FATE analysis* [Manuscript submitted for publication]. Learning, Design, and Adult Education Department, Indiana University.

Markoff, J. (2015). *Machines of loving grace: The quest for common ground between humans and robots.* Harper Collins

McMurtrie, B. (2023, January 5). Teaching: Will ChatGPT change the way you teach? *The Chronicle of Higher Education.* https://www.chronicle.com/newsletter/teaching/2023-01-05

McMurtrie, B. (2024, June 13). Professors ask: Are we just grading robots? *The Chronicle of Higher Education.* https://www.chronicle.com/article/professors-ask-are-we-just-grading-robots

Reynolds, T. H., & Bonk, C. J. (1996a). Creating computerized writing partner and keystroke recording tools with macro-driven prompts. *Educational Technology Research and Development (ETR&D), 44*(3), 83–97.

Reynolds, T. H., & Bonk, C. J. (1996b). Facilitating college writers' revisionary processes within a generative-evaluative prompting framework. *Computers and Composition, 13*(1), 93–108.

Salomon, G. (1988). AI in reverse: Computer tools that turn cognitive. *Journal of Educational Computing Research, 4*(2), 123–139.

Scardamalia, M., & Bereiter, C. (1982). Assimilative processes in composition planning. *Educational Psychologist, 17*(3), 165–171.

Scardamalia, M., & Bereiter, C. (1986). Research on written composition. In M. C. Wittrock (Ed.), *Handbook of research on teaching* (3rd edition, pp. 778–803). Macmillan Education Ltd.

Schroeder, R. (2023, August 30). Supporting faculty member fearing generative AI. *Inside Higher Education.* https://www.insidehighered.com/opinion/blogs/online-trending-now/2023/08/30/supporting-faculty-member-fearing-generative-ai

Swaak, T. (2024, February 26). AI will shake up higher ed. Are colleges ready? *The Chronicle of Higher Education.* https://www.chronicle.com/article/ai-will-shake-up-higher-ed-are-colleges-ready?sra=true

Terry, O. K. (2023, May 12). I'm a student. You have no idea much we're using ChatGPT. *The Chronicle of Higher Education.* https://www.chronicle.com/article/im-a-student-you-have-no-idea-how-much-were-using-chatgpt

Vygotsky, L. S. (1978). *Mind in society: The development of higher psychological processes.* (M. Cole, V. John-Steiner, & E. Souberman, Eds. & Trans.). Harvard University Press.

Vygotsky, L. (1986). *Thought and language* (rev. ed.). MIT Press.

Wang, C., Li, Z., & Bonk, C. J. (2024). Understanding self-directed learning in AI-assisted writing: A mixed methods study of postsecondary learners. *Computers & Education: Artificial Intelligence, 6.* https://doi.org/10.1016/j.caeai.2024.100247

Whitfield, N. (2014, January 3). Ten classic electronic calculators from the 1970s and 1980s. https://www.theregister.com/2014/01/03/ten_classic_calcutors/

Woodruff, E., Bereiter, C., & Scardamalia, M. (1981). On the road to computer assisted composition. *Journal of Educational Technology Systems, 10*(2), 133–148.

INDEX

Made in United States
Cleveland, OH
10 February 2026

33081305R00103